Conduct Unbecoming

Conduct Unbecoming

Fifteen Military Criminals, Rogues and Victims of Justice from the Revolutionary War to Vietnam

SCOTT BARON *and*
JAMES E. WISE, JR.

McFarland & Company, Inc., Publishers
Jefferson, North Carolina

ALSO OF INTEREST

At the Helm of USS America: The Aircraft Carrier and Its 23 Commanders, 1965–1996, James E. Wise, Jr., and Scott Baron (McFarland 2014)
James Arness: An Autobiography, James Arness with James E. Wise, Jr. (McFarland 2001; paperback 2013)

LIBRARY OF CONGRESS CATALOGUING-IN-PUBLICATION DATA

Names: Baron, Scott, 1954– author. | Wise, James E., Jr., 1930–2013, author.
Title: Conduct unbecoming : fifteen military criminals, rogues and victims of justice from the Revolutionary War to Vietnam / Scott Baron and James E. Wise, Jr.
Description: Jefferson, North Carolina : McFarland & Company, Inc., Publishers, 2016. | Includes bibliographical references and index.
Identifiers: LCCN 2015048992 | ISBN 9781476662695 (softcover : acid free paper) ♾
Subjects: LCSH: Trials (Military offenses)—United States—History. | Courts-martial and courts of inquiry—United States—History. | Military discipline—United States—History. | Military offenses—United States—History.
Classification: LCC KF7641 .B37 2016 | DDC 343.73/0140261—dc23
LC record available at http://lccn.loc.gov/2015048992

BRITISH LIBRARY CATALOGUING DATA ARE AVAILABLE

ISBN (print) 978-1-4766-6269-5
ISBN (ebook) 978-1-4766-2306-1

© 2016 Scott Baron. All rights reserved

No part of this book may be reproduced or transmitted in any form or by any means, electronic or mechanical, including photocopying or recording, or by any information storage and retrieval system, without permission in writing from the publisher.

On the cover: Camp Logan court-martial in session, 1917 (National Archives and Records Administration)

Printed in the United States of America

McFarland & Company, Inc., Publishers
Box 611, Jefferson, North Carolina 28640
www.mcfarlandpub.com

To Jim Falk in everlasting friendship.
—James E. Wise, Jr.†

In remembrance of James Wise, Jr.,
December 11, 1930, to July 7, 2013
—Scott Baron

Contents

Acknowledgments by Scott Baron   ix

Preface   1

1. Pvt. Thomas Hickey (Mutiny, Sedition—1776)   3
2. Lt. Col. Paul Revere (Disobedience of an Order—1782)   10
3. Commander Alexander Slidell Mackenzie (Murder, Illegal Punishment—1842)   26
4. Capt. John Patrick Reily (Desertion—1848)   34
5. Lambdin P. Milligan (*Ex Parte Milligan*) (Conspiracy, Inciting Insurrection—1864)   47
6. Maj. Henry Wirz (War Crimes, Murder—1865)   54
7. Cadet Johnson C. Whittaker (Conduct Unbecoming an Officer, Conduct Prejudicial to Good Order—1881)   69
8. Camp Logan Incident (Mutiny, Riot—1917)   88
9. Operation Pastorious (*Ex Parte Quirin*) (Treason, Sabotage—1942)   99
10. Fort Lawton Courts-Martial (Riot, Murder—1944)   128
11. Port Chicago Court-Martial (Mutiny—1944)   143
12. Freeman Field Mutiny (Disobedience of Orders—1945)   161
13. The Court-Martial of Pvt. Eddie Slovik (Desertion—1945)   177
    SIDEBAR: *Toth v. Quarles 350 U.S. 11*—1955   190

14. Sgt. Charles Robert Jenkins (Desertion and Aiding the
  Enemy—1965) 192
15. 2nd Lt. William Calley (War Crimes, Cover-Up—1968–1971) 204

Chapter Notes 239
Bibliography 249
Index 253

Acknowledgments
by Scott Baron

Special gratitude is owed to Natalie Hall (our superb editor of many years), Jay D. Smith, Paul Revai, Glenn Helm, Robert J. Tolle, Faye Haskins, Roger Cirillo, John Vernon, Scott Johnson, Diane Dellatorre Stevens, Kevin Reem, Murray Mullins, Tyrone Brown, Deborah Petranek; to staff members of the photo archives of the Naval Historical Foundation, the National Archives and Records Administration, and the Library of Congress.

Before this book could be published, my coauthor, friend, mentor, surrogate father—and one of the finest, most honorable, and decent people I have ever known—left this Earth to rejoin his beloved wife Carla. To say I will miss him is an understatement of biblical proportions.

Jim spent a career in the United States Navy, retiring as a captain. He worked for the CIA, contracted with the government, consulted, had a business, raised five children, and was always ready to lend assistance, especially to young people. (At eighty-three, Jim was among the few who considered me "young.")

Jim's good sense and calm reflection steered me safely through many a storm.

Captain James E. Wise, Jr., U.S. Navy.

We coauthored nine books together, and his steady hand at the helm as we navigated the literary seas taught me much, not just about writing but more importantly about life. How do you replace a friend whom you spoke with at least weekly? Jim had a way of making you feel as if he felt lucky to be in your company. Jim was a gentleman. To paraphrase Will Rogers, "I never met a man who didn't like him."

One of the last things he said to me was, "Scott, you'll do the next book by yourself. You're ready!" Like always, Jim called it—at least the "by yourself" part. But on reflection, he was wrong! Because I will always have him reading over my shoulder.

Godspeed, old friend, and smooth sailing. I await the day we meet again on the other side of the river.

Preface

As the writing of this book began in July 2013, the U.S. government has completed the trial of Maj. Nidal Malik Hasan on thirteen counts of premeditated murder committed on 5 November 2009 at Fort Hood. Found guilty, he was sentenced to death on 28 August 2013. With his conviction, he could become the first U.S. serviceman to be executed since World War II! The sensational nature of the crime, along with its political ramifications, has focused the national attention on the process of American military justice.

There have been many instances where the American military have counted among its members "criminals, rogues or victims of military justice," especially in times of war. The various accounts included in this book contain such cases. Although cases involving military justice have arisen in the recent actions in Iraq and Afghanistan, many identified cases are controversial or still in litigation; thus the authors have chosen to exclude them in this work.

Military justice differs in many significant respects from civilian justice, but this in no way suggests that it is superior or inferior, only that the procedures and applications differ. Military law, like all law, is in a constant state of transition. The Uniform Code of Military Justice, enacted by Congress in 1950, has evolved from the Articles of War adopted by the Continental Congress in 1775. That American military law is far from perfect is obvious to even the most ardent supporters, and military jurisprudence has both its admirers and detractors.

Military justice is sufficiently just for Warren Burger, former Chief Justice of the United States, to have called it "the most enlightened military code in history."[1] However, former Indiana senator Birch Bayh has argued, "It is a shameful fact that this nation, which prides itself on offering 'liberty and justice for all,' fails to provide a first rate system of justice for the very citizens it calls upon to defend those principles."[2] The authors have written about past courts-martial and military commissions, some little known or entirely unknown to readers, that have influenced the system of military law and justice in the course of our nation's history. When an incident occurs, officials sometimes, rather than accepting responsibility, resort to cover-ups. Some of the following true stories are so startling it is almost unbelievable that the American military would conduct itself in such a manner.

America since its founding has been a warlike nation, and justice in time of war is a tricky venture. To remain free the country has frequently had to take up arms. The challenge, then, is to sculpt military justice in such a way as to protect the nation's security while preserving individual rights.

1

Pvt. Thomas Hickey

Mutiny, Sedition—1776

> *The unhappy fate of Thomas Hickey, executed this day for mutiny, sedition and treachery, the General hopes will be a warning to every soldier in the Army.*—Washington's orders to the Army, 28 June 1776

On 9 July 1776, citizens of the city of New York and soldiers of the Continental Army stood in City Hall Park and listened as the Declaration of Independence was read aloud. Copies of the Declaration, printed four days earlier by John Dunlap, a Philadelphia printer, had been sent by horseback to the various assemblies, conventions, and committees of safety" and to the commanders of the Army. The United Colonies had declared themselves to be "free and independent states" and no longer bound either to Great Britain or to its king.

The reading itself was greeted with shouts, huzzahs, the firing of muskets, and the tearing down of British symbols. Following the reading, New Yorkers stormed to Bowling Green Park and tore down an equestrian statue of King George III erected by New York merchants in 1770 in gratitude for the repeal of the Stamp Act. Constructed of gilded lead, it would be melted down to make musket balls.[1] But not all of New York's 25,000 residents greeted the independence with joy and elation. New York City had a large loyalist population, which had been steadily departing the city following the arrival of the patriot army in May, but a large proportion remained, encouraged by rumors of the imminent arrival of the British fleet. By June 1776, the city was a place of frantic activity as the army of the United Colonies, under the command of Gen. George Washington, worked frantically to throw up earthworks in anticipation of the impending arrival of British regulars, sent to put down the rebellion and restore order to King George's

American colonies. The city was awash with rumors of a Tory uprising that would precede the British landings.

The taverns of New York, mostly owned by loyalist merchants, were centers for Tory plots and attempts to gather intelligence on patriot forces. The royal governor, William Tyron, had withdrawn to a British warship, the seventy-four-gun HMS *Duchess of Gordon*, anchored with two other Royal Navy warships in the harbor. He remained, however, active in organizing resistance to the patriots, and he remained in communication with David Matthews, the mayor, who was also sympathetic to the British. Soldiers and others were enlisted into a conspiracy to "take up arms for the King" upon the British landing in New York.

To finance the revolution, two million Continental dollars had been printed in May 1775 on rag paper by Hall and Sellers of Philadelphia, and counterfeiting was prevalent throughout the colonies.[2] On 15 June, Sgt. Thomas Hickey and Pvt. Michael Lynch, both soldiers of Washington's Life Guard, were imprisoned for passing counterfeit money. It was this involvement with counterfeiting that revealed a loyalist plot and led to the first court-martial for sedition in American history.

In February 1776, Henry Dawkins, newly released from the New York City Jail, entered into a conspiracy with Isaac and Israel Young of Huntington, Long Island, to counterfeit Continental currency, for which purpose a printing press was purchased and installed in the Young's attic. In the absence of the safeguards that modern currency enjoys, counterfeiting colonial money was relatively simple. The difficulty was in obtaining the correct paper, which was available only to printers. Dawkins persuaded another coconspirator, Isaac Ketcham, to travel to Philadelphia, the center of the American paper industry, to purchase a quantity of the necessary stock. Ketcham's activities raised suspicions, and he was arrested in May. At about the same time, Dawkins, while drunk, made incriminating statements and was likewise arrested, followed shortly by the Young brothers.[3]

While imprisoned, Ketcham learned of Tory plots to kidnap Washington from his headquarters and to stage an armed uprising by forces loyal to the king. In exchange for not being prosecuted, Ketcham agreed to serve as a spy in the prison. Apparently liquor wasn't difficult to obtain in the jail, and Ketcham overheard Hickey drunkenly boasting of being involved in both Tory plots. After two days of collecting information, he sent word to the Provincial Congress.

Ketcham's allegations were confirmed when a patriot businessman, William Leary, contacted New York authorities and informed them that a former employee, James Mason, had indiscreetly confided that he and others were already being paid by the British. Arrested, Mason implicated Hickey, Gilbert Forbes (a gunsmith), William Forbes, and three other members of Washington's Life Guard: Drummer William Green, Fifer James Johnson, and a soldier, John Barnes. Leary and Mason in turn implicated Mayor Matthews, who was accused of supplying one hundred pounds to pay conspirators.[4]

Hickey and Private Lynch were already in custody on the counterfeiting charge when Ketcham and Mason made their accusations of treason; Matthews was arrested in his home early on the morning of 22 June, as was Gilbert Forbes. The three other members of Washington's Life Guard were arrested on 23 June. Many conspirators fled New York, but between twenty and forty were taken into custody.

The British commander, Lt. Gen. Sir William Howe, had evacuated Boston in March 1776. Washington suspected correctly that Howe would now land his 11,000 troops, on board 150 ships, in the area of New York City, where there was a large loyalist population. This would serve two purposes. First, the welcome and support that it was anticipated Howe's troops would receive would help convince a doubting English population that Great Britain enjoyed the support of most of the American colonies against a radical minority. Also, the move would isolate New England, seen as the heart of the rebellion, from the rest of the colonies.

Washington had sent Maj. Gen. Charles Lee to New York City in January to prepare a defense. Lee had arrived on 4 February but departed for South Carolina in March. There were virtually no fortifications in place when Washington arrived on 13 April, and he set the army to work building them. New York City controlled the Hudson River, a key to the defense of the city and of the northern colonies.

Washington understood that the nature of the war was about to change. Under his command the army would change from a static and defensive force to a mobile force, marching to meet British initiatives. This movement would increase his vulnerability to Tory spies and sympathizers as well as the British army itself; with raids on his headquarters a real possibility. As a result, Washington ordered the formation of a personal guard[5]:

Head-Quarters, Cambridge 11 March 1776
  The General is desirous of selecting a particular number of men as a guard for himself and baggage. The Colonel or Commanding Officer of each of the established regiments, the artillery and riflemen excepted, will furnish him with four, that the number of wanted may be chosen out of them. His Excellency depends upon the Colonels for good men, such as they can recommend for their sobriety, honesty and good behavior. He wishes them to be from five feet eight inches to five feet ten inches, handsomely and well made, and as there is

nothing in his eyes more desirable than cleanliness in a soldier, he desires that particular attention be made in the choice of such men as are clean and spruce. They are to be at headquarters tomorrow precisely at twelve o'clock noon, when the number wanted will be fixed upon. The General neither wants them with uniforms nor arms, nor does he desire any man to be sent to him that is not perfectly willing or desirous of being in this Guard.—They should be drilled men."[6]

Capt. Caleb Gibbs, of the 14th Massachusetts Continental Regiment, was selected by Washington to command the Guard, and George Lewis, Gibbs' nephew, was commissioned its lieutenant. The commander in chief's guard (CinC Guard) was officially designated as "His Excellency's Guard" or "The General's Guard," but it was popularly known to the soldiers as "the Life Guards," "the Washington Life Guards," or "the Washington Body Guard." Besides Gibbs and Lewis, the CinC Guard comprised "four sergeants, four corporals, a drum and fife, and fifty rank and file." One of the sergeants was an Irishman known as Thomas Hickey.

Little is actually known about Thomas Hickey. Records show that he was Irish-born, assigned to the CinC Guard on 12 March 1776 with the rank of private, and that he was eighteen years old at the time of his enlistment. He is rumored to have deserted from the British army, and we can discern from his actions that he did not value highly the qualities of honesty or sobriety. He was recruited into the conspiracy to take up arms for the king by Gilbert Forbes while drinking in The Sign of the Sportsman, a tavern Forbes owned on Broadway. After being given five gold guineas for signing up, Hickey was paid fifteen shillings a week for his treason, as well as a bounty for other soldiers he brought into the conspiracy. If the rumor of a plot to kidnap Washington were true, Hickey and the other members of the guard would be in a good position to assist in its execution. In point of fact, Mayor Matthews later bragged to a royal commission in England that he had conceived of a plot to "take Mr. Washington and his Guard prisoner."[7]

It is unlikely that stories of Hickey attempting to poison Washington's peas, only to be saved by the innkeeper's daughter or a servant named Phoebe, are anything other than tales related at second and third hand. The innkeeper Sam Fraunces owned Fraunces Tavern, where Washington would years later bid farewell to his troops, but family baptismal records from Christ Church in Philadelphia and Trinity Church in New York make no reference to a child name Phoebe, nor is she mentioned in his will or in the 1790 census. Recent studies have suggested that "Phoebe" was a nickname for Samuel's daughter, Elizabeth, but no evidence exists to support that, and if so, she would have been ten years of age at the time of the court-martial.[8]

On the strength of Ketcham's and Mason's accusations, Hickey was brought before a court-martial at Richmond Hill, New York, on 26 June 1776. Col. Samuel H. Parsons was named president of the court, and William Tudor the judge advocate. Twelve officers—Lt. Col. William Sheppard, Maj. Levi Wells, and ten captains (Joseph Hoyt, Abel Pettibone, Samuel Warren, James Mellin, Warham Parks, William Reed, Joseph Pettingil, David Lyon, David Sill, and Timothy Purcival) constituted the jury. The warrant was read and the jury sworn.[9]

Hickey stood accused of "exciting and joining in a mutiny and sedition, and of treacherously corresponding with, enlisting among, and receiving pay from the enemies of the United American Colonies."[10] Significantly, the charges of attempting either to kidnap/assassinate Washington, capture American artillery, or attack the Continental Army from the rear are mentioned nowhere in the trial transcript. The judge advocate was so confident of his case that Lynch, Barnes, Johnson, and Mason were never called to testify. Hickey pled not guilty to the charges, and four witnesses were called to establish his guilt.[11]

William Green testified that he had been recruited by the gunsmith Forbes three weeks earlier. Forbes had stated the impossibility of successful resistance by the colonies to the power of Great Britain and had paid Green to "inlist [sic] into the King's Service." Green had asked where the money would come from to pay him, and Forbes had replied, "The mayor." Green testified that he had agreed from patriotic motives to take the money, with the intent to "dupe the Tories of their money" and "detect their scheme." Green had recruited Hickey to his plan to dupe the Tories. Green wanted then to go to Washington, but Hickey had persuaded him to wait while they gathered additional information. Doubtless, the jury viewed Green's testimony with skepticism.[12]

Gilbert Forbes, gunsmith and paymaster, testified next; however, he stated that it was Green who recruited him into the plot and that he himself, although initially resistant, had been persuaded by numerous solicitations to join the conspiracy. He testified that Hickey's name had been on a list of conspirators handed to him by Green, who had requested money to pay the men and had received eighteen dollars. Forbes later received "upwards of a hundred pounds" from Matthews.[13]

William Welch, a soldier not part of the conspiracy, testified that he had been approached by Hickey on the street and taken to a grog shop. There Hickey had sworn Welch to secrecy on a Bible, then advised him that the country had been "sold," that the enemy would be arriving soon, and that it would be best if "old countrymen" like themselves joined together and made peace before the enemy came. He offered Welch a dollar; Welch declined it and departed.[14]

The last to take the stand was Isaac Ketcham, who had encouraged Hickey's drunken boasts in jail. He testified, "In different conversations, [Hickey] informed me that the army was becoming damnably corrupted, that the fleet was soon expected, and that he and a number of others were in a band to turn against the American Army when the king's troops should arrive, and asked me to be one of them." Ketcham also testified that "eight of the General's Guard were concerned, but mentioned only Green by name. He further told me that one Forbes, a tavern keeper, was to be their captain."[15]

Hickey represented himself, and his only defense was that he had "engaged in the scheme at first for the sake of cheating the Tories, and getting some money from them, and afterwards consented to have his name sent on board the man-of-war, in order that if the enemy should arrive and defeat the Army here, and he should be taken prisoner, he might be safe."[16] The jury's verdict was unanimous. Hickey was ruled "guilty of the charge against him, and of a breach of the fifth and of the thirtieth articles of the Rules and Regulations for the government of the Continental Forces; and the court unanimously sentence and adjudge that the prisoner, Thomas Hickey, suffer death for said crimes by being hanged by the neck till he is dead." The following day, Washington met with seven general officers, who confirmed the sentence and set the time for the execution at 11:00 a.m. the following day.[17]

Four brigades, those of Generals Heath, Scott, Spencer, and Lord Stirling, were ordered to witness the execution, which, it was hoped, would set an example for American soldiers and British agents alike. An eighty-man guard, with "good arms and bayonets," twenty men from each of the four brigades, was ordered as an escort to prevent any rescue attempt en route to the gallows. Gallows were erected in a meadow owned by Col. Henry Rutger near Bowery Lane. Revolutionary justice was swift, and on the morning of 28 June, as musicians played the "Dead Man's March" on fife and drum, Hickey was escorted to the gallows, accompanied by a chaplain. The executioner was an unidentified drummer. Hickey, after being blindfolded and bound, was dropped to his death. His execution was witnessed by an estimated 20,000 spectators.

Washington's orders for the day read in part:

> The unhappy fate of Thomas Hickey, executed this day for mutiny, sedition and treachery, the General hopes will be a warning to every soldier in the Army to avoid those crimes and all others, so disgraceful to the character of a soldier, and pernicious to his country, whose pay he receives and bread he eats. And in order to avoid those crimes the most certain method is to keep out of the temptation

of them, and to particularly avoid lewd women who, by the dying confession of this poor criminal, first led him into practices which ended in an untimely and ignominious death."[18]

Why was Hickey, the first American soldier tried for sedition, the only conspirator brought to trial? The answer is suggested in a letter Washington sent to John Hancock, president of the Continental Congress, on the morning of the execution. He wrote, "I am hopeful this example will produce many salutary consequences and deter others from entering into like traitorous practices."[19] William Morony, the provost marshal, endorsed the death warrant: "By virtue of, and in obedience to, the foregoing warrant, I have this day, at the time and place therein ordered and directed, caused Thomas Hickey, the prisoner within mentioned, to suffer death in the way and manner therein prescribed, and accordingly return this warrant fully executed."[20]

This "example" came just in the nick of time. The next morning, 29 June, four British warships dropped anchor in New York Harbor, the 130-strong vanguard of ships carrying 34,000 troops that would arrive over the following week, initiating the battle of Long Island and beginning what one historian has called "Washington's long retreat to victory."[21]

2
Lt. Col. Paul Revere
Disobedience of an Order—1782

> *Listen my children and you shall hear of the Midnight Ride of Paul Revere. On the eighteenth of April, in Seventy-five; Hardly a man is now alive who remembers that famous day and year.*—Henry Wadsworth Longfellow

Every American schoolchild knows the tale of Paul Revere's Midnight Ride, however historically inaccurate Mr. Longfellow's poem may be, written as it was eighty-five years later on April 19, 1860. However few Americans are aware that this icon of the American Revolution was court-martialed at his own request for his actions during the Penobscot Expedition on July 25, 1779, considered by some the worst naval defeat in U.S. history.

In mid–June 1779, the focus of the American War of Independence shifted from New England to the southern colonies. British forces, seeking a base from which to combat American privateers and establish a trading post with Nova Scotia as well as provide refuge for displaced Loyalists fleeing the rebellious colonies, sent a small fleet into the upper reaches of Penobscot Bay, Maine, landing two regiments under the command of Brigadier General Francis McLean on the Castine Peninsula. The troops numbered approximately 700; 50 men of the Royal Artillery and engineers, 450 of the 74th Regiment of Foot (Argyle Highlanders) and 200 of the 82nd Regiment (Duke of Hamilton's). Enlisting support from the local population, construction began on Fort George in the area then known as Maja Bagaduce, now Castine, Maine.[1]

Alerted to this incursion, authorities in Boston, which maintained sovereignty over Maine until 1820, began plans for an expedition to oust the British from the area. Granted the use of three warships by the Continental Congress, then in Boston, the remainder of the ships was comprised of Massachusetts State Navy and private vessels, forty-three ships in all, under the command of Commodore Dudley Saltonstall.

Saltonstall, born in New London, Connecticut, on September 8, 1738, to a family prominent in British colonial affairs, was a direct descendant, on his mother's side, of John Winthrop, governor of Massachusetts Bay in the 17th century. He was an experienced sailor, having served as the captain of merchant ships and the privateer *Britannia* during the French and Indian War during which he made several successful voyages to the West Indies.

When hostilities broke out at the beginning of the American Revolution in 1775, Saltonstall enlisted in the Connecticut Militia and helped to defend New London's harbor. In October 1775, thirteen ships were authorized by the Congress for the newly-created Continental Navy, with Esek Hopkins of Rhode Island appointed as its commander in chief.

Through the influence of his brother-in-law, Silas Deane of the Naval Committee of Connecticut, Saltonstall was commissioned as the 4th senior captain in the new navy and given command of the *Alfred*, a 440-ton warship with a complement of 220 men and armed with twenty 9-pound cannon and ten 6-pounder smoothbore cannons, which served as Commodore Hopkins' flagship. Saltonstall chose a young Scottish immigrant, John Paul Jones, as his first lieutenant and second in command, but the two did not get along, Jones offended by Saltonstall's distant and superior demeanor and style of command. On its maiden voyage on March 1, 1776, the *Alfred*, accompanied by *Andrew Doria, Cabot, Columbus, Providence, Fly, Wasp* and *Hornet* set sail for New Providence (Nassau) in the Bahamas, where they met with limited success when a large quantity of gunpowder was spirited away to avoid capture. On the return, the fleet captured British ships on April 4 and 5, but the failure to engage and capture the warship *Glasgow* would result in censures of several captains for "cowardly behavior."[2]

By early 1779, Saltonstall was in command of the *Warren*, having replaced Hopkins as captain when the latter was suspended, and eventually dismissed from the service for breach of orders. As the senior Continental Navy commander present and captain of the *Warren*, Saltonstall was put in command of the naval forces for the Penobscot Expedition on July 2.

On June 26, command of the land forces accompanying the expedition was placed in the hands of Gen. Solomon Lovell, a farmer and militia general, with Brigadier General Peleg Wadsworth second in command. Among the rebel forces that seized Dorchester Heights in 1776 and in command of a militia unit at the Battle of Rhode Island in 1778, Lovell had little experience in amphibious operations. Perhaps not wishing to share credit in what was expected to be an easy victory, the Massachusetts Board of War did not consult with Gen. Horatio Gates for advice nor request troops. The three Maine militia units from York, Cumberland and Lincoln made up the land force, but were mainly inexperienced and ill-equipped farmers, loggers and fishermen, about 870 boys and old men, far less than the 1,500 expected. On July 8, 100 artillerymen were ordered to join the expedition, under the command of Lt. Colonel Paul Revere.[3]

Details of Revere's early life are unclear, and differ by source. It is likely that he was born on December 22, 1734, in Boston's North End to a French Huguenot father, Apollos Rivoire, and a Boston mother, Deborah Hichborn. Revere was the second of nine, possibly twelve, children. He apprenticed as a gold- and silversmith under his father, and inherited the business after his father's death in 1754. Two years later, at age 21, Revere volunteered to fight the French during the French and Indian War and was commissioned a second lieutenant in the colonial artillery, seeing combat at Lake George, New York, while attempting to capture the fortress at Crown Point.

In August 1757, back from the army, Revere married Sarah Orne with whom he had eight children. Upon Sarah's death in 1773, Revere, with six surviving children, married Rachel Walker with whom he had another eight children, five of whom would survive. During this period, his renown as a silversmith grew, and examples of his work exist today in museums and private collections as outstanding examples of early American art.

In 1765, the British passed the Stamp Act, a direct tax on the colonies, to help pay for the French and Indian War, a tax resented by the colonists who felt unfairly taxed without representation in Parliament. A friend of political activists James Otis, John Hancock, Samuel Adams and Dr. Joseph Warren, Revere became increasingly involved in resisting British authority by joining the Sons of Liberty, acting as a messenger for the Boston Committee of Public Safety and by drawing political cartoons which helped shape anti–British public opinion. His most famous engraving was of the Boston Massacre in 1770 entitled "The Bloody Massacre Perpetrated in King Street Boston on March 5th, 1770."

Possibly present at the Boston Tea Party in 1773, he carried the news by horseback to New York City. Revere's political activities increased after England closed Boston Harbor and began quartering large numbers of British regulars in homes around Boston to punish Boston with the so-called "Intolerable Acts." By early 1775, Revolution was in the air, as colonies began raising militias and stockpiling arms and powder. As a creator of the "mechanics," an early intelligence network that gathered information by

"The Bloody Massacre Perpetrated in King Street Boston on March 5th 1770 by a Party of the 29th Regt." by Paul Revere, 1770. A sensationalized portrayal of the skirmish, later to become known as the "Boston Massacre," between British soldiers and citizens of Boston on March 5, 1770. On the right a group of seven uniformed soldiers, on the signal of an officer, fire into a crowd of civilians at left. Three of the latter lie bleeding on the ground. Two other casualties have been lifted by the crowd. In the foreground is a dog; in the background are a row of houses, the First Church, and the Town House. Behind the British troops is another row of buildings including the Royal Custom House, which bears the sign (perhaps a sardonic comment) "Butcher's Hall."

observing British troop movements and vessels along the Charles River, Revere became aware of Gen. Gage's plan to move on Lexington to arrest patriot leaders Sam Adams and John Hancock and seize the stores of arms and powder at Concord.[4]

On the evening of April 18/19, Revere and another rider, William Dawes, were directed by Dr. Warren to ride to warn Adams and Hancock of the British Army's movement towards Lexington with the intent to arrest them. Revere crossed the Charles River by boat to Charlestown while Dawes proceeded overland. As previously arranged, Robert Newman, the sexton of the Old North Church, and Captain John Pulling held two lit lanterns aloft in the church steeple to signal Charlestown that the British were proceeding by crossing the Charles River. Riding through present-day Somerville, Medford and Arlington, Revere roused the villagers with cries of "The Regulars are coming out" and eventually as many as forty riders crossed Middlesex County rousing the militias, known as "minute-men."

Around midnight, Revere arrived at the Hancock-Clarke House at Lexington and roused and warned Adams and Hancock, with Dawes arriving thirty minutes later. The two riders took off west toward Concord around 1 a.m. and, as British troops were marching through Cambridge, they met up with an elegantly dressed young gentleman, Dr. Samuel Prescott, returning home to Concord from a late evening courting a Miss Lydia Mulliken of Lexington. Informed of their mission, Prescott immediately volunteered to help raise the alarm, and despite the danger of British patrols, the three roused all the houses they could as they proceeded toward Concord. Two miles beyond Lexington Green, they came upon the settlement of Lincoln, a cluster of four farmsteads. As Dawes and Prescott roused the inhabitants, Revere advanced several hundred yards and spied two horsemen lurking under some trees. Joined by his companions, they advanced on the two with hostile intent only to discover that the two were four British Regulars with drawn pistols and swords who ordered, "God Damn you, Stop! If you go an inch further, you are a dead man."[5]

Revere, Prescott and Dawes were herded at gunpoint to a pasture north of the Great Road by officers who swore to "blow their brains out" if they did not turn into the pasture. At a signal, Prescott turned left and galloped off, jumping a low stone fence, as Revere spurred his horse right. Although pursued by several horsemen, Prescott, familiar with the area, disappeared into the swamp and woods, and escaped. Contrary to Longfellow's poem, only Prescott arrived in Concord to warn the inhabitants. Revere was not so fortunate. Intercepted by six additional horsemen, he was surrounded by ten British Regulars aiming pistols at his heart, and his reins were seized. In the confusion, Dawes escaped to an abandoned farm, but his horse bolted in fright, unhorsing him, and galloped off. Dawes limped off back toward Lexington in the moonlight, avoiding British patrols.[6]

Angry at losing two of three suspicious colonials, the British forced Revere to dismount and he was abused until an officer intervened. He joined others detained by the patrol, including Elijah Sanderson and Jonathan Loring from Lexington, and Solomon Brown, a messenger sent to Concord. The prisoners were interrogated throughout the night, especially regarding the whereabouts of Adams and Hancock. Revere was frank in admitting he was aware of their mission and had spent the morning raising the alarm throughout the countryside. Angry, a rider returned with Major Edward Mitchell of the 5th Foot, menaced Revere with a pistol to his head, but un-intimidated, Revere self-confidently advised the soldiers that it was *they* who were in peril from the roused militia gathering in Lexington. Although militias were gathering throughout the countryside, Revere stressed the build-up at Lexington, aware that it was where Adams and Hancock were hiding.

At about a quarter past two, as Sanderson later recalled, they were led out of the pasture and the ten nervous regulars and four prisoners headed east toward Boston at a smart pace. Showing the strain, Major Mitchell warned, "We are now going toward your friends and if you attempt to run or we are insulted, we will blow your brains out." Revere answered, "You may do as you please."[7]

About a half mile from Lexington Green, the party heard first a shot, then a volley of musket fire, and the officers gave greater credibility to Revere's warnings. The impression was reinforced by the clanging of the town's bells. Alarmed, the British made their prisoners dismount, cut the bridles and girths, ran off the horses, and galloped off toward Cambridge to warn the advancing British column.

Revere, now free but horseless, walked across muddy pastures and a cemetery to Rev. Clarke's house, only to find Adams and Hancock still debating the proper course of action with Hancock desiring to join the Lexington men on the common to face down the approaching British troops while Adams argued that they could render greater service in the cabinet. With Revere's arrival, Hancock was persuaded that discretion was the wiser course since the large numbers of Tories in the area made it unlikely that their hiding place would long remain a secret. With Hancock finally convinced, the three departed at dawn in Hancock's heavy coach northwest to Burlington where Revere left them safe, then returned to Lexington, to Buckman's Tavern, to retrieve a trunk of Hancock's papers. The subsequent confrontation between Captain John Parker's militiamen and British Regulars at Lexington, the "Shot Heard 'Round the World," launched the American War of Independence.

Returning to Boston after the British evacuation, Revere was commissioned a Major of Infantry in the Massachusetts militia in late March 1776, but was wisely transferred to the artillery the following month and was promoted on November 27 to the rank of Lieutenant-Colonel. His 16-year-old son, Paul Jr., was given a lieutenant's commission in one of the companies. The ten companies in the artillery regiment he commanded were styled the "Massachusetts State's Train."[8]

Revere's military service included management of a gunpowder mill at Canton, Massachusetts, and taking command of Castle William, the principal fortification guarding Boston Harbor, on September 1, 1778. With the exception of a brief expedition to reinforce Gen. Sullivan against the British at Newport, Rhode Island, in July 1778, he saw little field service until his selection to command the artillery on the Penobscot expedition, his talents being better utilized in the production of powder and the casting of cannon. On June 26, 1779, Revere received orders to "hold yourself and a hundred matrosses (assistant gunners) and other officers in readiness to embark at an hour's notice for the defense of this state and to attack the enemy at Penobscot under the command of General Lovell." Here then was a second chance for battlefield glory as all expectations were that expelling the British from Maine would be an easy task.[9]

The armada that departed Boston's Nantasket Roads on July 19 consisted of three Continental Navy vessels, the 32-gun frigate *Warren*, the 14-gun brig *Diligent* and the 12-gun sloop *Providence* as well as three Massachusetts State vessels, the brigs *Hazard*, *Active* and *Tyranicide*, each mounting fourteen guns. A New Hampshire State vessel, the twenty-gun *Hampden*, and twelve

Paul Revere, circa 1887 (Library of Congress).

Massachusetts privateers, as well as twenty-four transports, accompanied the force. The assembled fleet, with about 2,000 seamen and Marines and nearly 1,000 artillerymen and militia aboard, was possibly the largest naval armada assembled during the Revolution.[10]

They sailed first to Boothbay Harbor where it was expected they would rendezvous with more troops, but none were found waiting. Lovell called a meeting of senior commanders aboard the *Warren* and it was evident from the beginning that Commodore Saltonstall and Gen. Lovell disagreed over tactics. As Revere recalled, "In the evening, he [Lovell] called a Council of War ... there was nothing proposed and consequently nothing done. It was more like a meeting in a coffeehouse than a Council of War ... they agreed upon nothing." With no additional troops forthcoming, and unwilling to delay, Satonstall set sail at 3 a.m. on Saturday the 24th.[11]

The Americans arrived at the mouth of the Penobscot on the afternoon of the 25th to find the earthwork fortifications still under construction, the walls only five feet high with only two guns mounted, one facing seaward, the other into the woods. Only three armed sloops, the 20-gun *North*, and 18-gun *Albany* and *Nautilus*, guarded the water approach to Castine Harbor, the remaining ships having sailed for Halifax.

The British were not unaware of the American expedition. Gen. McLean had heard rumors, and had sent for reinforcements from New York even as he hurried to improve his fortifications, establishing secondary batteries on the southern shore of the peninsula and on Nautilus Island. He also ordered Captain Henry Mowat, captain of the *Albany*, to moor the three sloops, mounting fifty-six guns, near the western entrance. Commodore Sir George Collier wrote from New York on July 28: "I received this morning certain intelligence that an armament sailed from Boston on the 21st instant to attack his Majesty's new settlement in Penobscot River.... I intend putting to sea daylight tomorrow."[12]

Upon arrival, Saltonstall deployed nine of his larger vessels against the three sloops guarding the entrance to the harbor and they exchanged ineffective fire for over three hours. At dusk, an attempt was made to land seven boats of militia to establish a beachhead on the peninsula, but strong winds and tidal currents created a concern that troops might be stranded on the beach and Lovell called off the landing. As Lovell reported by letter to the President of the Massachusetts Council three days later, "I the same evening attempted to make a lodgment on Maja Bagaduce, but the wind springing up very strong, I was obliged to desist, lest the first division might suffer before they could be supported by the second."[13]

The following day, the 26th, Lovell sent a force of 150 Marines, gathered from various ships, to capture the British battery on Nautilus (Banks) Island as the sloop *Providence* and the brigs *Pallas* and *Defence* provided covering fire. Meanwhile the militia was to land at Maja Bagaduce.

The Marines successfully drove off the British defenders, and Revere emplaced artillery placing the British anchorage within range and obliging His Majesty's sloops to move a half mile eastward into the harbor for protection. As Revere stated in a letter to the *Boston Gazette* dated August 9, 1779, "the Marines attacked an island where the enemy had a battery of 2 guns; they were commanded by Captain Welsh of the *Warren*. I sent one field piece to support them; they landed under cover of three vessels. The enemy quitted it with precipitation, left their colours flying and four pieces of cannon, two of them not mounted. We immediately built a battery there and mounted two 18 and one 12 pounder. This island is directly opposite to the enemy and commands the mouth of the harbour."

The militia landed on the southwestern shore of the peninsula and Gen. Lovell led between 600–750 militiamen, depending on source used, to within several hundred yards of the British fortifications. Here events would present the conundrum that would plague the expedition and lead to disaster—a lack of cooperation between the land and naval forces. General Lovell insisted that Commodore Saltonstall engage the vastly outnumbered British vessels to clear the way for the land forces to storm the garrison, however Saltonstall refused to hazard his fleet until Lovell's militia seized the fortifications and single battery overlooking the harbor. Unable to convince Saltonstall to attack, Lovell's men began construction on siege works, coming under fire from the British.[14]

On the morning of July 27, thirty-two lieutenants and masters of several privateers appealed to Saltonstall to engage the British before they could strengthen their fortifications, stating, "We would Represent to your Honour that the most spedy Exertions should be used to accomplish the design we came upon. We think Delays in the present Case are extremely dangerous, as our Enemies are daily Fortifying and Strengthening themselves & are stimulated so to do, being in daily Expectation of Reinforcement" and stated that they had no wish to advise or censure, but only "express our desire of improving the present Opportunity to go Immediately into the Harbour & Attack the Enemy's Ships." They clearly expressed the opinion that seizing the fort would be greatly facilitated by removing the ships that protected it.[15]

During the day, Revere's artillery bombarded the enemy fleet, wounding four seamen aboard the HMS *Albany*. By the evening, agreement had been reached on a plan for an amphibious assault on Maja Bagaduce by Marines the following morning under the cover of a naval bombardment.

At 3 a.m. on July 28, under heavy covering fire from the *Tyannicide*, the *Hunter* and the *Sky Rocket*, Gen. Wadsworth led a force of 200 Marines and 200 militia ashore with orders to capture the British fort. As Revere later wrote in a letter:

> We landed in three divisions, the marines on the right, Col. Mitchell on the left, and Col. Mc. Cobb, the volunteers and my corps in the centre. The land being so mountainous and full of wood that our cannon could not play, I landed with my small arms, the whole force under cover of two ships and three brigs, who drew near the shore and kept up a constant fire into the woods till we began to land. The enemy's greatest strength lay upon our right, where the marines landed; they had three hundred in the woods. As soon as the right landed they were briskly attacked. The enemy had the most advantageous place I ever saw; it is a bank above three hundred feet high and so steep that no person can get up it but by pushing himself up by bushes and trees, with which it is covered. In less than 20 minutes the enemy gave way and we pursued them. They left twelve dead on the spot, 8 wounded and about 10 prisoners. We lost about 35 killed and wounded. We took possession of a height near their fort and are now building a battery to play upon them.[16]

The Americans advanced on the fort, forcing the British pickets, who put up a stiff resistance, to retreat when the fort failed to send reinforcements, leaving the Americans in possession of the heights. It was to be the only significant American victory during the expedition. Once again, Lovell called for Saltonstall's fleet to engage the British ships before he ordered the final assault on the bastion, believing his exhausted force insufficient to take the fortifications unless Mowat's warships could be neutralized. Despite overwhelming naval superiority, Saltonstall refused to move against Mowat until Fort George was taken.

Lovell, instead of ordering an assault on the fort, ordered his men to entrench, having decided to build a battery "within a hundred rods" of the British lines and bombard them into surrender. Casualties were greater than Revere estimated with one hundred casualties, one out of four in the landing party, with the Marines taking the majority. The number of casualties appalled Saltonstall to the point that he refused to land any more Marines and threatened to recall those on shore.[17]

On the morning of the 29th, perhaps giving in to pressure from his own officers, Saltonstall sailed the *Warren* and three other ships against the British ships, and unfavorable winds led to a battle fought by long-range cannonades, at which the experienced British gun crews had a distinct advantage over the novice gun crews aboard the American vessels, with the *Warren* suffering the majority of damage.

Relations between the land and naval commanders deteriorated, with no one apparently in command, and frequent councils were held aboard the *Warren*, but little was accomplished and few decisions made. Americans and British skirmished even as improvements were made to Fort George's fortifications. The siege continued into early August with minor skirmishes and light casualties on both sides, but times was running out. On August 3, a fleet of 10 British warships departed New York under the command of Commodore Collier.

Still, the American commanders found themselves at an impasse. On August 6, Lovell noted in his journal, "I wrote a Letter to the Commodore desiring an answer whether he wou'd or whether he wou'd not go in with his Ships & destroy the Shipping of the Enemy, which consist only of three Sloops of war, when he returned for answer, if I wou'd storm the fort he wou'd go in with his Ships." Again, on the 11th, he wrote Saltonstall, "The destruction of the Enemy's ships must be effected at any rate, although it might cost us half our own."[18]

On August 11, 250 American militia advanced and occupied a recently abandoned battery about a quarter mile from the British fort. As expected, a sortie of about 55 British troops advanced from the fort to engage: but the poorly trained American troops fired only one volley at the attacking British troops and fled back to their fort, leaving behind all of their arms and equipment.

In a letter to Saltonstall from the Navy Board of the Eastern District dated August 12 they observed, "We have for sometime been at a loss to know why the enemy's ships have not been attacked.... Our apprehensions of your danger have ever been from a reinforcement to the enemy; you can't expect to remain much longer without one. Whatever, therefore, is to be done, should be done immediately, both to prevent advantages to the enemy and delays if you are obliged to retreat." The American naval and militia commanders had finally agreed to mount a joint operation on August 14, but like the instructions from the Council, it was too late to be of use.[19]

At about 2 p.m., two American ships, the *Active* and *Diligent*, patrolling the mouth of Penobscot Bay spotted a large naval force on the horizon. It was Commodore Collier's relief fleet, he aboard the 64-gun *Raisonable* accompanied by the 32-gun *Blonde* and *Virginia*, the 28-gun *Greyhound*, the 20-gun *Galatea* and *Camilla*, and the 14-gun *Otter*. Although some officers urged making a stand, a council was held at which it was decided the fleet was too strong to engage and pinned as they were within the bay, the only alternative was to make a run up the Penobscot River. A fog rolled up the river's mouth as darkness set in, delaying the British long enough for the Americans to make an orderly withdrawal onto the transports. At noon on the 14th, Saltonstall signaled his captains to retreat and deny the ships to the enemy, and ordered every man to be responsible for himself. Chaos ensued as discipline disappeared in the rush to safety.

For the next two days, the Americans raced upstream attempting to evade the British in pursuit. Two ships, the *Hampden* and a Massachusetts privateer, *Hunter*, were captured by the British, the remainder being run aground and burned to prevent their falling into British hands as crews and militia took to the woods and fled overland back to Boston, many without ammunition or provisions. (A contemporary account by John Calef placed the number at 26 American ships burned, 11 captured.) It was the worst U.S. naval disaster prior to Pearl Harbor.[20]

When the order had been given to evacuate, Revere had taken a boat to Grant's Mill to recover his men. Revere passed General Lovell aboard another transport who ordered him to bring up his cannon to engage the British. Revere attempted to comply with the order but was unable to locate sufficient artillerymen to man the guns. When ordered by General Wadsworth to give up his boat so that the crew of a drifting schooner could be evacuated, Revere initially refused, and argued before giving up the boat. Without orders, Revere then took two officers and eight soldiers into the woods, making their way overland to Fort Western at Augusta, Maine, arriving on August 16. By the 26th, Revere was back in Boston.[21]

That so small a force could defeat the much larger American force was a cause of great rejoicing by Loyalists and the British, and was met with embarrassment and chagrin, and a desire by the General Court to find someone upon whom to place the responsibility for the failure. The naval officers blamed the militia, as the militia officers blamed the sea captains and privateers. An investigation into the circumstances surrounding the Penobscot Expedition was ordered, and on September 9, a court of inquiry was appointed. Presided over by Gen. Artemas Ward, its members included Generals Michael Farley, Jonathan Titcomb and Timothy Danielson, Colonel Moses Little, Major Samuel Osgood, James Prescot, Esquire and the Hon. William Sever and Francis Dana, Esquire of the Council.[22]

On October 7, the court of inquiry issued its conclusions, finding that the destruction of the fleet was the result of Saltonstall "not exerting himself at all at the time of the retreat in opposing the enemy's foremost ships in pursuit" and blamed the failure on "want of proper spirit and energy on the part of the Commodore" and on Saltonstall's failure to engage the British naval forces early on, before reinforcements arrived. The investigation exonerated Generals Lovell and Wadsworth. Since Saltonstall was under orders to the Continental Congress and not Massachusetts, Saltonstall was tried by a court martial on September 28, 1779, aboard the 32-gun frigate *Deane* in Boston Harbor and was found guilty and dismissed from the navy.

Saltonstall returned to Connecticut and, financed by Adam Babcock, a relative of his wife, he converted a merchant ship into a privateer, the 16-gun brigantine *Minerva* and set out to sea again on May 21, 1781, as her captain. Within a month, he took the 10-gun *Arbuthnot* with a cargo of tobacco and the 16-gun *Hannah* with a cargo worth 80,000 pounds, the most valuable prize captured by a Connecticut ship during the war. After the war, he carried cargos of African slaves in the West Indies, where he died of a "tropical disease" in 1796.

Revere had returned to Boston on the 26th of August, weeks before Saltonstall, and he was the subject of gossip and rumors regarding his part in the fiasco, much of it based on a letter of Captain Todd who quoted Lovell as being "surprised at Col. Revere's inattention to his duty." Todd and Revere had previously had confrontations at Castle William. No official action was taken however and Revere resumed command of Castle (Fort) William on August 27.

Ten days later, Thomas Jenness Carnes, a captain of Marines aboard the *General Putnam*, a warship of the Penobscot Expedition, filed a formal complaint with the council regarding Revere's conduct, alleging;

> First For disobedience of orders from General Lovell in two Instances, Viz: When ordered to go on shore with two Eighteen pounders, One twelve, One four & One Howitzer, Excused himself.
> Second When ordered by Major Todd at the Retreat to go with his Men and take said Cannon from the Island, Refused, and said his orders was to be under the Command of Gen Lovell, during the Expedition to Penobscot; & that the Siege was raised, he did not consider himself under his Command.
> Thirdly For neglect of Duty in Several instances
> Fourthly For unsoldierlike behavior, During the whole expedition to Penobscot, which tends to Cowardice
> Fifthly For Refusing Gen. Wadsworth, the Castle Barge to fetch some men on shore from a Schooner, which was near the Enemy s ships on the Retreat up the River
> Sixthly For leaving his men and suffering them to disperse and taking no manner of Care of them
> T. J. Carnes. Sept 6. 1779.[23]

That same day, Revere was relieved of command of Castle William, and was placed under house arrest until the matter was investigated or "he be discharged by the General Assembly or Council." Released after three days, Revere actively sought a court-martial to clear his name and reputation. In a letter to the council dated September 9, he wrote: "Were I conscious that I had omitted doing any one thing to Reduce the Enemy, either thro fear, or by willful opposition, I would not wish for a single advocate. I beg your Honors, that in a proper time, there may be a strict enquiry into my conduct where I may meet my accusers face to face."[24]

In a second letter to the council, Revere attributed his difficulties to the malice and falsehoods spread by former officers in his regiment: "Your Honors must remember the difficulties that arose in our Regiment the last February when it was reduced to three Companies. Because I accepted the command (which was by desire of the Council) and did all in my power to hinder the men from deserting, and because I did not give up my Commission in the same way the others did, some of them propagated every falsehood malice could invent." Captain Todd had entered a complaint earlier alleging that Revere had drawn rations for more men then he was entitled to, charges that were never substantiated. In the same letter, Revere made a thorough and methodical defense of his actions at Penobscot.

The report of the Council's court of inquiry on October 7 was confined to assigning responsibility for the failure of the expedition, placing the blame fully on Saltonstall. This is not surprising when one considers that Saltonstall, an officer of the Continental Navy, was found responsible while Generals Lovell and Wadsworth, both officers of the Massachusetts militia, were both found blameless. No mention was made of Lt. Col. Revere.[25]

Revere was not satisfied by the report which had neither condemned nor acquitted his actions. Feeling his reputation had been unfairly maligned, he again wrote the Council on October 9 asking that either the court reconvene, or that a court-martial be constituted to try the charges against him. He urged expedience, as many witnesses were due to put to sea and would not be available. The House and Council complied and ordered the court of inquiry to reconvene, which it did on November 11. The committee re-examined Revere's actions and on November 16 reported to the Council:

> The Committee of both Houses appointed to make inquiry into the conduct of the officers of Train, and the Militia officers, employed in the late Expedition to Penobscot, have attended the Service assigned them; and the Opinion of your Committee on the subject mater will fully appear by the following questions and answers thereto;

1. Was Lt. Col. Paul Revere crityzable for any of his conduct during his stay at Bagaduce, or while he was in, or upon the River Penobscot? Answer. Yes.
2. What part of Lt. Col. Revere's conduct was critqzable? Answer. In disputing the orders of Brigadier General Wadsworth respecting the Boat; and in saying that the Brigadier had no right to command him or his boat.
3. Was Lt. Col. Paul Revere's conduct justifiable in leaving River Penobscot, and repairing to Boston, with his men, without particular orders from his Superior officer? Answer. No, not wholly justifiable.
4. Does anything appear in Evidence to the disadvantage of any Militia Officers during the Expedition to Penobscot? Answer. No. Excepting Col. Jonathan Mitchel, who by his own confession left the River Penobscot without leave from any Superior officer; and returned to North Yarmouth the place of his habitation.
All which is humbly Submitted. Artemas Ward[26]

If Revere was unhappy about the first court's findings, he was certainly less happy with the second court's conclusions, and on January 17, 1780, he wrote the Massachusetts State Council demanding a regular court-martial:

> Twice I have petitioned your Honors, and once the House of Representatives, for a Court Martial but have not obtained one. I believe that neither the Annals of America or Old England, can furnish an Instance (except in despotic reign) where an officer was put under an arrest and he petitioned for a trial (although the arrest was taken off) that it was not granted. The complaint …will remain an everlasting monument of my disgrace if I do not prove they are false; is there any legal way to prove them false, than by a Court-Martial?[27]

Ignored, Revere again requested a trial on March 9, 1780, and on April 13, his request for a court-martial was granted, and the court, presided over by Col. Edward Proctor, was ordered to sit on the 18th at the County Courthouse, Boston, but for unknown reasons, the court was never convened. Clearly frustrated, Revere again petitioned the Council on January 22, 1781, complaining, "Your Petitioner petitioned the Hon. Council and House of Representatives six different times between the 6th of Sept. 1779, and the 8th of March 1780, for a trial by a Court-Martial, but did not obtain one, till about a fortnight before the time expired for which said Corps was raised.... Your Petitioner therefore most earnestly Prays this Hon. Assembly, to … order either a Court-Martial, or a number of Officers … properly qualified, who may enquire into his conduct on said expedition, and report."[28]

Revere was again disappointed when the petition was held over to the following session, but finally, on February 19, 1782, a second court-martial was ordered with Brigadier General Wareham Park appointed president and Joshua Thomas as judge-advocate, with a court consisting of twelve captains. The charges were reduced to two:

1. For his refusing to deliver a certain Boat to the Order of General Wadsworth when upon the retreat up Penobscot River from Major Bagwaduce
2. For his leaving Penobscot River without Order from his Commanding Officer.

Upon reviewing the evidence, the court issued the following judgment:

1. The Court finds the first charge against Lt Col. Paul Revere to be supported (to wit) "his refusing to deliver a certain boat to the order of Gen. Wadsworth when upon the retreat up Penobscot River from Major Bagwaduce." But the court taking into consideration the suddenness of the refusal, and more especially, that the same boat was in fact employed by Lt. Col. Revere to effect the purpose ordered by the General as appears by the General's deposition, are of the opinion, that Lt. Col. Paul Revere be acquitted of this charge.
2. On the second charge, the Court considering that the whole Army was in great confusion, and so scattered and dispersed, that no regular orders were or could be given, are of opinion, that Lt. Col. Revere, be acquitted with equal honor as the other officers in the same expedition.

The findings of the court were officially approved by the President of the Council, John Hancock. After a three-year struggle, Revere had his vindication.

In the economic depression that followed the war, Revere found difficulty in making a living as a silversmith, and opened a hardware and home goods shop, then opened an iron and brass foundry in Boston's North End in 1788. In 1801, Revere was a pioneer in producing copper plating and the company he founded, the Revere Copper Company, is still in operation. He died at home at the age of 83 on May 10, 1818, and is buried in the Old Granary Burying Ground on Tremont Street in Boston.

3

Commander Alexander Slidell Mackenzie

Murder, Illegal Punishment—1842

> *I learn, Mr. Spencer, that you aspire to command of the* Somers.—
> Commander Mackenzie to Acting Midshipman Phillip Spencer
> aboard the USS *Somers*, August 26, 1842

On December 1, 1842, three sailors of the United States Navy were hung at sea aboard the USS *Somers* for mutiny, without the benefit of a trial. The resulting public outrage would lead to the court-martial of a 27-year veteran officer for murder and would indirectly lead to the creation of the U.S. Naval Academy at Annapolis, Maryland, on October 10, 1845.

In the early years of the American republic, there was no training school for naval officers, and young men, mostly teenagers, were commissioned as midshipman (student officers) and trained in nautical skills through on-the-job training aboard sea-going warships.

On May 7, 1842, Commander Alexander Slidell Mackenzie was given command of the soon-to-be-commissioned USS *Somers* at the Brooklyn Navy Yard in New York. The ship was launched on April 16 and commissioned on May 12, 1842. The *Somers* was a brig, 100 feet in length with a 25-foot beam, which displaced 259 tons and the ship operated as a training ship for midshipmen. Armed with ten 32-pound carronades, short, smoothbore cannons, she carried a crew of 120 officers and men.[1]

Alexander Slidell, who added the name Mackenzie in 1832 to please a maternal uncle, was born in New York City on April 6, 1803, and was from a large family that included older siblings Thomas Slidell (later chief justice of Louisiana's state supreme court), John Slidell (later U.S. senator from Louisiana), and Jane Slidell (later the wife of Commodore Matthew C. Perry, brother of Oliver Hazard Perry).

He was commissioned a midshipman in January 1815, at the age of eleven. To improve his seamanship, he took command of a merchant vessel in 1822. Promoted to lieutenant in January 1825 and commander in September 1841, he saw active service combating pirates in the West Indies, the Mediterranean, and the West Indies and was in command of the USS *Dolphin* off the Brazilian coast 1838–1839. In 1842, he transferred to the *Somers*.

Mackenzie was an author of some renown and wrote several books, including biographies of John Paul Jones (2 vols., 1841), Commodore Oliver Perry (2 vols., 1841) and Commodore Stephen Decatur (1846). He later served as an emissary to Mexico for President Polk and served in the War with Mexico as an ordnance officer during the siege of Veracruz and was one of only two naval officers to receive its surrender on March 27, 1847. He then commanded a division of artillery in the second storming of Tabasco on June 15. He died in Tarrytown, New York, shortly after the end of the war on September 13, 1848.[2]

His two sons also rose to some prominence in the military. Ranald Slidell graduated from West Point in 1862 and served valiantly in the Civil War, rising to the rank of major general. His other son, Alexander Slidell, served as a naval officer during the Civil War. He rose to the rank of lieutenant commander and lost his life leading a charge against natives at Formosa, China, on June 13, 1867.

The *Somers* went on a shakedown cruise to Puerto Rico and back between June and July 1842, then departed New York Harbor on September 13 on her maiden voyage to the Atlantic coast of Africa. Her mission was to carry dispatches and deliver them to the frigate USS *Vandalia*. Along on the voyage was a nineteen-year-old midshipman, Philip Spencer.

Spencer was born to a prosperous family at Canandaigua, New York, on January 28, 1823, and was described by contemporaries as handsome with high intelligence, but also wild and uncontrollable with a fondness for pirate stories. He spent three years (1838–40) at Geneva (now Hobart) College in New York, quit, then briefly attended Union College before leaving school for the sea, running away to sign aboard a whaler at Nantucket, Massachusetts. Located by his father, Secretary of War John C. Spencer, he was persuaded that life at sea would be better as an officer and gentleman in the U.S. Navy, and in November of 1841, Spencer Sr. procured a commission for his son as an acting midshipman.

Assigned to the USS *North Carolina*, a 74-gun ship of the line, he twice assaulted a superior officer while under the influence of alcohol. He was reassigned to the USS *John Adams* and sailed for Brazil in June 1842, but his involvement in a drunken brawl with a Royal Navy officer while on shore leave in Rio de Janeiro led to his resignation rather than face a court-martial. He returned to the United States aboard the USS *Potomac*, arriving on July 31. Most likely due to his father's influence, Spencer's resignation was not accepted and he was ordered to report aboard the *Somers* on August 13, 1842.[3]

After departing New York, the *Somers* made port calls at Madiera, Portugal, Tenerife, Spain and Praia, Cape Verde before arriving at Monrovia, Liberia, on November 10. Finding that the *Vandalia* had already departed, the *Somers* made sail the following day, November 11, for St. Thomas in the Virgin Islands in the hope of catching up with the *Vandalia*.

As the voyage progressed, the officers noticed morale was low and heard rumors of discontent among the crew. On the evening of August 25, Midshipman Spencer approached purser's steward J.W. Wales and invited him to join him on the booms, where they could converse without being overheard. After having Wales take an oath of secrecy, Spencer revealed that there was a plan, supported by approximately 20 members of the crew, to take control of the ship. Rising in the night, they would throw the officer of the watch overboard, murder the remainder of the officers and any who opposed them and sail in Spanish waters as pirates, "robbing the defenseless, ravishing the females, and murdering the men he might overcome." Also involved in the conversation was Seaman Elisha Small, who threatened Wales with death if he revealed the plan to anyone.[4]

On the morning of November 26, Wales reported the conversation up the chain of command to Purser H. M. Heiskill, who in turn reported it to the first mate, First Lieutenant Guert Gansevoort, the only other commissioned officer aboard besides the captain. Already a 19-year veteran of the navy in 1842, Gansevoort commanded the USS *Roanoke* during the Civil War, and retired afterwards with the rank of rear admiral. His first cousin, Herman Melville, would use elements of the *Somers* story when writing the novel *Billy Budd*.

Gansevoort reported the matter to Commander Mackenzie who ordered him to keep a close but discreet watch on Spencer. During the day, Spencer was observed examining a chart of the West Indies, asking about the error rate on a chronometer (necessary for accurate celestial navigation), asking questions about the Isle of Pines, a notorious haunt for Caribbean pirates, and sketching a sailing ship flying a black flag.[5]

Upon Gansevoort's report, Mackenzie had Spencer brought to his cabin where he confronted Spencer with plotting a mutiny. Spencer replied it was a "joke." Mackenzie, not amused, ordered Spencer placed in chains, under guard on the quarterdeck.

A search made of Spencer's locker revealed a list of names of the crew in Greek lettering, and divided into columns labeled "certain," "doubtful" and "Nolens Volens" (unwilling-willing, i.e., undecided). The list was deciphered by Henry Rodgers, a midshipman who spoke Greek. Among those listed as certain were Spencer, Wales, D. McKinley, and E. Andrews (believed to be Samuel Cromwell).

The following day, Sunday, November 27, while the crew was aloft in the masts hoisting the sails, a topgallant mast failed and rigging was damaged. Suspecting sabotage, possibly as a diversion to free Spencer, Boatswains Mate Samuel Cromwell was questioned and he implicated Seaman Small, and both joined Spencer in chains on the quarterdeck.

Later that evening, a number of crewmen rushed onto the quarterdeck as a new topgallant mast was being hoisted into place, and again suspecting an attempt to free the prisoners, Lt. Gansevoort pulled a colt revolver and pointed it at Seaman Charles Wilson, until Midshipman Rodgers moved the men aft.

On November 28, wardroom steward Henry Waltham was flogged for stealing brandy to give to Spencer, after which Mackenzie advised the crew of the plot by Spencer to seize the ship and murder the loyal crewmen.

The following day, two men, Landsmen Mckinley and Apprentice Green missed muster and failed to show up for their watch, and two others, Sailmaker Charles A. Wilson and Apprentice Alexander Mckee, were caught attempting to access the weapons locker. All four were placed in chains on the quarterdeck, bringing the total number of crew under arrest to seven. Mackenzie had inadequate resources to secure the men and felt a growing concern for the safety of the ship.

On November 30, after arming the petty officers with pistol and cutlass, Mackenzie convened a panel of ship's officers, to include Lt. Gansevoort, Asst. Surgeon L.W. Leecock, Purser Heiskill, Acting Master Matthew Calbraith Perry, and three senior midshipmen, Henry Rodgers, Egbert Thompson and Charles W. Hayes, and asked their advice on the best way to proceed. They spent November 29 and 30 interviewing the ship's company, then submitted their recommendation in writing on the evening of November 30.

The document, dated December 1 read:

Sir: In answer to your letter of yesterday, requesting our counsel as to the best course to be pursued with the prisoners, Acting-Midshipman Philip Spencer, Boatswain's Mate Samuel Cromwell, and Seaman Elisha Small, we would state that the evidence which has come to our knowledge is of such a nature as, after as dispassionate and deliberate a consideration of the case as the exigencies of the time would admit, we have come to a cool, decided, and unanimous opinion that they have been guilty of a full and determined intention to commit a mutiny on board of this vessel of a most atrocious nature; and that the revelation of circumstances having made it necessary to confine others with them, the uncertainty as to what extent they are leagued with others still at large, the impossibility of guarding against the contingencies which "a day or an hour may bring forth," we are convinced that it would be impossible to carry them to the United States, and that the safety of the public property, the lives of ourselves, and of those committed to our charge, require that (giving them a sufficient time to prepare) they should be put to death in a manner best calculated as an example to make a beneficial impression upon the disaffected. This opinion we give, bearing in mind our duty to God, our country, and to the service.[6]

The decision was unanimous, and so advised, Mackenzie made the decision to hang the men the afternoon of December 1, and the prisoners were so advised. On that date, at 1:45 p.m., the crew was assembled on deck, and the condemned men were brought forward. The charges were read and the defendants were secured to ropes hoisted over the ship's yardarm. At 2:15 p.m., the condemned were hoisted aloft underneath the ship's ensign (flag) and all hands were ordered to give three cheers as a salute to the flag. The three men were left hanging until 3:30 p.m., and then lowered and their bodies turned over to shipmates to be prepared for burial. That evening, they were buried at sea.

Mackenzie was later criticized for not returning with the three men to the United States for courts-martial, as at the time of the hanging, the ship was only thirteen days distant from its home port, but Mackenzie cited the lack of facilities to confine the mutineers, the lack of personnel to guard them, the fatigue of the crew and his fear for the safety of his ship.

The *Somers* landed at St. Thomas, Dutch Virgin Islands, on December 5, and then returned to New York on December 15. Mackenzie had already sent a report of the incident ahead, when he was in St. Thomas, in case the brig never arrived in New York. Upon landing in New York, he sent a second report with his clerk, Oliver Hazard Perry, Jr., to Washington, D.C. He also arrested eight additional crewmen: Apprentices Goldenham, Hamilton, Kneavels, Sullivan, Warner and Van Velzer and Seamen Galia and Wiltham who at 23 years was the oldest of the group. Along with the other four under arrest, the group of twelve was taken aboard the warship USS

North Carolina for confinement. Mackenzie wrote a third report on December 19, consisting of some 13,000 words which would serve as the basis for his defense later on.

The hanging death of the son of the Secretary of War for the first mutiny aboard ship in the history of the U.S. Navy was not something to go unnoticed and Secretary of the Navy Abel P. Upshur ordered a court of inquiry to be convened on December 28, 1842, to both investigate the affair and report its opinion as to the propriety of the captain's actions. The court was composed of Commodore Jacob Jones, Commander of all Navy vessels in New York, Commodore A.J. Dallas, Commander of the Pensacola Navy Yard, and Captain Charles Steward, Commander of the Home Squadron. The Judge Advocate was the Hon. Ogden Hoffman, U.S. Attorney for the Southern District of New York.

On January 20, 1843, Mackenzie was unanimously exonerated of all blame in the matter; however, the court had no legal standing and Mackenzie requested, and was granted, a court martial. This might have been done to avoid a civil trial which Spencer Sr., and the families of the other two sailors were pressing for. On January 23, Mackenzie was formally charged with murder, oppression, illegal punishment, conduct unbecoming an officer and oppression of the brig's company.

Mackenzie's legal difficulty was this; in 1800, Congress enacted the "Act for the Better Government of the Navy" which enumerated certain punishments that could/must be punishable by death upon conviction by a court martial. Article 13 provided that "If any person in the Navy shall make or attempt to make any mutinous assembly he shall, on conviction thereof by a court martial, suffer death." The key was "upon conviction by a court martial." No court martial was, or could have been, convened aboard the *Somers* because there were not a sufficient number of officers aboard to constitute a court.[7]

The meeting in the wardroom called by Commander Mackenzie wasn't a court martial and didn't offer the most basic constitutional protections. Witnesses were not sworn and the accused were not allowed to be represented by counsel, nor were they afforded an opportunity to confront and cross-examine the witnesses against them.

Mackenzie's court martial opened on January 28, 1843. A panel of officers was convened, consisting of Captains John Downes, George C. Read, William C. Bolton, Daniel Turner, John D. Sloat, Joseph Smith, Isaac McKeever, John Gwinn, Thomas W. Wyman, George W. Storer, and Benjamin Page; and Commanders Henry W. Ogden and Irvine Shubrick. Captain Smith was later excused for poor health. The Judge Advocate was

William H. Norris, Esq. of Baltimore. Mackenzie represented himself and pleaded not guilty to all charges.

The fact that Mackenzie ordered the execution of the three seamen was never in question and he openly admitted giving the order, but he argued that the executions were proper given the circumstances and "justified by necessity." He acknowledged that he had lacked the resources (officers) for a court martial and that he lacked authority to inflict death as a punishment without a court martial.

However under the laws in effect, a commander had the right, *and the duty*, to use deadly force in suppressing an actual mutiny, and Mackenzie argued that the executions were necessary to prevent against further mutiny.

To support his argument, Mackenzie quoted a letter from Gen. George Washington to the Hon. John Laurens, Esq. dated January 30, 1781, when in referring to a revolt among New Jersey troops, he wrote: "I did not hesitate a moment, upon the report of it, in determining to bring matters to a speedy issue by adopting the most vigorous exertions; accordingly a detachment marched from the posts below, and on the morning of the 27th surrounded their quarters, and brought them, without opposition, to unconditional submission. Two of the principal leaders were immediately executed on the spot."[8]

Critics argued as to whether the actions of Spencer and the others could reasonably be considered as mutinous. No overt acts to take over the ship occurred, and while some words might have been seditious, some events like the broken mast, or the rush by the men to the quarterdeck, were ambiguous at best, and might have been misunderstood. Does sketching a ship with a black flag constitute mutiny?

If a mutiny was indeed imminent, and the executions were necessary to suppress it, then Commander Mackenzie was within his rights and duty, and his actions were justifiable. For several weeks the court interviewed crewmen and other witnesses. On March 31, the court issued its findings. It concluded that the charges and specifications were not proven, but the decision wasn't unanimous. On the charge of murder, nine of twelve voted to acquit. On the charge of oppression, eight voted to acquit versus four in favor of a conviction, and all twelve voted for acquittal on the charge of illegal punishment. The fourth and fifth charges were abandoned (dropped). Perhaps to assuage the powerful Secretary of War, the findings were simply "confirmed and carried into effect without any expression of approbation."

Although Cromwell's widow and Spencer's father attempted to have Mackenzie and Gansevoort indicted in U.S. District Court for murder, they were unsuccessful because once acquitted by court martial, Mackenzie was prevented from further prosecution under the U.S. Constitution's 5th Amendment prohibition against double jeopardy.

Prior to the verdict in the court martial, Lt. John West assumed command of the *Somers* on March 20, 1843. For the next three years, the *Somers* patrolled the Atlantic seaboard and the West Indies, assigned to the Home Squadron. She served blockade duty during the Mexican-American War under the command of Lt. Raphael Semmes, later of the Confederate Navy in command of the commerce raider CSS *Alabama*.

On one notable occasion, while assigned to the blockade of Veracruz, the *Somers* boarded and captured the Mexican schooner *Criolla*, but calm winds prevented the crew from sailing their prize out to sea, so they set the ship afire, and returned to the *Somers* with seven prisoners. Only later did they learn that the *Criolla* was a U.S. spy ship operating under the orders of Commodore David Conner.[9]

On December 8, 1846, while chasing a blockade runner off Veracruz, the *Somers* capsized and sank with the loss of 32 crewmen. Semmes and six others were captured by the Mexicans. The U.S. Navy has since commissioned four other USS *Somers*, all destroyers.

The *Somers* affair was the last instance of an execution aboard a U.S. Naval warship.

4

Capt. John Patrick Reily

DESERTION—1848

> *Bring the damned son of a bitch out! My order was to hang 30 and by God I'll do it!*—Col. William S. Harney, upon being told by the medical officer that one of the condemned San Patricio prisoners, Francis O'Connor, had had both legs amputated the previous day.

On 2 October 1835, in the Mexican state of Tejas, the northernmost province of Mexico, a rebellion broke out in the town of Gonzales, beginning a fight for independence that culminated with the signing by General Santa Anna of the treaty of Velasco, Texan independence, and the creation of the Republic of Texas, on 21 April 1836. The Mexican government, however, refused to recognize the treaty. As early as 1837, Texas sought annexation by the United States, but fear over a war with Mexico and northern concerns over the addition of another slave state kept the American Congress from approving the union. Finally, on 29 December 1845, after more than nine years of conflict between Texas and Mexico and debates in Congress, Texas was formally admitted into the United States. The annexation of Texas put a strain on relations between the United States and Mexico, made worse by the lack of agreement on the location of the border between Texas and Mexico. The United States claimed the border as the Rio Grande, while Mexico maintained that the border was the Nueces River, approximately 150 miles to the north.

After taking office on 1 March 1845, President James K. Polk sent an agent, John Slidell, to Mexico City in November to meet with Mexican officials. Slidell was authorized to offer Mexico $25 million dollars for California and New Mexico, on the condition that Mexico accept the Rio Grande as the border of Texas. In exchange, the United States would assume Mexico's debts to U.S. citizens. Mexican officials refused to meet with Slidell. On 4 January 1846, Mariano Parades y Arrillaga, a Centralist leader who desired war with the United States in order to regain Texas, overthrew President Jose Joaquin Herrera and ordered Slidell to leave Mexico. Hoping to provoke Mexico into declaring war, Polk ordered Gen. Zachary Taylor to take an army of 3,500 men (almost half of the entire U.S. regular army) that had been assembled in Corpus Christi, Texas, and move south across the Nueces River into the disputed territory.[1]

A large part of Taylor's forces—indeed, a large proportion of the American army at the time—was made up of foreign-born immigrants, mainly Catholics from Ireland and Germany. Located mostly in the eastern and northern cities, immigrants, especially Catholics, were discriminated against by nativists. An anti–Catholic, anti-immigrant political party, the "Know Nothings," was formed, and immigrants, in part to escape the violence in the cities, joined the army in large numbers. They found conditions little better in the army and were often subjected to harsh discipline for minor offenses.[2]

Taylor's army arrived at Santa Isabel, Texas, on 25 March, causing panic among its Mexican inhabitants, then proceeded south to the mouth of the Rio Grande, across from Matamoros, Mexico, on 28 March 1846. The army began construction of an earthworks fortress they nicknamed Fort Texas. Avoiding a direct confrontation, Mexican authorities began a propaganda campaign aimed at creating dissention in the ranks of the American army, appealing to immigrant and Catholic soldiers to desert.

The first proclamation was issued on 2 April by Gen. Pedro de Ampudia, the commanding general of Mexican forces in Matamoros. Written in English, it appealed to soldiers of English and Irish birth to resist American aggression. It cited the threatened seizure by the United States of the Oregon country, a territory both countries laid claim to. They saw it as similar to America's annexation of Texas, which had been Mexican territory. It also appealed to soldiers of German, French, and Polish birth to cross the lines and fight for their shared "sacred imperiled religion." The proclamation concluded by offering good treatment and paid passage to Mexico City for those who deserted.[3] A second proclamation, this one by Gen. Don Mariano Arista, who replaced General Ampudia as commander, was circulated on 21 April urging English and Irish soldiers to battle the "Protestant tyrants" who sought to destroy Catholicism. It offered 320 acres of land and Mexican citizenship to all privates who deserted, more for deserters of higher rank, and additional bounties for bringing along others.[4]

Desertion was not uncommon in the armies of the nineteenth century. Many of the foreign-born soldiers who deserted from the American army had previously deserted from the British and other European armies. Of the 31,000 regulars in service during the Mexican War, 2,850 deserted, and of 59,000 volunteers, mainly southern militiamen, 3,900 deserted—the highest rate of desertion for any U.S. war. Unlike the regulars, few if any volunteers defected to the Mexican army.[5] For many Irish immigrant soldiers serving in the regular army, the idea of a Protestant nation seizing the lands of its Catholic neighbor was not an unfamiliar one, and a surprisingly large number began to desert even before war was declared. One of these was an Irish sergeant named John Patrick Reily.

John Patrick Reily (aka O'Riley, Reilly, and O'Rily) was born Seán O'Raghailligh in Clifden, County Galway, Ireland, around 1805. An article in the *Niles National Register*, a weekly newspaper published from 1811 until 1849, described "Ryley" on 9 October 1847 as "a man of very large frame, more than six feet high" and as a "sergeant in the 66th regiment of the British army, stationed in Canada, from which he deserted." He crossed into Michigan in September 1845 and enlisted in the U.S. Army, where it is rumored, he served as a drillmaster at West Point before joining K Company, 5th U.S. Infantry.

Reily was by all accounts an able soldier, skilled in the use of artillery, and a competent noncommissioned officer—but one who was better at enforcing discipline than at taking it. After receiving a reprimand for disobedience of orders, and possibly a demotion to private, Reily requested a pass to attend Mass, crossed the Rio Grande, and deserted to the Mexicans. Thirty others also deserted. Their reasons varied from religion-based discrimination or mistreatment to opposition to the invasion or to the economic incentives offered by the Mexican government. Very few of the deserters were U.S. citizens.

On 4 April Reily led a number of deserters, dressed in their old U.S. uniforms, back across the Rio Grande, distributed proclamations encouraging desertions among the American troops. He repeated this action later that month. Impressed with his daring, General Arista promoted Reily to lieutenant and authorized him to raise a company among the foreign expatriates in Matamoros, including deserters from the U.S. Army.[6]

Reily recruited a company of volunteers numbering forty-eight, composed primarily of Irishmen and four *esclavos negroes* (escaped slaves). Included were at least five non-Irish deserters—Thomas Millet, Hezekiah Akes, John Hartley, Alexander McKee, and John Bowers—all from Battery H, 3rd U.S. Artillery. The men were still training with artillery when Arista announced that war had been declared against *"La Injusta Invasion Norteamericana."*

When General Arista replaced General Ampudia as commander of the Army of the North, he brought with him orders to attack the U.S. forces that had invaded Mexican territory. On 25 April, Mexican cavalry crossed the Rio Grande and ambushed a detachment of the 2nd U.S. Dragoons, commanded by Capt. Seth B. Thornton. Fourteen U.S. soldiers were killed and another seven wounded, including Thornton.[7] It was this skirmish to which President Polk referred in his war message to Congress on 11 May 1846, declaring that "American blood had been shed on American soil." Congress responded two days later, on 13 May, by voting to declare war on Mexico. Although many were enthusiastic, others saw the war as unjust aggression, including former president John Quincy Adams, the writer Henry David Thoreau, and Congressman Abraham Lincoln. Six more Americans lost their lives from an ambush near Point Isabel on 28 April. Mexican attacks struck Palo Alto, on 8 May, and at Resaca de la Palma, on 9 May; both were repulsed. Present during these battles was the Legion de Extranjeros (Legion of Foreigners), troops recruited from foreigners living in Mexico.[8]

Concurrently, from 3 May through 9 May, Mexican forces laid siege to Fort Texas. During this siege Reily and his troops manned artillery, targeting their former comrades. Ruddy in complexion, with red hair and sunburned skin, Reily's men earned the nickname *"Los Colorados Valientes"* (Red Heroes) for their valor in battle. However, General Arista lifted the siege and withdrew his forces to Monterrey.

Deserters continued to drift south over the summer, including soldiers from the 1st, 2nd, 3rd, and 4th U.S. Artillery; the 2nd, 3rd, 4th, 5th, 6th, 7th, and 8th U.S. Infantry Regiments; and the 2nd Dragoons. Many of these men joined up with Reily. In September 1846 the Saint Patrick's Battalion (Las Companias de San Patricio) was formed as an artillery battery, with the addition of the Legion de Extranjeros and additional deserters and expatriates. The force was called by the Americans "The Irish Deserters"—a misnomer. The unit comprised primarily Irish and German Catholics, but it included Canadians, Frenchmen, Englishmen, Italians, Poles, Scots, Spaniards, and Swiss immigrants, native Mexicans, and escaped slaves. Many of its men were neither Irish, nor deserters from the American army. The unit served as artillery for much of the war and kept its artillery pieces after being designated as infantry later.

Taylor advanced on Monterrey and gave battle on 21 September. For three days the fighting raged, and by all accounts the San Patricios performed brilliantly and valorously, defeating several assaults on the city with accurate and devastating fire before a withdrawal by the Mexican forces was ordered. It was in this battle, some sources state, that Reily was given his commission as a lieutenant. Regardless, after three days a cease-fire was worked out between Taylor and Arista.

After six weeks, an agreement was reached whereby Taylor took control of Monterrey and Arista's troops withdrew south with full military honors. Reily and the San Patricios retreated with the rest of the army to San Luis Potosí, where Gen. Antonio Lopez de Santa Anna, once again in command of Mexico's army, was mustering a large force and making plans to expel the *norteamericanos* from Mexico. It was also at San Luis Potosí that the San Patricios gained their famous banner. Sewn by the nuns of San Patricio, it was made of green silk, with "*Libertad por la Republica Mexicana*" (Liberty for the Mexican Republic) above a golden harp and the words "*Erin go Bragh*" (Ireland Forever) underneath.[9]

The San Patricios next fought at the battle of Buena Vista, on 23 February 1847, near Coahuila, an engagement known as the battle of Angostura in Mexico. The San Patricios were supplied with the army's heaviest cannons, eighteen- and twenty-four-pounders, and were trained under Lt. Ned McHerron (McHeran), formerly a sergeant in Battery G of the 4th U.S. Artillery. McHerron, a deeply religious man in his sixties, had deserted after witnessing the desecrations of Catholic churches, leaving behind a son, a sergeant, who refused to desert. His guns were positioned on the high ground overlooking the battlefield.[10]

Early in February, Santa Anna marched his army north across the

Banner of the San Patricios Battalion, with the words "*Erin go Bragh*" translated as "Ireland Forever" (Library of Congress).

desert, with rations and forage in short supply. Santa Anna's advance was observed by Capt. Ben McCulloch, of the Texas Rangers, and his force lost the element of surprise. Taylor deployed his 4,700-man army into defensive positions facing Santa Anna's force of 15,000.[11] As the battle opened, the San Patricios fired on U.S. forces with deadly accuracy as the Mexicans advanced. They broke up a charge by the 1st Dragoons, whom General Taylor had ordered to "take that damn battery!" They then targeted an artillery battery directly opposite their position—Battery D, 4th U.S. Artillery, under Lt. John Paul Jones O'Brien. Their accurate fire decimated the battery, silencing the unit's six-pounders, killing the horses, and wounding or killing most of the men, allowing troops under Gen. Manuel Lombardini to capture two intact pieces.[12]

Unable to dislodge the Americans, however, and taking heavy casualties, Santa Anna abruptly ordered a retreat, covered by the guns of the San Patricios, who repelled assaults and skirmished with two "flying batteries" under the command, respectively, of Capt. George Davis and Capt. Braxton Bragg. Suffering roughly one-third casualties, the San Patricios were later cited for bravery by Gen. Francisco Mejia; several members were awarded the War Cross. Reily was promoted to captain and was awarded the Angostura Cross of Honor.[13]

Following Buena Vista, the focus of the war shifted to the Gulf Coast, as Gen. Winfield Scott bombarded, then landed at, Veracruz with nine thousand troops and moved into the interior. The San Patricios were shifted south to Jalapa, where on 18 April 1847 they fought an effective holding action in the mountains during the battle of Cerro Gordo, again taking heavy casualties and adding to their fame. The attack on Cerro Gordo was led by units under Gen. William J. Worth. U.S. engineers, including Robert E. Lee, George B. McClellan, Joseph E. Johnston, and P. G. T. Beauregard, found a trail that allowed the Americans to envelop and rout Santa Anna's forces. Mexican losses during the battle were one thousand casualties and three thousand taken as prisoners, while American losses were sixty-four killed and 353 wounded. Again, the Mexicans were forced to retreat.[14]

In June 1847, Santa Anna created the Mexican Foreign Legion as part of the army. The San Patricios were redesignated as infantry and assigned to it (but retaining, as noted above, their field pieces). Known as the 1st and 2nd Militia Companies of San Patricio, they were commanded by Col. Francisco Moreno, with Captain Reily in command of the 1st Company and Capt. Santiago O'Leary of the 2nd Company. The two companies were often referred to as the "Foreign Legion of San Patricio."[15]

As Scott advanced his army west toward Mexico City, Santa Anna ordered Gen. Gabriel Valencia to take up defensive positions on the west side of the lava beds near the town of Contreras. Disobeying subsequent orders to retreat, Valencia engaged the Americans on 20 August and was outflanked, costing Santa Anna an opportunity to counterattack. Attacking from the rear, the Americans inflicted over one thousand casualties and captured eight hundred prisoners, two hundred artillery pieces, and a herd of mules. American losses were one hundred men. Santa Anna retreated to Churubusco, where he ordered Valencia shot.[16]

It was on 20 August 1847, during the battle of Churubusco, that the San Patricios went from heroes to legends. The road west from Contreras bottlenecked at a bridge over the Rio Churubusco, overlooked by the massive Convento (Monastery) de San Pablo. There Santa Anna ordered a delaying action by approximately 1,500 veteran troops, including the San Patricios, as the main army retreated to Mexico City. Surrounded by thick stone walls, the monastery was a natural defensive position, and artillery manned by the San Patricios was emplaced along the parapets. Other San Patricios placed guns at the bridgehead in support of two infantry companies, the Bravos and Independencias. They inflicted heavy casualties upon successive American assaults until they were outflanked by infantry under Franklin Pierce and were forced to withdraw to secondary positions inside the monastery.

Hopelessly surrounded, the defenders fought on until their supply of ammunition was expended, then fought hand to hand. When a Mexican officer tried to raise a white flag, it was torn down by Capt. Patrick Dalton, a San Patricio, and Gen. Pedro Anaya ordered his men to fight on. Eventually they were overcome by sheer numbers. Capt. James Smith of the 3rd U.S. Infantry, the first American officer inside the monastery, had a hard time preventing his troops from immediately bayoneting the deserters. Incredibly, Reily refused to surrender until he could present his sword to Gen. David Twiggs himself. Later, when asked by General Twiggs where his ammunition was stored, General Anaya replied, "If I had ammunition, you would not be here." A young lieutenant, Ulysses S. Grant, would later recall the battle as "the severest battle fought in the valley of Mexico.... [T]he gunners who stood their ground were deserters from General Taylor's Army on the Rio Grande."[17] Mexican losses were estimated at more than four thousand killed and wounded and more than 2,500 prisoners; by contrast, American losses were slightly more than one thousand. According to General Anaya's written report, thirty-five San Patricios were killed in action, eighty-five were taken prisoner, and another eighty-five managed to escape to rejoin the retreating Mexican army.

Seventy-two prisoners were charged with desertion. General Scott issued General Orders 259 and 263 on 22 August convening courts-martial at Tacubaya and San Angel.[18] None of the men were represented by counsel, nor were transcripts kept of the trials. Some of the defendants would claim, in what was a common defense at the time, that drunkenness had led them to desert. Others would testify that they had been kidnapped and forced to serve in the Mexican army, testimony that was impeached by other witnesses. Most either would offer no defense or offer defenses of which there is no record. In any event, desertion during time of war was punishable by death, and the men had all been found under arms and in the uniform of the enemy.[19]

Brevet Col. John Garland, who commanded a brigade under General Worth, convened the first court-martial, at Tacubaya at noon on 23 August 1847. (Garland, whose daughter had married Maj. James Longstreet in 1848, would remain loyal during the Civil War and serve briefly as a Union general before dying in New York City in mid–1861.) During the court-martial, forty-three deserters were brought before twelve officers sitting behind a long table. Colonel Garland served as president of the court. Col. Robert Buchanan of the 4th Infantry, a bigoted officer despised for his harsh discipline, served as both the trial judge advocate and the defense counsel and voted with the other twelve on the verdicts.[20]

Of the forty-three tried at Tabacuya, those who pled guilty were quickly sentenced to hang by their neck until dead. Thirty-seven pled not guilty, twenty-seven citing drunkenness, in hopes that a general order issued allowing drunks who had gone absent without leave back into the ranks would work in their favor. It didn't. Others claimed coercion, which was only slightly more successful. Buchanan called two prosecution witnesses, Englishman John Wilton, a former San Patricio sergeant, and Irishman Thomas O'Connor, a muleteer, who would testify that the defendants had served in the legion and fought against the Americans. The motivations of the two men, neither of whom was on trial for desertion, to testify against their former comrades has never been explained. The last man tried, Abraham Fitzpatrick, a former noncom in the infantry, was ordered shot by firing squad, in deference to his years of service. In all, forty-one men were tried, found guilty, and sentenced to death.

Col. Bennet Riley of the 2nd U.S. Infantry, an Irish Catholic officer, convened the second court-martial at San Angel on 26 August. Colonel Riley, a career army officer, had undergone his own court-martial, called at his own request, at Puebla on 28 July regarding his conduct at Cerro Gordo. The verdict had declared him "deserving of the highest praise" and had been affirmed by General Scott. (He would later serve as the last military governor of California before convening a constitutional convention at Monterey, California, in September 1849 and turning over executive power to the new state government. Fort Riley, Kansas, would be named in his honor.) Capt. Samuel Chase Ridgeley, a battery commander in the 4th U.S. Artillery, served as prosecutor at San Angel. Twenty-nine men, including John Reily, were sentenced to hang.[21]

In total, seventy of the seventy-two men charged with desertion were convicted and condemned to death, and the cases went to General Scott for his review. (Edward Ellis, a dragoon, was found to have been improperly enlisted, so could not technically have deserted. Lewis Preifer, or Pieper, who was mentally deficient, was also spared.) While the prisoners waited under guard in city warehouses, further attempts to negotiate a peace were under way. During those negotiations Santa Anna argued with President Polk's envoy that the San Patricios should be treated as prisoners of war. Scott received appeals for clemency for the San Patricios from the Archbishop of Mexico; from Charles Bankhead, the British minister to Mexico; and numerous foreign citizens living in Mexico City, including Americans. Scott assured all parties that he would carefully review the verdicts, with scrupulous fairness and in strict accordance with the rules of war and the enormity of the offenses.

Upon review, Scott upheld fifty of the death sentences, reduced the sentences of fifteen deserters, and issued five pardons. German immigrant Henry Neuer, who had served as a stretcher bearer, had never taken up arms and had risked his life to aid wounded American soldiers; he was pardoned and ordered returned to the 4th U.S. Artillery. Two soldiers, fifteen-year-old David McElroy and sixteen-year-old John Brooke, were spared because of their age. Abraham Fitzpatrick, formerly a sergeant in the 8th U.S. Infantry, was pardoned because of his "prior honorable service"; he was demoted to private and returned to his unit. Lieutenant McHerron was unconditionally pardoned because of the gallantry and "loyalty to the flag" his son had displayed during the war; he was ordered returned to his unit. (Ironically, McHerron's son, William, would desert on 1 February 1848, be rapidly caught, and be dismissed from the service on 21 August 1848.[22])

Scott accepted drunkenness or coercion as mitigating circumstances in the cases of nine soldiers: Hezekiah Akles, John Bartley, Alexander McKee, John Bowers, Roger Duhan, W. Thomas, John Daly, Thomas Cassady, and Martin Miles. Six men—John Reily, James Kelley, John Murphy, John Little, Thomas Riley, and John Mills—were found to have deserted the army prior to the declaration of war and thus not liable to execution under the Articles of War. The men whose sentences were reduced were ordered to be stripped to the waist and to "receive fifty lashes each on their naked backs, and to be branded with the letter D high up on the cheekbone, near the eye but without jeopardizing its sight." They were then to be "kept a close prisoner as long as the army remains in Mexico, and then to be drummed out of the service." They were also forced to wear spiked iron yokes.[23]

Just as some had beseeched Scott for Reily's life, now many, especially officers of the army, including Generals Twiggs and Worth, passionately argued to Scott that Reily should be hanged, "lest it [i.e., leniency] be attributed by the enemy to fear on our part" and produce "a more stubborn resistance and increase our difficulty in taking the city of Mexico." Captain Davis wrote, "It would be far preferable that every one of the rest of the condemned deserters should be pardoned rather than Riley should escape death." Scott listened politely but remained adamant that given the Articles of War, hanging the men "would be nothing less than judicial murder."[24]

On 8 September, Scott issued General Order No. 281, which confirmed twenty of the San Angel death sentences and ordered that they be carried out on 10 September, with General Twiggs in command. It rained throughout the night of the 9th, but stopped shortly before dawn. At 6:00 a.m. the condemned men were awakened and sixteen of them were bound and marched from the warehouse; the other four were left behind under guard. Reily and six others, also bound, accompanied the condemned men.

The men were marched to a park in San Jacinto Plaza, adjacent to the Catholic Church of San Angel, where a forty-foot-long gallows had been erected, with sixteen nooses dangling from the crossbeam. Several hundred soldiers were formed in ranks to witness the execution; numerous civilians were also present, including seven priests dressed in full vestments. Since no platform had been constructed, the men were placed two apiece in the beds of eight mule-drawn wagons.

Prior to the hangings, punishment was meted out to the seven men present whose death sentences had been commuted: John Reily, Thomas Riley, James Mills, Hezekiah Akles, John Bartley, Alexander McKee, and John Bowers. All were bound to trees and received fifty lashes from two Mexican muleteers wielding whips that, with six eighteen-inch-long knotted rawhide tails, left their backs looking like what one witness described as a "pounded piece of raw beef, the blood oozing from every stripe." The letter *D* was then branded on their cheeks with red-hot branding irons; the plaza was filled with the screams of the men and the smell of burning flesh. When it was discovered that the brand had been applied upside down on Reily, he was revived and branded a second time, correctly. The seven were now forced to dig the condemned men's graves.

Then, after last rites were administered by the priests, the eight mules were whipped forward, leaving the sixteen men hanging. All died quickly except for Capt. Patrick Dalton, whose noose, by accident or design, had been misapplied; he died slowly by strangulation. The four condemned men left behind were hanged the following day in Mixcoac. That same day, 11 September, Scott issued General Order No. 263, which confirmed the thirty death sentences issued at Tacubaya and ordered the sentences to be carried out at Mixcoac on 13 September, with Col. William S. Harney in command.

On 24 August Scott had granted an armistice of Tacubaya in order to permit negotiations for a peace treaty, but Santa Anna had used the time only to muster troops and fortify his defenses. On 7–8 September, Shortly before the executions, Scott, charging that Santa Anna had violated the truce, had renewed hostilities at Molino del Rey. The Americans forced the Mexican position and moved west toward the capital. The key to Mexico City's defense was the fortress at Chapultepec. At dawn of 13 September, as U.S. forces prepared to make the assault, Harney in Mixcoac, which was nearby, ordered the thirty condemned men brought forward. Harney pointed his sword at the embattled castle and told the men that at the moment the Stars and Stripes, "the flag you have dishonored," replaced the Eagle and Snake of the Mexican flag, they would die.

The men waited throughout the morning under the hot sun, hands tied and nooses around their necks. Despite a heroic defense by teenage cadets of the Mexican Military College, the Mexican flag was finally lowered, and Lt. George Pickett raised the Stars and Stripes at 9:30 a.m. The condemned men gave a cheer that resounded across the valley—whether in defiance, remorse, or just relief that their torment was over will never be known. The signal was given, and thirty pairs of legs danced in the air.

The deserters whose sentences had been commuted were placed at hard labor for the remainder of the occupation. The sentences imposed on the San Patricios were met with outrage among the Mexican public. In

Opposite: **Memorial plaque dedicated to the soldiers of the San Patricios Battalion, which is on the wall of the former monastery at Churobuscomo in Mexico City. The inscription reads, "In memory of the Irish soldiers of the heroic San Patricio Battalion martyrs who gave their lives for the cause of Mexico in the unjust American invasions of 1847—With the gratitude of Mexico for 112 years of your sacrifice, September 10, 1959 (National Archives and Records Administration).**

Toluca, authorities narrowly prevented rioters from hanging American prisoners in retaliation. Although considered deserters and criminals in the United States, in Mexico the San Patricios were held as national heroes, and efforts were made to achieve their release.

Following the occupation of Mexico City by Scott's forces, Santa Anna resigned the presidency on September 16. He was forced to resign command of the army on 7 October, after which he fled the country. The new acting president, Pedro Maria Anaya, began negotiations with the American peace commissioner, Nicholas Trist, in November. The Treaty of Guadalupe Hidalgo was signed on the main altar of the old basilica of Guadalupe at Villa Hidalgo on 2 February 1848. According to the last issue of *The American Star*, the army newspaper, dated 30 May 1848, the San Patricios were taken to New Orleans and dishonorably discharged.[25]

As to the fate of the released San Patricios, an article in the 11 October 1848 edition of the *Niles National Register* reported, "We are informed that many of the San Patricio deserters are wandering about Vera Cruz in a state of extreme destitution, neither Americans nor Mexicans being willing to aid them." This is confirmed by other contemporary accounts.

As for Reily, the author Robert Ryal Miller, in his book, *Shamrock and Sword* (1989), reports finding the following death certificate in the Book of Burials in the cathedral of Veracruz: "On the thirty first of August of eighteen hundred and fifty, I, Don Ignacio Jose Jimenez, curate of the parish church of the Assumption of Our Lady, buried in the general cemetery the body of Juan Reley, of forty five years of age, a native of Ireland, unmarried, parents unknown; died as a result of drunkenness, without sacraments."[26]

The memory of the men of Saint Patrick's Battalion continues to be revered in Mexico. They are memorialized twice a year: on 12 September, the accepted anniversary of their execution, and on 17 March, Saint Patrick's Day.

5

Lambdin P. Milligan (Ex Parte Milligan)

CONSPIRACY, INCITING INSURRECTION—1864

> *We think that the power of Congress, in such times and in such localities [where ordinary law no longer adequately secures public safety] to authorize trials for crimes against the security and safety of the national forces, may be derived from its constitutional authority to raise and support armies and to declare war, if not from its constitutional authority to provide for governing the national forces.*—Ex Parte Milligan 71 U.S. 2 (1866)

At what point does opposition to a war become treason? In 1866, the fate of a man sentenced by a military commission in 1864 to hang for his plan to free Confederate prisoners and take over the government would decide the constitutionality of the wartime suspension of habeas corpus and clearly define the circumstances permitting the trial of civilians before military tribunals.

Lambdin Purdy Milligan was born on 24 March 1812 in Belmont County, Ohio, the oldest son of Moses Milligan, a Pennsylvanian, farmer, and veteran of the Revolutionary War. His mother was Mary Purdy, a Virginian. Although his formal education ended at the age of eight, he had a swift, sharp mind and left home at seventeen after his mother refused him permission to attend college. He went to work in a law office in St. Clairsville, the Belmont County seat, and educated himself in matters of the law. On 27 October 1835 he led his class of nine, including future secretary of war Edwin M. Stanton, in his law examinations, after which he was admitted to the bar of the supreme court of Ohio. Milligan married Sarah L. Ridgeway the same day he graduated in 1835. He raised three sons, moving the family to Huntington County, near Fort Wayne, Indiana, in 1845.[1]

A Presbyterian, Milligan remained with the "Old School" Presbyterians, who favored slavery when the denomination split over the issue in 1837. Though he preferred farming, ill health forced his return to the law in 1853. Hospitable, generous, and articulate, he became a prosperous attorney, representing the Wabash and Erie railroads in northeastern Indiana, and in the early 1850s he began to have political ambitions. A zealous Democrat who admired Jefferson and Jackson, he ardently believed in states' rights and became more fanatical as the clouds of civil war gathered in the east.[2]

Too outspoken to be successful as a politician, Milligan nonetheless publicly spoke out against the war, the Lincoln administration, Indiana governor Oliver P. Morton, and the Emancipation Proclamation. In the early part of the war, with events going poorly for the North, opposition to the war was seen there as disloyalty. On 24 September 1862, Lincoln issued a proclamation stating that "all Rebels and Insurgents, their aiders and abettors within the United States, and all persons discouraging volunteer enlistments, resisting militia drafts, or guilty of any disloyal practice ... shall be subject to martial law and liable to trial and punishment by Courts Martial or Military Commission."

At some point following Lincoln's Emancipation proclamation, Milligan's opposition to the war went from verbal to active.[3] Democrats in the North were angered by the proclamation, fearing that liberated blacks would flood into Ohio, Indiana, and Illinois. Although Democrats bore their share of sacrifice in holding the Union together, they were not necessarily aligned with the Republican administration's new goals of ending slavery and establishing a stronger central government. Additionally, high tariffs were enriching eastern industry while simultaneously injuring western agriculture, even as eastern bankers grew rich on war contracts. Some in the west spoke of creating a "Northwestern Confederacy," at a time when any expression of sympathy for the South or criticism of the war was seen as treason.

The government, unable to fill the army's ranks through enlistments, began conscription in the summer of 1862. By late 1862, Milligan was openly opposed to Indiana's participation in the war and spoke out publically discouraging enlistments, attracting the attention of federal agents. The subsequent investigation was to allege that on 1 October 1863 Milligan conspired with William A. Bowles, Andrew Humphreys, Stephen Horsey, Horrace Heffren, and other Indiana "copperheads" (as antiwar Democrats were known) to organize a secret society, the Order of American Knights (or Order of the Sons of Liberty), with members drawn in large part from an earlier, discredited group, Knights of the Golden Circle. Other conspirators identified by the government included Kentuckian Joshua F. Bullit and Missourian J. A. Battett, suggesting a broad northwestern involvement.[4]

Federal agents gathered evidence that the group was stockpiling arms and distributing them to individuals resisting the draft. A speech by Milligan at a meeting of Democrats in Fort Wayne on 13 August was monitored by a Mr. Bush, a federal detective. A critical report was sent to Governor Morton, who was then running for reelection. Morton resolved to have Milligan arrested.

On 20 August 1864, federal authorities raided the print shop of Harrison H. Dodd, Grand Commander of the Sons of Liberty in Indiana, and uncovered thirty-two crates labeled "Schoolbooks" filled with revolvers and ammunition. Dodd and a number of others were arrested. In September, the newly appointed military commander of the district of Indiana, Brevet Maj. Gen. Alvin P. Hovey, appointed a military commission of seven officers to try Dodd and "such other prisoners as may be brought before it." Hovey subsequently added another five officers to bring the number on the tribunal to twelve. The court consisted of Brevet Brig. Gen. Silas Colgrove as president of the court and Colonels William McLean, John T. Wilder, Thomas T. Lucas, Charles D. Murphy, Benjamin Spooner, Richard Dehart, Ambrose Stevens, Ansel D. Wass, Thomas W. Bennett, Reuben Williams, and Albert Heath. All except Wass were officers of the Indiana Volunteer Infantry.

Gen. Henry Carrington, who had been the military commander in Indiana when Dodd and the others were apprehended, favored trying them in civilian courts, but Governor Morton and Secretary of War Stanton, perhaps doubting the reliability of Indiana juries, favored a military trial, and Carrington was replaced by Hovey.

Pursuant to Special Order No. 129 dated 17 September, Dodd's trial began on 19 September, but he escaped from prison and fled to Canada while being tried. He was convicted in absentia and sentenced to death on 10 October.[5] On 5 October 1864, at 11:00 p.m., a company of soldiers under the command of a Captain Case and at the direction of General Hovey arrived by train at Huntington, surrounded Milligan's home, and, without warrant or affidavit, placed him under arrest. He was confined at his home until 4:00 a.m., when he was conveyed in secret to the railroad depot, and transported to Indianapolis. When the party arrived at 3:00 p.m. it was met by a large, hostile crowd. Milligan was confined in prison until charges were preferred by Maj. Henry L. Burnett, the judge advocate for the Northwest Military District.

On 21 October 1864, Milligan was brought before a twelve-officer military commission convened in Indianapolis by order of General Hovey. Milligan was accused of conspiring with four others—Bowles, Humphreys, Horsey, and Heffren—to steal Union weapons and invade a Union prisoner-of-war camp. It was alleged that they planned, after arming the freed Confederates, to liberate other camps, raise an army, and take over the state governments of Indiana, Ohio, and Michigan. When their plan was discovered, the men had been arrested.

The five were charged with:

- Conspiracy against the government of the United States
- Giving aid and comfort to rebels against the authority of the United States
- Inciting insurrection
- Disloyal practices
- Violation of the rules of war.

They pled not guilty. During the trial, Heffren agreed to testify for the prosecution, and charges against him were withdrawn. Fourteen prosecution witnesses testified that the accused were members of the Order of the Sons of Liberty and established that some, including Dodd, had been in communication with Confederate government representatives in Canada. There was testimony about plans to link up with Confederate guerrillas in Kentucky and take Louisville, and also to assassinate Governor Morton and seize the state government of Indiana.[6]

In early December, the commission found each of the defendants guilty on all charges and sentenced Bowles, Horsey, and Milligan to be hanged on 19 May 1865. Humphreys was sentenced to imprisonment at hard labor until the end of the war. General Hovey approved the sentences but commuted Humphrey's sentence and paroled him, stating that the evidence failed to show that he had taken an active role in inciting insurrection or aiding the conspiracy. Lincoln might have commuted the other sentences as well, but he was assassinated in April 1865, and his successor, Andrew Johnson, approved the executions for 19 May.

Once the proceedings of the military commission came to an end, the Circuit Court of the United States for Indiana met in Indianapolis on 2 January 1865 and empaneled a grand jury to inquire whether any laws of the United States had been violated. The grand jury found no bill of indictment and made no presentment against Milligan. The Circuit Court adjourned on 27 January, after discharging the grand jury.[7]

On 10 May 1865, Milligan and the others petitioned the Circuit Court of the United States for Indiana for a writ of habeas corpus asking to be discharged from unlawful imprisonment, arguing that as citizens of the United States and of Indiana, a state that was not and had never been in rebellion against the United States, they were entitled to a trial by jury, as a right guaranteed to them by the U.S. Constitution. Additionally, Milligan argued that a military tribunal lacked the jurisdiction to try him—since he was not, and had never been, a member of the military—upon the charges preferred or upon any charges whatsoever. Milligan's hope was either to have the charges dismissed or to be brought before a civilian court for trial.

Their case was heard by District Court Judge David McDonald and Justice David Davis of the U.S. Supreme Court. Unable to reach agreement on whether the writ should be issued, whether the petitioners should be discharged, or on the jurisdiction of the military commission in the case before them, they certified (referred) the case to the U.S. Supreme Court. In the interim, President Johnson, at the urging of Governor Morton, commuted the three sentences to life imprisonment at hard labor.

The case came before the U.S. Supreme Court on 5 March 1866 as Ex Parte Milligan. The question before the Court was whether the government in time of war could suspend a citizen's constitutional rights under the Fifth and Sixth Amendments and set up military courts in areas in which civilian courts were still operating.

The government was represented by James Speed of Kentucky (who had replaced Edward Bates as attorney general under President Lincoln), Benjamin Butler of Massachusetts (former general and future governor), and Henry Stanbery of Ohio (who would later serve as President Johnson's attorney general). The petitioners were represented by David Dudley Field of New York, a lawyer and the older brother of Justice Stephen Field; Jeremiah Black of Pennsylvania, a former Pennsylvania Supreme Court justice and attorney general under President Buchanan; and Rep. James A. Garfield, a former general, a sitting member of Congress, and future president of the United States. The written briefs submitted by both sides were unusually succinct by modern standards: eight pages for the petitioners and fifteen pages for the government. Oral arguments lasted six days, between 5 and 13 March 1866.

The government argued that military commissions were necessary during times of war and insurrection and that the executive authority during a war should be the "sole judge of the exigencies, necessities and duties of the occasion, their extent and duration" and that "during the war, his powers must be without limit." The government also argued that the men were prisoners of war and therefore not covered by the 1863 Habeas Corpus Act. Finally, it argued that even if the petitioners could not be tried by military commission, it had been proper and legal to hold them in military detention until the end of hostilities.[8]

The defense argued that a military commission had no jurisdiction in this case, as the petitioners were civilians in a state not in rebellion and in which the civil courts were functioning. Additionally, they argued, the petitioners had been denied due process in that the Fourth Amendment to the Constitution protected them from unreasonable search and seizure without probable cause to issue a warrant. Further, the Fifth Amendment declared that "no person shall be held to answer for a capital or otherwise infamous crime unless on presentment by a grand jury, except in cases arising in the land or naval forces, or in the militia." Finally, the Sixth Amendment guaranteed them the right to trial by jury.[9]

On 3 April 1866, the Court issued its decision. In a unanimous decision (nine to none) the Court held that the suspension of habeas corpus was lawful but that it was unconstitutional to try civilians in military courts when civilian courts were functioning, even in time of war. Justice Davis, in the majority decision, called the Constitution "a law for rulers and people, equally in time of war and peace." The Court further held that, absent prior congressional legislation, the president was not empowered to suspend habeas corpus or impose martial law even in time of war or insurrection and that when habeas corpus was suspended, citizens could only be held, not tried or executed, by military tribunals.

In a concurring opinion, Chief Justice Salmon P. Chase, joined by Associate Justices James Wayne, Noah H. Swayne, and Samuel F. Miller, argued that Congress had intended to ensure civil trials to civilians when it adopted the Habeas Corpus Act of 1863 and that therefore Milligan had been wrongly tried. He insisted, however, that Congress had the authority to enact martial law under its war powers, even in areas removed from the theater of war.

Davis, writing for the majority, wrote, "Martial law cannot arise from a threatened invasion. The necessity must be actual and present, the invasion real, such as effectually closes the courts and deposes the civil administration." The Constitution prohibited military trials of civilians where civil courts remained open. Martial law was permissible only, Davis insisted, in "the theater of active military operations," where civil courts could no longer function. Davis further asserted that neither the president nor the Congress could authorize the trial of civilians by military commission as long as the civil courts were open.

The Court's opinion was controversial. The petitioners were released from military custody on 10 April. By late 1866, violence against former slaves was increasing, but President Johnson used the *Milligan* decision as justification to reduce military authority in the occupied states, angering Republicans, who feared that the Court would declare unconstitutional the Reconstruction Act of 1867, which authorized military trial of civilians in the rebel states. Regardless, *Ex Parte Milligan* is seen as a landmark civil rights case, one in which civil liberty was protected from military authority.

6
Maj. Henry Wirz
War Crimes, Murder—1865

He would frequently give way to paroxysms of rage so violent as to verge closely on insanity.—Former Yankee prisoner describing Major Wirz

[It] is loose, indefinite, and for the most part, contradictory.—Wirz's attorney Louis Schade, describing testimony for the prosecution

This is too tight.—Last words of Capt. Henry Wirz prior to being hanged

Henry Wirz was not an easy man to like. Described as a "stooped frail fellow" with dark hair, hazel eyes, and a full black beard, he was foul-mouthed and short-tempered and displayed a nervous energy as he went about his duties. Following the Civil War, he was tried for war crimes as the commandant of Camp Sumter, commonly known as Andersonville; he was the only Confederate so charged. Demonized by the public, he came to personify all that was evil in the defeated Confederate states. He was executed for war crimes resulting from circumstances over which he had had little or no control. Nonetheless, it would be difficult to find a less sympathetic character.

Henry Wirz was born Heinrich Hartmann Wirz in Zurich, Switzerland, on 25 November 1823. Versions of his early life differ, and it is disputed whether he graduated from the University of Zurich and studied medicine at universities in Paris and Berlin. Though frequent in his use of profanity, Wirz was well educated; he was fluent in German and Dutch, as well as English, though he spoke it with a thick accent.[1]

Wirz began practicing medicine in Switzerland, married in 1845, and had two children before the death of his wife. In 1849 he left his two children, Paul and Louisa, with his parents to raise and immigrated to the United

States, possibly as a result of the failed revolution in the German states the previous year. After working briefly as a weaver in Lawrence, Massachusetts, Wirz moved to Hopkinsville, and later Cadiz, Kentucky, where he began to practice medicine.[2] In Cadiz Wirz married Elizabeth Wolfe, a well-to-do widow of good family and the mother of two young daughters, three-year-old Susan Jane and two-year-old Cornelia, on 27 May 1854. By all accounts, they had a strong marriage. A third daughter, Cora, was born on 25 February 1855.

Some sources allege that Wirz departed Kentucky over some scandal regarding his credentials, while others suggest that he as a Catholic foreigner he was unwelcome in the predominantly Anglo-Protestant community. He resettled in Milliken's Bend, in Madison Parrish, Louisiana, where Catholics were more welcome, and obtained work on the Marshall Plantation doctoring slaves. Since the importation of slaves had been banned in 1808 the price of slaves had risen dramatically, with the result that plantation owners were more willing to pay for their medical care. History is silent on how Wirz felt about his new patients, but at three dollars per slave per year, and with hundreds of slaves on the Marshall and neighboring plantations, Wirz led a prosperous life.

On 16 June 1861, following the outbreak of the Civil War in Charleston, South Carolina. Wirz enlisted as a private in the Madison Infantry, Company A, 4th Louisiana Battalion, at Richmond, Louisiana. The battalion, also known as the 4th Battalion Louisiana Infantry, was ordered to Richmond, Virginia, and then to guard sea-coast defenses along the South Carolina shores. The battalion was part of the force under Gen. Joseph E. Johnston that opposed the Union army's Peninsula Campaign and fought at the battle of Seven Pines, in Henrico County, Virginia, between 31 May and 1 June 1862. Known as the battle of Fair Oaks by Union troops, the engagement marked the culmination of Gen. George B. McClellan's advance on Richmond and the beginning of his retreat back across the James River following the Seven Days battles, 25 June–1 July. Losses for both sides at Seven Pines exceeded 11,000 killed and over 8,300 wounded.[3]

During the battle Wirz, now a sergeant, was severely wounded in the right arm by two Minié balls, which shattered the bone and left him with limited use of the arm. On 12 June 1862, after several weeks in the hospital, he returned to his unit and was promoted to captain for "bravery on the field of battle." Unfit for frontline duty, however, Wirz was detailed to the acting adjutant general, Gen. John Henry Winder.[4]

Winder, the son of Gen. William Henry Winder, who had been disastrously defeated by the British at the battle of Bladensburg during the War of 1812, had graduated from West Point in 1820. He then served on the western frontier and during the war with Mexico. He had resigned his commission as a major in the artillery in April 1861 to accept a commission as brigadier general in the Confederate army, which assigned him as provost marshal and commander of military prisons in Richmond, Virginia.[5]

After the First Battle of Bull Run, the capture of a large number of Union prisoners prompted the creation of a prisoner-of-war compound on Belle Isle, near Richmond. Located in the middle of the James River and surrounded by rapids, the compound was virtually impossible to escape, a fact attested by the number of would-be escapees who drowned. Designed for a population of three thousand to be housed in tents, the prison actually held almost twice that number when Captain Wirz assumed command on 26 August 1862. Because he had a limited number of guards and an overcrowded compound, Wirz enforced discipline strictly, earning a reputation as a martinet.[6]

On 26 September, Wirz was ordered to Montgomery, Alabama, to search for missing records of prisoners captured in 1861 and early 1862 and to report the results of his investigation to the Confederate agent of exchange, Col. Robert Ould. Upon the completion of his task in December 1862, Wirz was given command of the Confederate prison at Tuscaloosa, Alabama.[7] His health failing, Wirz applied for leave. In mid–1863 he was directed to report to Richmond, where he met with the Confederate president, Jefferson Davis, who appointed him as a special representative of the government. Wirz carried secret messages to Paris and Berlin, his proficiency in languages no doubt having prompted his selection for the mission, returning to the Confederacy in February 1864. On 12 April 1864, Wirz reported to Lt. Col. Alexander Persons of the 55th Georgia Volunteers, the commander of troops at Camp Sumter, near Andersonville, Georgia. Command at Camp Sumter was divided between the commanders of the troops, of the post, and of a prison recently established there. Wirz was placed in command of the prison.

In the mid-nineteenth century, the problem of what to do with captured enemy soldiers was a new one for Americans. In the nation's previous wars, captured enemy soldiers had been paroled or exchanged, and Americans hadn't faced the problem of interring large numbers of them. This inexperience led to indifference, which led to neglect on both sides; no concerted effort was made to address the problem. Over 430,000 men (220,000 Confederate and 211,000 Union) were prisoners during the Civil War, four times more than in any other American war, and 56,000 of these died in captivity.[8]

At the beginning of the war, the facilities that existed for the confinement of prisoners were mostly jails or makeshift warehouses, where prisoners were briefly detained until exchanges could be arranged. In 1863, the Union army issued General Order No. 100, "The Rules of Land Warfare," which specified the treatment of prisoners of war (POWs) and enemy civilians. But in March 1864, when Lt. Gen. Ulysses S. Grant took overall command of the Union army, prisoner exchanges were halted. This action, which would greatly increase the suffering of prisoners on both sides, has been attributed to Northern outrage over the abuse by the Confederacy of captured African American soldiers. Ken Burns states, "Grant ordered an end to the prisoner exchange in effect since early in the war, until and unless the South formally agreed to recognize 'no distinction whatever in the exchange between white and colored prisoners.'"[9]

Although that rationale is certainly at least partially true, it is informative to examine statements made by other senior officials that might suggest other motivations for ending the exchange of prisoners. Gen. Benjamin F. Butler had told Grant that "by the exchange of prisoners we get no men fit to go into our army, and every soldier we give the Confederates goes immediately into theirs, so that the exchange was virtually so much aid to them and none to us." Secretary of War Edwin Stanton declared, "We do not propose to reinforce the rebel army by exchanging prisoners." Grant himself would write in his memoirs that the "exchange meant reinforcement of the rebel army, and that the exchanged rebel soldier behind brigades and fortifications fighting on the defensive was equivalent to three Union soldiers attacking him." Clearly, Grant understood that continuing the prisoner exchange would sustain the Southern war effort.

With the cessation of prisoner exchanges, both sides scrambled unsuccessfully to provide for an increasing number of enemy soldiers they held. Poor and inadequate food, lack of sanitation, poor medical care, inadequate protection from the weather, and second-echelon, poor-quality guards were common on both sides. The result was sickness, epidemic disease, malnutrition, mental disease, and deaths in large numbers.

The Confederate government made the decision to erect a prison camp in Sumter County, Georgia, away from the front lines and the possibility of Union cavalry raids. Camp Sumter, popularly known as Andersonville, due to its proximity to the town, opened in February 1864. Prisoners began arriving before the camp even formally opened; originally encompassing 16.5 acres, it was quickly expanded, in June, to twenty-six acres.

The prison itself was bare ground, devoid of any foliage or structures and surrounded by a stockade of pine logs that varied in height between fifteen and seventeen feet. Sentries were posted every ninety feet along the fence in small towers, called "pigeon roosts" by the prisoners. There were two entrances on the west side; a stream, a branch of Sweetwater Creek, flowed through the prison yard and was the only source of water for most prisoners.[10] To prevent prisoners attempting to tunnel under or climb over the palisade, a light fence of post-and-rail design was constructed nineteen to twenty-five feet inside the stockade wall, demarcating a prohibited area between the two. Prisoners who crossed over the inner fence—or, on at least one occasion, reached over it—were shot by sentries.

Designed to hold ten thousand, the prison held a population of 26,000 by the end of June and more than 33,000 by August 1864. This overcrowding, as well as malnutrition, disease, and exposure would result in the deaths of almost 13,000 prisoners, the largest number of any military prison on either side during the Civil War. Andersonville was also, however, the largest POW camp on either side; at one point, it was the fifth-largest "city" in the Confederacy. Conditions inside the camp were horrific. Having no shelter from heat, cold, or rain, the men dug holes in the ground and covered themselves with ponchos, coats, or whatever other clothing had not been stolen by the guards or fellow prisoners. Overcrowding was extreme, and there was little food, nothing to cook in, and no wood for fires. The only water, the stream that bisected the compound, was used as a latrine and soon was foul smelling and a breeding pool for disease.

If disease, malnutrition, exposure, and starvation were not troubles enough, theft of personal property was a constant problem among the pris-

Andersonville POW camp, 1864 (Library of Congress).

oners. Sgt. Samuel Boggs, 21st Illinois Infantry, had been captured at Chickamauga, Georgia, in March 1864. He described his arrival at Andersonville: "Two guards seized me, took my knife, hat, blanket, and shoes; this was done quickly, and I was ordered to keep quiet and go to the further end of the pen, where some guards had my stripped comrades herded in a corner like a flock of shorn sheep; some had lost all but their shirts and drawers; they skinned us of all the clothes that were not too much worn."[11]

The guards, because of the shortage of fit men, were expected only to prevent escape, not maintain order within the compound. New prisoners were victimized on arrival by a gang of Union prisoners (led by Pennsylvanian William "Mosby" Collins), who beat and stole food, money, and anything else of value from their fellow prisoners. Calling themselves the "Raiders," they made life hell for sick and weak prisoners until another group, calling themselves the "Regulators," organized itself and overwhelmed the "Raiders." With Wirz's knowledge and consent, a prisoners' court-martial was held, presided over by Peter "Big Pete" McCullough as judge; a group of new prisoners was the jury. Six men were hanged on 12 July 1864 by the south gate, and others were punished by being forced to run a gauntlet of prisoners armed with clubs, which killed another three. Following this confrontation, a police force was organized, and the amount of crime diminished greatly.[12]

Following the war, numerous accounts by former prisoners of Andersonville detailed the daily horrors prisoners had endured, many of them likely sensationalized to enhance sales. However, an account published in 1908 by James Madison Page, a former Union lieutenant, was surprisingly sympathetic to Wirz; it debunked many of the myths regarding Andersonville. Page, then a Union lieutenant, had been captured in 1863 and sent to Andersonville; surviving the war, Page would attend Wirz's trial.[13]

On 2 September 1864, after the capture of Atlanta by Gen. William T. Sherman, Confederate authorities decided to move Andersonville's ambulatory prisoners to other camps to prevent their rescue by Union cavalry. The men were sent to Millen, Georgia, and Florence, South Carolina, leaving only 1,359 prisoners at Andersonville, where conditions dramatically improved. Although many prisoners later returned, the numbers at Andersonville remained significantly lower than before.

Wirz, promoted to major prior to the previous winter, and his command were included in General Johnston's surrender to General Sherman in April 1865, and he returned to civilian life. The war ended on 9 April 1865, and on 20 April Union troops under Maj. Gen. J. H. Wilson entered Georgia and set up headquarters near Macon. Union soldiers arrived at

Andersonville in early May to find 12,884 graves and the surviving prisoners in a skeletal and emaciated condition. Photographs of the prisoners published in Northern newspapers created outrage and calls for retribution.

On 2 May, Wilson's aide-de-camp, Capt. Henry E. Noyes, was traveling south by train carrying information for Gen. Benjamin Grierson at Eufaula, Alabama, when the train made a stop for wood and water. Dismounting, Noyes observed large numbers of very sick former Union prisoners being paroled, but he had to reboard the departing train before he could make any inquiries. He reported his observations to General Wilson upon his return to Macon. On 6 May, Noyes departed Macon with a Lieutenant Rendelbrook and a party of soldiers with orders to arrest Wirz.[14]

Differences exist in accounts of how Wirz came to be in Federal custody, but later Wirz would attempt to gain immunity from prosecution by alleging that Captain Noyes, who escorted him to Macon and subsequently arrested him, had promised him safe passage to General Wilson's headquarters in Macon and back home again. That motion to dismiss would be denied by a commission late that summer, mainly on the basis of the testimony of Noyes and Wilson. Noyes would testify,

> When I got back to Macon, I reported to General Wilson what I had seen, who told me I must go there again and arrest Captain Wirz. I left that day, or the next day, about the 6th of May, and I took a party of men with me.... I remained overnight [in Americus, Georgia,] coming back to Andersonville the next morning. There I accomplished my mission, that is, I arrested Captain Wirz and gathered all the records I thought important.... The immediate circumstances of Captain Wirz's arrest were these: I went to his house and saw him there, the family was about him, that is his wife and two daughters. It is a very hard thing to take a man from his family.... Mrs. Wirz and one of her daughters ... were crying and having considerable trouble. To pacify them and do the thing as quietly as I could, I told Mrs. Wirz, and also the captain, that they need not distress themselves at all, that on his arrival at Macon, if General Wilson was satisfied that he had done no more than his duty and had simply acted in accordance to his orders, he would probably be released.... General Wilson did not direct me to make any promise to the prisoner, or to give him any safe conduct, and I do not consider that I did.[15]

After his interview with General Wilson, Wirz was placed under arrest and remained in custody at Macon until 20 May, when he was transported under guard by rail to Washington, D.C. He was escorted by Captain Noyes, who carried the Andersonville records to turn over to investigators at the War Department. Several times during the journey Wirz was accosted by angry groups, and only the presence of Noyes and guards allowed him to reach Washington without serious injury. His splendid Confederate uniform was reduced to rags by the time he arrived at the Old Capital Prison.

General Wilson too would testify: "I ordered his arrest for the purpose of bringing [Wirz] to trial, and for no other purpose, and with the special intention that he should not have the benefit of the amnesty or armistice between Sherman and Johnston, so far as I could prevent it."[16]

Early in August, Secretary Stanton ordered a military commission to be convened, and a court was empaneled consisting of Maj. Gen. Lew Wallace (as president), brevet Maj. Gen. (and adjutant general of the armies) Lorenzo Thomas, brevet Maj. Gen. Gersham Mott, Brig. Gen. Francis Fessenden, Brig. Gen. E. L. Bragg, brevet Brig. Gen. John F. Ballior of the 148th Pennsylvania, brevet Col. Thomas Allcock of the 4th New York Artillery, and Lt. Col. John H. Stibbs of the 12th Iowa. Col. Norton Parker Chipman was named as judge advocate, assisted by Maj. A. A. Hoener.[17]

On 21 August Wirz's chief defense attorneys, Louis Schade and Otis T. Baker, filed a series of motions with the commission, citing five reasons for dismissal. First, they argued that the military commission had no general jurisdiction. Second, as mentioned above, they argued that he had been arrested in violation of a promise of safe conduct. Third, they asserted that because he was a naturalized U.S. citizen and had never served in the land or naval service of the United States, now that peace had been declared the commission had no authority to try him. Fourth, they argued that he was included in the lenient terms of surrender agreed upon by Generals Johnston and Sherman. Finally, they argued that the charges were indefinite and vague, that he was not guilty of any offense punishable under the laws of war.[18]

The defense motions were denied, and the court commenced on 21 August 1865 in the courtroom of the U.S. Court of Claims, in the Capitol Building in Washington, D.C. The trial was well attended by the press, which gave it extensive, if not unbiased, coverage. One reporter for the *Boston Advertiser* described Wirz as "scorned, loathed, despised, hated of all men" and as "the miserable creature" without any vestige of the presumption of innocence. Other papers called him a "bloodthirsty monster" and "the demon of Andersonville."[19]

Wirz was charged with one count of "Maliciously, willfully and traitorously, and in aid of the then existing rebellion against the United States ... conspiring to injure the health and destroy the lives of soldiers ... then held and being prisoners of war ... in violation of the laws and customs of war."[20] The charge listed his coconspirators as Jefferson Davis; James A. Seddon, the Confederate secretary of war; Howell Cobb, commander of Georgia's Reserve Corps; Gen. John H. Winder, who had commanded all Confederate prison camps east of the Mississippi River; Josiah H. White,

R. R. Stevenson, and S. P. Moore, all surgeons at Andersonville; Capt. William S. Winder, the former assistant adjutant general, and General Winder's son; Capt. Richard B. Winder, camp quartermaster and second cousin to General Winder; Capt. W. Shelby Reed, Andersonville provost marshal; Benjamin Harris, a local farmer whose dogs had hunted escaped prisoners; and W. J. Kerr, a hospital steward. Initially, the list also included Robert E. Lee, but the secretary of war had ordered him, as well as Davis and Seddon, removed from the indictment. The court adjourned, only to reconvene two days later, on 23 August, with an amended charge replacing the three with the phrase "others whose names are unknown." (Wirz's attorneys would later claim that the adjournment and reconvening of the court constituted double jeopardy, but the court would reject the argument.[21]) In addition, Wirz himself was charged with murder, with thirteen specifications. Wirz pled not guilty to all charges. Over 160 witnesses, mostly former prisoners, would be called over the sixty days that the trial lasted. The record would fill over 2,300 pages.[22]

The prosecution was presented by Colonel Chipman, a thirty-one-year-old native of Ohio who had graduated from law school in Cincinnati and moved to Iowa, where he had practiced law before the war. Commissioned a major in the 2nd Iowa Infantry, he had risen to the rank of brevet brigadier general before being selected for the Wirz panel. Chipman later served as the District of Columbia's delegate to the Forty-Second and Forty-Third Congresses (1871–75) and as a commissioner of the California Supreme Court in April 1897. He would write a book about the trial in 1911, *The Tragedy of Andersonville: Trial of Captain Henry Wirz, the Prison Keeper* (see note 14).

To support the first charge against Wirz, conspiracy to injure the health and destroy the lives of his prisoners, Chipman called a succession of former prisoners to testify. Much of the testimony was repetitive, as he questioned each about rations, water, the hospital, sickness in camp, the stocks, the chain gang, the shooting of prisoners by the guards, and the cruelty of Captain Wirz. The horrible conditions of the camp were described, but no written diaries, records, telegraph messages, or other written documents were presented to support a claim of conspiracy, nor did any witness testify to overhearing conversations that would indicate knowledge of a conspiracy. Rations had been poor even among the Confederates, and sickness prevalent among the guards as well as the prisoners, suggesting that the cause of the high numbers of dead may have been the collapsing Southern economy rather than intentional cruelty. However, the testimony regarding malnutrition and sickness among the guards was not allowed into the record.[23]

In fact, the court appeared to display a bias against the defendant in the motions it sustained almost from the beginning. Anything that tended to reflect poorly on Wirz, however prejudicial, irrelevant, or unreliable, was admitted in the interest of "getting at the truth." Evidence and witnesses favorable to the defense were excluded or saw their subpoenas revoked by Chipman. When defense attorneys attempted to impeach the fictions and hearsay of prosecution witnesses, they were denounced for questioning the integrity of Union soldiers; Union soldiers favorable to the defendant, when allowed to testify, were characterized by Chipman as disloyal, deserters, or bounty jumpers. Testimony that Wirz had allowed a delegation of prisoners to travel to Washington, D.C., with a petition to President Lincoln was disallowed on the grounds that it could damage the reputation of the martyred president.[24]

The cases for the thirteen specifications of murder were even weaker. Specifications one, three, and four accused Wirz of shooting prisoners "with his own hand" on 8 July, 13 June, and 30 May 1864, respectively. However, none of the witnesses called could identify the victims by name. In fact, the prosecution could not put a name to any of the thirteen "victims." As for specifications five and six, in which Wirz was accused of ordering men placed into stocks, resulting in death, on 20 August 1864, and 1 February 1864, Wirz had been on sick leave in August and had not yet reported for duty in February. Additionally, the use of stocks was accepted punishment in the Union army at the time.[25]

With regard to specification seven, that Wirz had ordered men chained together on 20 July 1864, resulting in one man's death, the prosecution was unable to provide the name of the dead man or any of the others involved. Specifications eight, nine, ten, and twelve referred to Wirz ordering a sentry to shoot a prisoner, resulting in his death, on 15 May, 1 July, 20 August, and 27 July 1864. In all four instances, the prisoners had crossed the "dead line" in violation of standing orders. "Dead lines" had been common practice in prison camps on both sides during the war, and in any case, Wirz had been on sick leave during the time that specification ten was alleged to have occurred. Specification eleven accused Wirz of allowing bloodhounds to attack and wound a prisoner on 1 July 1864, resulting in his death, but again the prisoner was never identified. Specification thirteen accused Wirz of beating a prisoner to death with his pistol on 3 August 1864, an act he had been physically incapable of committing.[26]

One of the prosecution's most damning witnesses was a former Union prisoner, Felix de la Baume, a native of France and the grandnephew of the Marquis de Lafayette. Intelligent and articulate, he witnessed to almost every transgression of which Wirz stood accused, holding the court and gallery enthralled as he recounted details of Wirz's inhuman cruelties. He testified that he had witnessed Wirz shooting two prisoners and threatening countless others. So impressed were certain members of the government that de la Baume was given a commendation and appointed to a position in the Department of the Interior on 19 October, while the trial was still in session. It was only on 21 November 1865, eleven days after Wirz's execution, that it was revealed that de la Baume was really a Union deserter, Felix Oeser, formerly of the 7th New York Volunteers, who had never been to Andersonville. It is doubtful that his had been the only perjured testimony.[27]

Wirz's lawyers tried to put on a defense, hindered by the court's open bias. They tried to enter testimony from senior Confederate officials stating that the conditions in the camp had been beyond Wirz's ability to control, that the whole South had lacked food and medicine, but it was excluded. Comparisons with other prison camps weren't permitted. Key witnesses, including Robert Ould, the former Confederate commissioner in charge of prisoner exchanges, were not allowed to testify. Several former prisoners, like Martin S. Harris of the 5th New York Cavalry and Augustus Kleich of the 8th Pennsylvania Cavalry, testified that they had never heard or seen Wirz shoot or hurt anyone and told of his efforts to try to help the prisoners. Wirz's lawyers pointed out that he was too frail and ill to have carried out the attacks of which he was accused. But it was all to no avail. The court appeared predisposed to find Wirz guilty.

Testimony was completed in mid–October. By that time all of Wirz's lawyers, who had volunteered to defend him without pay, had resigned in protest over the conduct of the trial, and Wirz was reduced to making his own closing statement in writing. He wrote, "Every respectable and reliable witness, either for the government or for myself, who was in a position to know anything about the everyday history of Andersonville, has stated before this court in the most positive and unequivocal terms that all the stories about my cruelty were entirely new to them when they came to Washington, and had never reached their ears before."[28]

On 6 November, the commission issued its preordained verdict, finding Wirz guilty of conspiracy and guilty of ten of the thirteen specifications of murder, and not guilty of specifications four, ten, and thirteen. On specifications five and six, for which Wirz had not been present at Andersonville, they merely amended the dates before finding him guilty.[29]

On 3 November, President Johnson approved the findings of the court, and the following day Wirz was sentenced to death, to be hanged by the neck until dead, the sentence to be carried out six days hence. On 6 November, Gen. C. C. Augur, commanding the Department of Washington, accompanied by Maj. George B. Russell, Washington provost marshal, and Capt. George R. Walbridge, commandant of the Old Capital Prison, went to Wirz's cell to read him the death sentence. They informed him of the time and date set for his execution, 10 November 1865, between 6:00 a.m. and noon.

The day before the execution, 9 November, Schade called on President Johnson to ask him to commute the sentence, but no pardon or stay was offered, and Wirz's former defense lawyer returned to the Old Capitol Prison to tell him that his appeal had been turned down. The Swiss consul came to visit Wirz and obtained information about his family so that they could be officially notified. Wirz ate supper, retired to bed, and slept soundly through the night.[30]

Wirz arose early the following morning, ate a moderate breakfast and met with Richard Winder, his comrade from Andersonville. They reminisced until half past eight, Winder declaring that they were equally guilty—or rather, equally innocent—and that if Wirz was guilty enough to hang, then so was he. Winder then bade Wirz an emotional farewell. Schade then met with Wirz for the last time. Wirz expressed his thanks and presented him with a letter:

> Mr Schade, Dear Sir,
> It is no doubt the last time I address myself to you. What I have said to you often and often, I repeat. Accept my thanks, my sincere heartfelt thanks, for all you have done for me. May God reward you—I cannot. Still I have something more to ask of you, and I am confident that you will not refuse to receive my dying request. Please help my family, my dear wife and children. War, cruel war, has swept everything from me, and today my wife, my children are beggars. My life is demanded as atonement, I am willing to give it, and I hope that after awhile, I will be judged differently from what I am now. If anyone ought to come to the relief of my family, it is the people of the South for whose sake I have sacrificed all. I know you will excuse my troubling you again. Farewell Dear Sir. May God bless you. Your thankful—
> H. Wirz.[31]

With Schade's departure, two clergymen, Fathers Boyle and Wiget, entered the cell and remained with Wirz until his departure to the gallows.[32] Major Russell and Captain Walbridge had worked throughout the previous night supervising the erection of the scaffold in the southern portion of the Old Capitol Prison yard, where the Supreme Court building currently stands. Four companies of soldiers mustered in the yard that morning to serve as guard over two hundred spectators who had been issued tickets of admission. Others watched from the top of the Capitol dome a quarter-

Major Wirz about to be hanged (Library of Congress).

mile distant, from nearby rooftops, or the tops of trees on the grounds of the Capitol.

Since the time of the execution was indefinite, ticket holders began assembling early, around 7:00 a.m., although none were admitted into the yard until 10:00 a.m. Many were former Andersonville prisoners. At about the same time, Russell, Waldridge, and several guards entered Wirz's cell, where they found the prisoner calm and prepared, even joking that he hoped to trade soon the black shroud he was dressed in for a white robe. His arms could not be pinioned because of his injured right arm, so Wirz was allowed to proceed unbound to the scaffold. Taking a last gulp of whiskey and a plug of tobacco, he took his place in the procession.[33]

Major Russell led, followed by Wirz, flanked by Fathers Boyle and Wiget, then the guard, with Captain Waldridge in the rear. The group mounted the scaffold, and Wirz was seated upon a stool resting atop the trapdoor, a noose hanging above his head. Russell read aloud the execution order, the findings of the court, and the approval of sentence by the president. The reading was finished at 10:20 a.m.

When Russell asked if he had any last words, Wirz replied, "No Sir, only that I am innocent and will die like a man, my hopes being in the future. I go before my God, the almighty God, and he will judge between me and you." As the priests performed the last rites, shouts of "Hang him!" and "Remember Andersonville!" were chanted by the crowds.

Wirz was directed to stand in front of the stool, and his arms and legs were pinioned by straps as L. J. Richardson, a military detective, adjusted the noose around his neck. Wirz thanked Captain Walbridge, saying, "Well, Captain, Good-Bye. I thank you and the other officers of the prison as I have been well treated." He then warned Major Russell that this was what came of following orders (or words to that effect). At exactly 10:32 a.m., at a signal from Major Russell, Sylvester Ballou, another detective, sprang the trap, and Wirz fell through to dangle in the air. His shoulders convulsed, and his limbs drew up; and it was several minutes before he hung still, indicating that his neck had failed to snap and he had apparently strangled to death. After fifteen minutes he was taken down and examined by Dr. Ford, the post surgeon, who pronounced him dead.[34] Father Boyle, in a letter to Jefferson Davis, wrote, "I attended the Major to the scaffold, and he died in the peace of God and praying for his enemies. I know that he was indeed innocent of all the cruel charges on which his life was sworn away, and I was edified by the Christian spirit in which he submitted to his persecutors."[35]

The scaffold and rope used to hang Wirz fell victim to relic hunters and souvenir seekers. The government refused to release the body to Wirz's widow and buried him without ceremony in the Old Capitol Prison yard, beside the bodies of the Lincoln conspirators. On 2 March 1869, Wirz was reinterred at Mount Olivet Cemetery in northwest Washington, D.C. The reburial, presided over by Father Boyle, was attended by Louis Schade, the Wirz family, and friends.

In its 1905 convention, the United Daughters of the Confederacy voted to erect a memorial to Captain Wirz on the site of the prison to "rescue his name from the stigma attached to it by embittered prejudice." The memorial, dedicated on 12 May 1908, states in part, "Discharging his duty with such humanity as the harsh circumstances of the times, and the policy of the foe admitted, Captain Wirz became at last a victim of a misdirected popular clamor. He was arrested at a time of peace under the protection of parole. Tried by a military commission of a service to which he did not belong, and condemned to an ignominious death on the charges of excessive cruelty to federal prisoners."

While it is possible to argue and debate the degree of guilt that should be attached to Wirz for the horrendous conditions at Andersonville, not even his most ardent detractors would argue that he received anything even close to a fair trial under the American system of justice. The Fifth Amendment to the Constitution guarantees, "No person shall be held to answer for a capital, or otherwise infamous crime, unless on a presentment or indictment of a Grand Jury, except in cases arising in the land or naval forces, or in the Militia, when in actual service in time of War or public danger." Yet Wirz was never brought before a grand jury, nor had he ever served in the U.S. military.

Additionally, the Supreme Court case *Ex Parte Milligan 71 U.S.2 (4 Wall)* (*1866*) (see chapter 3) held that trying civilians in military courts is unconstitutional when civilian courts are in operation and is constitutional only when there is no power except the military and trial is absolutely necessary. Had the government tried Wirz in Georgia, where no civilian courts were in operation, the trial might have been valid. In fact, however, he was tried in Washington, D.C., where the civilian courts were functioning.

His trial was filled with circumstances that would have resulted in appeals under normal circumstances: insufficient evidence, perjured testimony, questionable jurisdiction, lack of due process, and the absence of opportunity to appeal, given the short period, only three weeks, between sentencing and the execution of the sentence. Also, despite being one of many named conspirators, Wirz was the only man tried and convicted—for the first time in American history—of war crimes.

Was Wirz the monster that the Northern press made him out to be? Consider that at the Union prison at Elmira, New York, 2,963 Confederate prisoners died of the 12,123 confined there, roughly 24 percent, compared with the 13,200 of 52,300 Andersonville prisoners who died, roughly 25 percent. Or consider the boast of Elmira's surgeon who bragged that he "had killed more Rebels than any soldier at the front." The commander of the Rock Island Prison, on an island of the Mississippi River between Iowa and Illinois, ordered Confederate prisoners to sleep outside on reduced rations during the winter, in retaliation for reports about Andersonville. There 1,960 prisoners died of starvation and exposure, deaths for which the commander of the prison was never charged.[36]

In 1977, at the National Convention of the Sons of Confederate Veterans, Wirz was declared a Confederate martyr and hero and awarded a posthumous medal of honor, which is on display at the visitors center at Andersonville.

7

Cadet Johnson C. Whittaker

CONDUCT UNBECOMING AN OFFICER,
CONDUCT PREJUDICIAL TO GOOD ORDER—1881

> *West Point is an institution of learning designed to serve the government, not the individual. The survival of the fittest is the rule of its conduct.*—Maj. Asa Bird Gardiner, judge advocate at Whittaker court-martial

On 24 July 1995, in a ceremony held in the Roosevelt Room of the White House, President Bill Clinton signed papers granting a commission as second lieutenant in the U.S. Army to Johnson Chesnut Whittaker. What made this particular commission unique was that it was awarded posthumously more than a century after Whittaker was court-martialed and dismissed from West Point.

Along with the gold bars of a second lieutenant, Clinton presented Whittaker's seventy-seven-year-old granddaughter, Cecil Whittaker Pequette, with a Bible that had been given to Whittaker by his mother when he left for West Point. Seized as evidence in his court-martial in 1881, it had been stored in the National Archives until its return to the family.[1] Whittaker had found comfort in reading the Bible, scribbling his inner thoughts about his loneliness and isolation, such as, "Forgive as soon as you are injured and forget as soon as you forgive," and "Do right at all times, under whatever circumstances and at whatever cost." Ultimately, the cost would be high, and there would be a lot to forgive and forget.[2]

Although the American Civil War ended slavery in the United States, racism survived in both the north and south, and Reconstructionist politicians discovered that neither could equality be legislated nor social integration mandated. However, Reconstruction, along with the Thirteenth, Fourteenth, and Fifteenth Amendments to the Constitution, did result in the election of twenty-eight African Americans to Congress, making possible for the first time the nomination of black males to attend the U.S. Military and Naval Academies.

Between 1870 and 1887, African American congressmen nominated twenty-seven blacks to the U.S. Military Academy, at West Point, New York. Twelve candidates were able to pass the academic and physical exams, but of those only three completed the four-year course of study and graduated. Of the three black midshipmen admitted to the Naval Academy at Annapolis, Maryland, none graduated.[3]

By all accounts, Johnson Whittaker was a good bet for success, despite humble beginnings. He and his twin brother Alex were born on 23 August 1858, at Mulberry Plantation, the plantation home of the Chesnut family just outside of Camden, South Carolina. The Chesnut family was prominent in southern society, and the patriarch, Col. James Chesnut, was active in South Carolina politics. James Jr., a U.S. senator, would serve as a Confederate general during the Civil War, and Jefferson Davis was a family friend.

Whittaker's mother, Maria J. Whitaker (so spelled), was the personal slave of the daughter-in-law, Mary Boykin Chesnut, the noted Civil War diarist. His father, James, was a free black who had worked as a tailor and bought his freedom. He had abandoned his family upon the birth of twins, whom he refused to recognize as his own, twins not being common in his family. Both boys and their older brother worked from an early age, cleaning the big main house with its twelve bedrooms, where their mother worked, until the end of the war. Liberated, Maria moved her family to Camden, where she found work as a maid for the W. C. Reynolds family, relatives of the Chesnuts. The boys attended Freedmen's Bureau schools, where Johnson showed such promise that he was tutored by a local minister. At the age of sixteen, in 1874, Whittaker added an additional *t* to his name and entered the University of South Carolina. Integration of the university had resulted in an exodus of many of the faculty and white students. Teachers from the north had been hired, and the school now served to prepare freedmen for higher education. Whittaker excelled academically his first two years.[4]

One of Whittaker's professors was Richard T. Greener, himself the first African American graduate of Harvard in 1870, who recommended Whittaker for admission to West Point and tutored him in preparation. Rep. Solomon Lafayette Hoge, a northern Republican from Ohio representing South Carolina in Congress, was persuaded to make the appointment, and in August 1876 Whittaker arrived at West Point. Although he would spend the majority of his time at the academy as the only black cadet, Whittaker was not the first African American to arrive at West Point. It is instructive in understanding the attitudes of the nation at the time to note that the first postwar southern cadets were admitted to West Point in 1868, only three years following the end of hostilities, but blacks would wait an additional two years for the first African Americans to pass through its gates.[5] On 31 May 1870, two black candidates, James Webster Smith of South Carolina, and Michael Howard of Mississippi, entered West Point and waited to take their entrance examinations, scheduled in June. The fact that they were denied a meal at the government owned Rose Hotel might have served as an indication of the treatment they could expect.

Smith and Howard were roommates, and both suffered minor harassment during the days of testing. A person or persons unknown emptied slop pails on them one night while they were sleeping, and several days later a white cadet suspected of the offense, Robert McCord, struck Howard because he did not move out of the way when McCord entered the bootblack shop. Smith reported McCord, who was restricted to quarters. Both McCord and Howard failed their entrance exams and were dismissed from the academy, but Smith was among the thirty-seven candidates who passed. He officially entered the Corps of Cadets on 9 July 1870.[6]

Smith, born of mixed-race parents, had been enrolled by his father in a Freedmen's Bureau school in Columbia, South Carolina, following the Civil War. Like Whittaker, Smith showed promise and came to the attention of benefactors, including David Clark, a former Union officer and now a philanthropist, who took an interest in Smith and paid for him to attend a white high school in Hartford, Connecticut. Within six weeks Smith had progressed to senior-level classes, and Clark tutored him in foreign languages. A letter from Clark to Gen. Oliver O. Howard, chief of the Freedmen's Bureau, led Howard to convince Congressman Hoge (the same legislator who would later nominate Whittaker) to nominate Smith for an appointment to West Point. Although Clark had reservations regarding Smith's ability to succeed in the all-white academy, Howard persuaded him that Smith would receive fair treatment and a quality education.[7]

After Howard's dismissal, Smith found himself totally isolated, as no cadet would room with him, and his only conversations with others were in the line of duty. The senior class pledged to display no support for Smith. Several of the faculty also seemed predisposed against him. Professor George L. Andrews (class of 1851) said of Smith, "Possibly a worse selection for the first colored cadet could not have been made. He was malicious, vindictive and untruthful. Instead of contenting himself with manfully meeting trouble when it came, he diligently and successfully sought it." A Captain King, a tactical officer, characterized Smith as a "low, tricky, vindictive biped."[8]

Perhaps Andrews and the cadets mistook Smith's determination to receive equal treatment as a desire for controversy. His father had advised him upon entering the academy that he had been "elevated to a high position, and you must stand it like a man. Do not let them run you away for then they will say the 'nigger' won't do. Show your spunk and let them see that you will fight. When they find you are determined to stay, they will let you alone. You must not resign on any account, for it is just what the Democrats want."[9]

Faced with almost continuous harassment and social isolation, Smith unburdened himself to his sponsor David Clark in letters in which his bitterness showed through. In what he later expressed as a motivation to publicly reveal the challenges faced by black cadets, Clark had Smith's letter published in the *Hartford Courant*. Picked up by other newspapers, the letter caught the attention of the American public, all the way to President Grant, who assured Clark in a private interview that he would do everything to protect Smith's rights as a cadet. Meanwhile, the superintendent of West Point, Gen. Thomas G. Pitcher, was initiating an investigation and requesting that a formal court of inquiry be ordered by Secretary of War William W. Belknap. Belknap appointed General Howard to preside over the board of inquiry to investigate Smith's allegations of harassment.[10]

During the inquiry, initiated on 16 July, Smith informed the court that the published letter was not the one he had sent Clark and that it had never been his intent for his letter to be published. The board determined, through interviews conducted by Emery Upton, the commandant of cadets, that there had been minor harassment, and the guilty cadets—one the son of Gen. Quincy Adams Gilmore and another the nephew of the secretary of war—were reprimanded but not otherwise punished. On 21 July, the court found that of the allegations made by Smith either "unfounded or exaggerated" and recommended that he be court-martialed for making false statements. Belknap approved the court's findings but declined to order a court-martial, instead ordering General Pitcher to reprimand Smith.[11]

Three weeks after the reprimand, on 13 August, Smith got into an altercation with another cadet, John W. Wilson, when Smith was blocked from getting water, and the two struck each other. General Pitcher ordered an investigation. On 18 August, while it was being conducted Cadet Cpl. Edgar Beacon put Smith on report for being disrespectful to a cadet during drill, calling him "a file closer" (that is, short). Smith denied it, but three cadets verified Beacon's account, and Upton preferred charges against Smith for making false statements. Pitcher requested, and Belknap ordered, a court-martial, which convened on 20 October.

General Howard again presided, and Smith pleaded "not guilty" to the charge of assault on Cadet Wilson, and also to the charge of submitting a false report, proving that there had been no drill on the 18th and that the "witnesses" had had guard duty that day. Both Smith and Wilson were found guilty of assault and sentenced to three weeks confinement and extra duty; Smith was acquitted of the second charge, of making false statements. Feeling the punishment too light in comparison to the charges, Belknap disapproved the sentence, angering the rest of the Corps of Cadets, who perceived his actions as favoring Smith because of his race. As a result, the harassment continued and increased.

On 13 December, Smith was put on report by Cadet Cpl. Thomas Bailey after an altercation in the ranks between Smith and Cadet George Anderson, who had, Smith was convinced, deliberately stepped on Smith's toes. Bailey and Anderson's accounts conflicted with Smith's, and Commandant Upton charged Smith with "conduct unbecoming a cadet and a gentleman." Smith's second court-martial began on 6 January 1871, but this time the court rendered a verdict of guilty, and Smith was sentenced to dismissal from West Point; however, no action was taken pending a review by Edward Townsend (the army judge advocate general), Secretary of War Belknap, and President Grant. In the interim, Smith completed the first-year examinations, ranking high in his class, and public attention was drawn to the case; Smith's sentence was reduced from dismissal to being held back a year.

The new class of 1875 arrived on 11 June 1871, bringing with it a second black cadet, Henry Alonzo Napier, a former classmate of Smith's from Howard University. The two roomed together, but the harassment continued. Napier was dismissed in June 1872 for failing his examinations in math and French. Smith's rankings during his second plebe year were respectable, but he began having academic difficulties in his third year.

In 1872, black cadets James Elias Rector of Arkansas and Thomas Van Rensselaer Gibbs of Florida arrived at West Point, but Rector failed to gain entrance, and Gibbs left in 1873 after failing math. Two more black cadets arrived in 1873, Henry O. Flipper of Georgia on 20 May and John Washington Williams of Virginia on 26 May. Both passed the entrance exams, but Williams was dismissed after failing French on 19 January 1874. Flipper would go on to become the first black to graduate West Point on

15 June 1877. Upon his arrival, Flipper roomed with Smith, possibly gaining insight from his roommate's experiences. Where Smith seemed to push for equal treatment, Flipper appeared inclined to endure silently.[12]

In June 1874, Smith was given his final examination in natural and experimental philosophy in private by Professor Peter S. Michie, who found Smith deficient in deductive reasoning. With no recommendation to retain him made by the Academic Board, Smith was dismissed from the Corps of Cadets in June 1874. He personally appealed to Secretary of War Belknap, accompanied by Republican senator John J. Patterson of South Carolina, but Belknap declined to intervene, stating that Smith had used his "second chance" after his court-martial in January 1871. Smith finished his college degree at the all-black South Carolina Agricultural and Mechanics Institute at Orangeburg, Carolina. He died of tuberculosis sixteen months later, at age twenty-six.

So it was that when Johnson C. Whittaker arrived at West Point on 23 August 1876, the ninth black to be admitted, none had yet graduated. He roomed with Flipper but found himself alone and isolated when Flipper graduated on 15 June 1877. Another black cadet, Charles Augustus Minnie, entered West Point that June but was discharged in January 1878 after failing mathematics.[13]

Whittaker's academic performance was marginal, and he was close to academic disqualification when he was put back a year. By 1880, Whittaker, now a second classman, was at the head of the sixth (lowest) section academically. Ostracized by the rest of the Corps of Cadets, who refused to speak to him except officially, Whittaker's only friends were two black workers, Louis Simpson and Mitchell, who worked the grounds. He studied, wrote letters, and read the Bible.

Like Smith and the others before him, Whittaker endured daily insults, harassment, and humiliations as cadets refused to sit near him at meals or to stand next to him in formations. Once when a cadet from Alabama, John C. McDonald, struck Whittaker for looking him in the eye, Whittaker refused to strike back and instead reported the offender, who was court-martialed and suspended for six months. His refusal to fight, however, was perceived as cowardice by many cadets.

On Sunday, 5 April 1880, Whittaker returned from supper to find a post commissary envelope on a chair inside his room. Inside was a note that read, "Mr. Whittaker, You will be 'fixed.' Better keep awake. A friend." He showed the note to Simpson, who advised him to ignore it. The next day, in a letter to his mother, he mentioned the note and his intent to take it to the superintendent, Gen. John M. Schofield, but he failed to do so before turning in that night.[14]

On the morning of 7 April, Whittaker failed to show up at reveille, and the cadet officer of the day, George R. Burnett, went to Whittaker's room looking for him. When there was no answer to his knock, Burnett opened the door to find Whittaker unconscious on the floor in his underclothes, his ankles tied to the bed rail. There was blood in his hair, chunks of which were missing, his earlobes were slashed and bloody, and there was blood on the floor and the wall above the middle of his bed. On the floor were clumps of hair, burned scraps of paper, a smashed mirror, and an Indian club stained with blood. Whittaker's wrists had also been restrained. Burnett ordered another cadet, Frederick G. Hodgson, to secure the room while he summoned help.

Burnett returned with an officer and pushed through the crowd of cadets gathered at the door. They released Whittaker from his bonds; the post surgeon, Maj. Charles T. Alexander arrived shortly afterward. He checked Whittaker's pulse and temperature and found them normal but could not rouse him. Whittaker was left undisturbed until the arrival of the commandant of cadets, Lt. Col. Henry M. Lazelle, when both he and the surgeon again attempted to wake him. Regaining his senses, Whittaker called out, "Oh, don't cut me. I never hurt you." To which Lazelle replied, "Get up, and be a man," after which, Lazelle stated, Whittaker appeared "restored to perfect and complete sensibility."[15]

After Dr. Alexander treated his wounds, Whittaker walked to the post hospital, where he was fed breakfast and given a cursory physical examination. He was then dismissed to return to class. Later that day Whittaker was examined a second time, by the assistant post surgeon, Dr. Henry Lippencott. Both doctors described his injuries as "incised wounds on the anterior surface of the lobes of both ears ... with a small piece of flesh missing from the tip of the left lobe[;] ... a "thin scratch" along the left hand and "two parallel cuts" about five inches long across the big toe of his left foot."[16]

Whittaker reported that he had been awakened from sleep at approximately 2:00 a.m., when he had been dragged from his bed by three masked figures dressed in civilian clothes. He had struggled but had been choked, struck on the temple, given a bloody nose, and warned, "If you don't be still, you will be a dead man; don't you holler." Then one of the men stated, "Let's mark him as we mark hogs down south," whereupon he was pushed to the floor, and his feet tied. His earlobes were slashed, as was the back of his left hand when he tried to protect himself from being cut. One man used scissors to cut away clumps of his hair, as another held up a hand mirror to force Whittaker to look at himself. Then he was struck on the forehead with the mirror, shattering the mirror. His hands were tied in front of him, his feet secured to the bed rail. One of the assailants, who didn't take part in the attack, noticed all the blood and said, "Look out, don't hurt him"; he handed over a handkerchief to put on Whittaker's wounds.

The attackers placed a pillow under Whittaker's head, warned him to keep silent, and left. The last words he heard were, "then he will leave." Whittaker called out for help, but not loudly, fearing the men would return and carry out their threat to kill him. Besides, he later said, he didn't believe anyone would come to his aid. At some point he lost consciousness, remaining so until revived the next morning.

In the subsequent investigation by Lieutenant Colonel Lazelle, Whittaker, though asked several times, was unable to identify his attackers. None of the cadets questioned admitted any knowledge of the incident, and Lazelle concluded that they must be telling the truth, since lying would be a violation of the Cadet Code of Honor. On 8 April, after consulting with the two physicians, Lazelle reported his conclusions to General Schofield: Cadet Whittaker's assault had been faked and his wounds self-inflicted. In part, the report stated:

> I do not believe it possible that three cadets can be found in the Corps who would so utterly falsify as they must have done in the total denial of all knowledge of the outrage on Cadet Whittaker, had they taken part in it; prompted to such a thing as they must have been if at all, by the spirit of mere mischief.... I am compelled to the belief that Cadet Whittaker has himself inflicted or consented to the infliction of all his apparent injuries, and himself arranged all the striking surrounds of his position when found at reveille on the morning of the 6th. I respectfully recommend that Cadet Whittaker be given the choice of resignation, or asking for a court of inquiry or of a court-martial.

When Schofield informed Whittaker later that day of the conclusion of the investigation, Whittaker denied having any reason to injure himself and demanded a further investigation. Schofield agreed and immediately published Special Order No. 55, dated 8 April 1880, setting up a court of inquiry "to examine into and investigate the facts and circumstances connected with the assault upon Cadet Whittaker and the imputation cast upon his character in relation thereto."[17]

The court of inquiry convened the next day, 9 April, in the Military Academy library. It consisted of three officers: Maj. A Mordecai, an instructor of ordnance and gunnery; Capt. Charles W. Raymond, an instructor in practical engineering; and 1st Lt. Samuel E. Tillman, assistant professor of chemistry, mineralogy and geology. First Lt. Clinton B. Sears, an assistant professor of natural and experimental philosophy, would act as the recorder of the court, a role that combined prosecutor, investigator, and custodian of the official record. Appointed to West Point from Sherman's army during the Civil War, Sears had graduated to take a position on the faculty. First Lt. John G. D. Knight, class of 1874 and an assistant professor of mathematics at West Point for ten years, would act as defense counsel. The library was filled with spectators and reporters.

As the court of inquiry opened, events outside the courtroom were occurring that would affect the proceedings. That morning, Maj. Thomas F. Barr, representing the secretary of war, had arrived and met with General Schofield, who upon being shown the warning note and an example of Whittaker's writings commented to Schofield upon the similarity. Richard T. Greener also arrived from South Carolina, to assist in Whittaker's defense, although he was permitted only to observe, but not ask questions. Finally, the academy adjutant, Col. William Wherry was dispatched to New York City to obtain the services of a detective. Three days later, on 12 April, James Gayler, the superintendent of delivery for the New York Post Office and a handwriting expert, arrived to examine the handwriting on the warning note. He was the first of what would be five handwriting "experts" retained by West Point.[18]

Whittaker was the first witness called to testify, and from the beginning the inquiry seemed to center on Whittaker's social and academic life as bore on his credibility and character. On the second day of testimony,

Woodcut of court of inquiry for West Point Cadet Johnson C. Whittaker (inset), 1881 (Library of Congress).

Lieutenant Sears told Whittaker, "You are aware that the opinion held by some is that this assault is entirely an imaginary one and that you alone were involved. Now for your own benefit I have here this Bible which you state you are accustomed to reading, which has been in your possession for some years, in whose sacredness I presume you have every belief, and I want you to put your hand upon that Bible and take an oath that you do not have any knowledge of and were not involved in the attack." Whittaker placed his hand on the Bible and said, "I do, Sir." With that, Whittaker was excused.

The case was garnering attention, both in the press and in the higher reaches of the government. General Schofield had sent a detailed telegram to the adjutant general of the army in Washington, D.C., reporting the incident, stating that Whittaker's injuries were not serious, and complimenting the Corps of Cadets on its cooperation. A second telegram the next day reported that the cadets had disclaimed any responsibility in the attack. In a letter to Gen. William T. Sherman on 11 April, Schofield called the attack "a perplexing mystery" but asserted his confidence that no cadet had been involved.[19]

At the same time, Schofield was granting newspaper interviews and making statements prejudicial to Whittaker's case. In an interview with the *New York Herald*, Schofield indicated his belief that Whittaker had committed self-mutilation so as to spend time in the hospital and avoid the upcoming examinations, fearing failure. In an article in the *New York Tribune*, Schofield wondered why no one in the adjoining rooms had heard any sounds of struggle and what the motive for an attack could have been. "He has no enemies, because the other students have no intercourse with him." It appears that much of the press accepted Schofield's view.[20]

The hearing was front-page news, and editorials appeared both favorable to and critical of Whittaker. For many the trial became as much an examination of West Point's treatment of African American cadets as of the circumstances surrounding the assault itself. There were debates in both the House and Senate, and even the president, now Rutherford B. Hayes, sent a personal representative, Martin Townsend, the U.S. attorney for the District of New York, to function as "Assistant Counsel and Advisor to the Recorder." Upon his arrival on 14 April, Townsend stated to the assembled reporters, "I don't say the cadets did it, but if it was not a hostile attack, then the world is a farce." This did not endear him to Sears or the West Point authorities, and his presence created additional controversy.

On 12 April Sears took the investigation in a new direction when he informed the court that he had provided Gayler, twenty-five sheets of paper containing writing examples from twenty-five different cadets for comparison with the warning note. When Gayler failed to note any similarities, he was given seven additional examples (all suspected to be Whittaker's), but again Gayler stated there were no matches.[21]

A good part of the court's time was spent considering the testimony of the various handwriting experts and investigating a rumor, reported in the *New York Times*, that three cadets had been overheard plotting the attack the night it occurred. The conversation had allegedly taken place at Ryan's Tavern, a bar popular with cadets (though it was officially off limits to them), much as the legendary Benny Havens had been for an earlier generation of cadets. Ryan, called to testify, denied that cadets patronized his bar. His testimony was discredited after several cadets, who testified under immunity, admitted to frequenting the bar to change into civilian clothes before going into town. In the end, a lot of time was wasted on testimony that neither proved nor disproved anything.

But in the newspapers it was asked how trustworthy the cadets could be if the honor code they so highly touted was habitually broken in violations of curfew, imbibing of alcoholic beverages, and overt racial discrimination. In response, General Schofield issued a General Order No. 14 on 21 April 1880, commending the Corps of Cadets and expressing "confidence in their honor and integrity." Although he subsequently characterized the order as "a simple act of justice to the Corps of Cadets," its issuance while the inquiry was still in session revealed a bias against Whittaker and would lead to Schofield's eventual replacement as superintendant.

On 12 May, Townsend failed to appear in court, later telegraphing to inform the court that he would no longer be attending the hearings. Convinced of Whittaker's innocence, he had been highly critical of how West Point was handling the inquiry; Townsend's departure was most likely to the relief of Sears and the court. Sears would later describe Townsend as "Assistant Counsel to the Recorder de jure, but a virulent and partisan counsel for Whittaker de facto." Greener, concerned that Whittaker's interests were at risk, wrote a petition to the secretary of war asking for permission to question witnesses, but permission was denied.[22]

On 15 May, Whittaker was recalled to the stand, where he was directly confronted by Sears, who asked if Whittaker had written the warning note. Whittaker replied, "No." Sears then asked, "Why then, did experts agree the writing on the note matched his?" (In truth, there was never any consensus, and opinions changed.) Whittaker replied that perhaps someone had forged his handwriting. One expert, Albert G. Southworth of Boston, had matched the edges of the warning note with the edge of a letter from

Whittaker to his mother, and a requisition slip, concluding that they had all come from the same piece of paper. Whittaker had no answer.

This last evidence lost Whittaker some support from the public and the press, some blaming the ostracism at West Point for driving Whittaker to the desperate act. Other papers, less sympathetic, like *The Nation*, characterized Whittaker as "a tricky rascal" and called the inquiry "a vulgar and unsuccessful attempt at imposture on the part of audacious young rogue." Most Americans, both for and against him, seemed convinced of his guilt.

On 28 May, both sides offered their summations. Sears began by stating his belief that the trial had been conducted fairly, that he was personally without racial prejudice and liked Whittaker, and that his only interest was in doing his official duty. He then presented four theories regarding the attack. First, it might have been conducted by cadets out of spite or to get him to leave, but this was unlikely, as all had sworn no knowledge of the attack and to lie would violate the Code of Honor. Additionally, no evidence had been uncovered implicating any cadet. Besides that, the cadets had offered a thousand-dollar reward. His other theories were that the cadets hired someone to commit the assault or that the assault was committed, with or without Whittaker's knowledge, to aid the Negro cause. Sears considered either scenario unlikely, and that left the last theory—that Whittaker's assault was self-inflicted.

Sears believed the last theory to be the truth. Besides the strong circumstantial evidence provided by the handwriting experts and the numerous small inconsistencies and contradictions in testimony by Whittaker, the defendant had never been able to provide a motive for the attack, and many of his answers had been evasive. Sears identified Whittaker's motives as fear that he would fail the exams and as an attempt to garner the sympathy of his instructors and the public. He concluded by stating that "the circumstantial evidence against him is so strong that the merits of the case stringently demand that he be tried by a General Court Martial under Charges and Specifications, for Conduct unbecoming a Cadet and Gentleman and for Perjury."

Knight, in his summation, cautioned the court not to consider Whittaker's "brooding" as an indication that he had perpetrated the incident or that he had been "warped" from reading the Bible too much. As for the inconsistencies in Whittaker's testimony, he said it was unreasonable to expect a man assaulted in the night to possess a clear, complete, and unerring recall of events. As for the testimony of the handwriting experts, he reminded the court that experts had been proven wrong in the past. He finished, "Should the opinion you render be unfavorable ... the mystery surrounding the cause of this investigation will yield to another equally great[:] ... what could make one at the very threshold of manhood, of Christian training and principles, apart from all contaminating influences, what could make one a wretch to whom perjury is as easy as the truth?"

The following day, 29 May, the court issued its conclusions and opinions. The court declared itself unable to believe that Whittaker's slight wounds had been inflicted in the manner and under the circumstances he had alleged, or to understand why he had submitted to the assault without calling out for help either during the attack or afterward. The court believed that if he had been tied up as he described, he ought to have been able to free himself, and that the post surgeons' testimony, as well as that of others, indicated that Whittaker was feigning unconsciousness when discovered the morning of 7 April. Additionally, the court stated that only Whittaker had had a motive for the assault, that there was no evidence that anyone else had been involved, and that the hair clipping, cuts, and binding could have been accomplished by Whittaker himself. Finally, the court gave great weight to the testimony of the handwriting experts that Whittaker himself had written the warning note.

Based on those conclusions, the court issued the following opinion: "From the strong array of circumstantial evidence, from the testimony of the experts in handwriting, and from the conflicting statements of Cadet Whittaker and the lack of truth evinced by him in certain cases during the investigation, as shown by the evidence, the Court is of the opinion that the imputation upon the character of Cadet Whittaker referred to in the order convening the Court, and contained in the official reports of the Commandant of Cadets and the Post Surgeon is fully sustained."[23] In essence, the court had found that Whittaker had staged the assault and that his injuries were self-inflicted. Greener immediately vowed to appeal the decision to the secretary of war, even as Whittaker was placed on room arrest but allowed to continue to attend class in preparation for the June examinations. The press reacted along partisan lines, Whittaker's supporters questioning the fairness of the hearings and supporters of the academy rejoicing in West Point's vindication. Although the press was distracted by the 1880 presidential campaigns, the matter was far from put to rest; the treatment of blacks at West Point remained in the public's mind, and interest in Whittaker's case continued as it was forwarded to Washington, D.C., for review.

Whittaker did well in his exams but was failed in philosophy by the same professor, Peter S. Michie, who had years earlier failed Smith. Despite an Academic Board ruling that Whittaker had failed, General Schofield was notified by the War Department that all action in the Whittaker case was suspended pending review, and Whittaker was neither dismissed nor restored. Suspension was chosen as the best method to preserve Whittaker's military status for trial by court-martial, should a review of the records make such actions necessary.

Political pressures continued for the next few months, as advocates pressed for a court-martial and detractors lobbied for Whittaker's dismissal. Others argued for his restoration to West Point without a court-martial. There was also pressure to replace Schofield as superintendant of West Point. On 17 August, General Schofield was called to Washington, D.C., for a meeting with President Hayes, who informed him that a change of command at West Point had been decided upon to ensure fair treatment of black cadets. He inquired as to the general's thoughts on black cadets in general and on Whittaker's request for a court-martial in particular.

Schofield expressed the opinion that blacks were closer to whites at West Point than in general society but that an "enforced association" led to greater rather than less prejudice. Why, he asked Hayes, should not cadets who chose not to "mingle" with blacks enjoy the same rights as those who favored it? How could West Point force social intimacy when the rest of the country opposed it? As to Whittaker, he thought Whittaker should get his court-martial and suggested that Whittaker be put on an indefinite leave of absence until that time, thereby removing him from West Point. Hayes did so shortly after their meeting.[24]

Whittaker himself wrote a personal letter to President Hayes in early December 1880, requesting justice and the opportunity to restore his character through a fair hearing by an impartial court-martial. President Hayes showed it to General Howard, his choice to replace General Schofield as superintendent of West Point. He also discussed the letter with his cabinet, the members of which were divided between those wanting to grant Whittaker's request for a court-martial and those who advised resolving the question by simply dismissing him for failing philosophy. They also felt that replacing Schofield with Howard would send a positive demonstration of the administration's position on racial discrimination at West Point.

Howard was a West Point graduate (1854) and career soldier who had lost an arm while commanding a brigade at the battle of Fair Oaks, Virginia, on 1 June 1862. He would later be awarded a Medal of Honor and given command of the Army of Tennessee during Sherman's "March to the Sea." Following the war, from May 1865 until July 1874, he was appointed commissioner of the Bureau of Refugees, Freedmen, and Abandoned Lands, known commonly as the Freedmen's Bureau. It was a federal agency set up to assist refugees following the war, most notably in assisting former slaves with health care, education, and employment. He also helped found Howard University, which offered African Americans an opportunity for higher education. He was known for promoting the welfare of blacks.

After reading Whittaker's letter, Howard advised the president to convene the court-martial and suggested that it be composed primarily of officers not graduates of West Point and that it be held off the academy grounds. He also recommended that should Whittaker be found not guilty, he should be "placed in the class below his own," that is, the senior class. Hayes took Howard's advice and on 20 December 1880, ordered the War Department to begin proceedings for a court-martial.[25]

The actual order establishing the court-martial was issued on 31 December, setting the first meeting for 20 January 1881. The court would meet in the Army Building in downtown New York City. The following day, even as Schofield was called by the court to testify, Howard assumed command as superintendent of West Point. The court-martial board comprised nine officers, all northerners, five of whom had not graduated from West Point. Most prominent of the nine was the president of the court, Gen. Nelson A. Miles. Awarded a Medal of Honor for his actions at Chancellorsville, Miles had risen from a volunteer at the start of the Civil War to the rank of general following the Indian wars. He would later serve in the Spanish-American War and become commanding general of the army, a position later renamed chief of staff.

The next most senior officers were Col. H. A. Morrow of the 21st Infantry and Lt. Col. John M. Brannon of the 1st Artillery. Morrow, not a West Point graduate, had the most court-martial experience, but an illness caused his absence from the deliberations. Brannon, who was part of the class of 1841, in which he had graduated twenty-third of fifty-two, was a veteran of the Mexican War and served as a brigadier general of volunteers during the Civil War. He had also helped put down the railroad riots in Pennsylvania in 1877.[26]

Other officers on the court included Maj. Edwin Vose Sumner, Jr., of the 5th Cavalry. He was the son of Maj. Gen. E. V. Sumner, the oldest field commander on either side during the Civil War. The junior Sumner had served during the war, rising to the brevet rank of brigadier general of volunteers. He would later serve in the Indian wars and, as a general of volunteers, during the Spanish-American War.[27] Pinckney Lugenbeel, newly promoted colonel of the 5th Infantry and a graduate of the class of 1840, saw service against the Seminoles, during the War with Mexico and commanding a battalion at Lookout Mountain during the Civil War. Maj.

Lewis Merrill of the 7th Cavalry and Capt. Merritt Barber of the 16th Infantry were the other two West Point graduates on the court. (Barber would later serve as defense counsel in the court-martial of Lt. Henry O. Flipper.)[28]

Two other officers, Capt. J. N. Craig of the 10th Infantry (Colored) and Capt. R. T. Frank of the 1st Artillery, completed the court. Craig, decorated for gallantry at Gettysburg, was experienced in commanding black troops. The prosecution would be headed by Maj. Asa Bird Gardiner, assisted by Capt. Clinton Sears, prosecutor during the inquiry. Gardiner (whose Medal of Honor awarded for actions during the Civil War was later to be rescinded), was the first professor of law at West Point. Later, as district attorney of New York, he would be tried for corruption and, despite being acquitted, removed from office by Theodore Roosevelt.

The defense would be handled by Daniel H. Chamberlain, a Harvard Law graduate, a former officer in the all-black 5th Massachusetts Cavalry Regiment during the Civil War, and a "carpetbagger" ex-governor of South Carolina. He was also a trustee of the University of South Carolina, where Richard T. Greener taught and Whittaker attended classes. Chamberlain would be assisted by Professor Greener.

The court officially began on 20 January at 11:45 a.m. with the reading of Special Order No. 278, the convening order. Whittaker was then asked if he had any objections to any member of the court. He having none, the court was sworn in, then immediately adjourned for two weeks, until 3 February, to allow both sides time to review the three hundred pages of records of the court of inquiry and to prepare their cases. Both sides expressed the opinion that the case would last about two weeks. Actually, the trial would last until 10 June 1881.[29]

The court-martial resumed at 11:00 a.m. on 3 February. Whittaker was charged with two violations of army regulations. The first charge was conduct unbecoming an officer and a gentleman—specifically, that Whittaker had faked the assault, mutilated himself, and written the warning note in order to gain sympathy from the public, discredit the Military Academy, and escape having to take the June examinations, which he expected to fail. The second charge, false swearing to the prejudice of good order and military discipline, referred to his lying under oath during the court of inquiry. Whittaker replied "not guilty" to both charges.

Little new evidence would be presented during the court-martial, which was essentially a repeat of the court of inquiry. The prosecution based its case on the testimony of handwriting experts, the inconsistencies and errors in Whittaker's testimony, and the supposed lack of motive on the part of anyone except Whittaker. This time, in the hands of a more energetic advocate, Whittaker's defense attacked the credibility of the government's handwriting experts and called its own experts to rebut their conclusions. It also called five physicians to counter Dr. Alexander's testimony that Whittaker had been feigning unconsciousness the morning he was discovered. It also denied that Whittaker had had any motive to fake an assault on himself.

During the trial, numerous letters written by Whittaker were entered into evidence as examples of his handwriting, over the objections of the defense, which was damaged more by the content of the letters—which were critical of the cadets, professors, and West Point itself—than by the style of handwriting. Rather than trying to prove that others had involved in the assault, Chamberlain's strategy seems to have been largely reactive. He apparently felt that raising doubt regarding the government's case would be sufficient to win an acquittal. Defense experts spent most of the trial rebutting government witnesses. The defense rested on 17 May, and the court recessed until 1 June 1881, when closing arguments would be heard.

Chamberlain began by reminding the court that it was not the defense's burden to prove innocence but the prosecution's to prove his guilt and that Whittaker was "a youth of singularly irreproachable character." He stated that the prosecution had to prove three basic issues: that Whittaker had tied and mutilated himself, that he had feigned unconsciousness, and that he had himself written the warning note. It had to prove not just that Whittaker *could* have done those things but that he *had done* them. And why, he wondered, if the argument was being made that no cadet would act in such a manner, did it not apply to Cadet Whittaker?

On 6 May, Gardiner began the prosecution's closing argument by stating that the prosecution wasn't required to prove their case beyond a doubt but only beyond a reasonable doubt. He reiterated the view that Whittaker was the only person with a motive for the assault, suggesting that social ostracism might have created a desire for revenge or to gain sympathy. He also asserted to the court that "Negroes are noted for their ability to sham and feign.... [T]he colored person is, according to all anthropologists, endowed with cunning and the power of mimicry." He finished by focusing on the inconsistencies in Whittaker's account and declaring his belief in Whittaker's guilt.

The court rendered its decision at noon on 10 June. The court deleted the part of the first charge, which had accused Whittaker of committing the act to gain public notice, discredit West Point, and avoid June examinations, but it found him guilty of self-mutilation and of writing the warning note. In essence, Whittaker was guilty of the acts, but without any proven motive. The court recommended that he was "to be dishonorably dismissed from the military service of the United States, and to pay a fine of one dollar, and to be thereafter confined at hard labor for one year in such penitentiary as the reviewing authority may direct."[30]

But on the back of the last page of the transcript, six members of the court, including General Miles, had signed a recommendation that because of Whittaker's youth and inexperience, the fine and imprisonment be remitted. The case was forwarded to the reviewing authority, D. E. Swain, the army judge advocate general, on 1 December 1881. In a 101-page report, Swain cited deficiencies in the proceeding, including the fact that the president had had no authority to convene a court-martial, that the admission of Whittaker's letters had been illegal, and that the prosecution had failed to prove its case (i.e., that Whittaker had written the note or mutilated himself). Swain recommended that the proceeding, the findings, and the sentence be disapproved.

After some research, the secretary of war and the attorney general concurred with the judge advocate's opinion as to the admissibility of the letters, and on 22 March 1882, President Chester A. Arthur disapproved the court-martial due to improper admission of evidence. Whittaker was released from arrest and his sentence voided. Whereas Swain had found that the guilty verdict was in error, however, Arthur had simply thrown it out on a technicality. On the same day, the secretary of war, Robert Todd Lincoln, ordered Whittaker dismissed from the academy for failing the June 1880 examination. By this time the public had tired of the Whittaker case, and there was little public comment. On the same day, Congressman D. Wyatt Aiken, the representative from Whittaker's home district in South Carolina, nominated a white youth to take Whittaker's place at West Point. Once again there were no blacks cadets at the U.S. Military Academy. Johnson C. Whittaker was now a civilian.

After a short series of speaking engagements, Whittaker put West Point behind him and refused to speak of it for the rest of his life. He earned a law degree from South Carolina College, practiced law, raised a family, and moved his family to Oklahoma in 1908 to escape Jim Crow, only to return to South Carolina in 1925. He took work as a teacher, later as principal of the Colored Normal, Industrial, Agriculture and Mechanical College, teaching chemistry, psychology, and military science. He passed away from a bleeding ulcer on 14 January 1931.

Although denied a commission, Whittaker showed no bitterness, rather embracing education as a way to raise his race. Whittaker's sons,

Johnson Jr., and Miller, served as commissioned officers during World War I—Miller as a second lieutenant with the 368th Infantry, 92nd Division, and Johnson Jr., as a captain in the 317th Ammunition Transportation Battalion. Johnson became the first African American engineer in South Carolina, and Miller became president of South Carolina State College. A grandson, Peter, served as an officer and fighter pilot during World War II, flying with the Tuskegee Airmen. A great-grandson, Ulysses Boykin, a Harvard educated lawyer, served as a first lieutenant during Vietnam before rising to the bench of the Third Judicial Circuit Court in Detroit, Michigan.

A book, *Assault at West Point*, published in 1972, and a TV movie of the same name in 1994 raised awareness of Whittaker's case, undoubtedly contributing to President Bill Clinton's decision to commission Whittaker posthumously. Additionally, in October 1997, James Webster Smith was granted a posthumous commission as a second lieutenant, 123 years after being expelled from West Point. As the secretary of the army, Togo D. West Jr., observed, "It's never too late to right a wrong."[31]

8

Camp Logan Incident

MUTINY, RIOT—1917

Major, I think we're going to have trouble tonight.—Sgt. Vida Henry to Major Kneeland Snow in the early evening of 23 August 1917

With the declaration of war on 6 April 1917, the United States rapidly mobilized for the world war taking place in Europe. Segregation and racial discrimination was still legal in America; African Americans hoped that by enlisting in the military and participating in the struggle to "Make the World Safe for Democracy" they might be able to increase the fruits of democracy for themselves at home.

Black Americans had been serving in segregated units since the Civil War and had played a significant role in winning the war and then in taming the western frontier. Conflict between black soldiers and white civilians was all too common, especially for black soldiers posted in the south and southwest. Many of them were from the north and were outraged by the treatment afforded blacks in their new localities.

Known as "Buffalo Soldiers," black troops often had violent confrontations with the local populations they were assigned to protect. At Fort Hays, Kansas, where the black 10th Cavalry was sent to keep order, there were over thirty homicides between August 1867 and December 1873. Black soldiers of the 25th Infantry stationed at Fort Meade, near the town of Sturgis, in the Dakota Territory, were so angry about a recent lynching of a fellow soldier by townspeople that on 20 September 1885 they shot up two saloons, killing one townsman. The black 9th Cavalry, sent to Wyoming in 1892 during the Johnson County War, built Camp Bettens near the rail town of Suggs. Unwelcomed by either side of the conflict, the troopers remained for over a year despite a hostile and racist population. One soldier was killed, and two were wounded in gun battles with locals.[1]

But for black soldiers the worst place to be stationed was Texas, where segregation was strictly enforced by racist police and sheriffs and the local populations were hostile toward their presence. Many saw armed blacks as a challenge to white supremacy. On their part, black soldiers reacted strongly to unfair treatment, often escalating tension by openly violating Jim Crow laws; the result was conflict. In 1870, near Fort McKavett, Texas, one John Jackson murdered Pvt. Boston Henry, Cpl. Albert Marshall and Pvt. Charles Murray among the unit sent to capture him. Finally arrested, he was set free by a local jury. In 1875, two black soldiers in a five-man patrol were killed in an ambush near Rio Grande City; nine men were indicted for the murder, but only one was brought to trial, and he was acquitted. In 1878, when locals assaulted a black sergeant in a saloon in San Angelo, Texas, and stripped him of his chevrons, troopers from nearby Fort Concho stormed the saloon, starting a gunfight.[2]

Black troops fought a gun battle with police in Texarkana in 1899. That same year, black troops stationed at Rio Grande City fired on the town after receiving reports that a mob was gathering. In Laredo, a law officer was assaulted in retaliation for the police beating of a black soldier. In 1900, after two black soldiers were arrested for drunkenness and disorderly conduct, other black soldiers attempted to break them out of an El Paso jail; one black trooper and one lawman were killed in the attempt. Local prosecutors convicted one soldier on little evidence; he was sentenced to life in prison.[3]

By 1917, many in Texas recalled the Fort Brown riot at Brownsville, Texas, in 1906, in which soldiers of the 25th Infantry had been accused of going into town on a shooting spree in which one white had been killed. The whole regiment had been discharged without honor by President Theodore Roosevelt. The 1st Battalion, 24th Infantry too got a Texas "welcome" in April 1917 when, refused service at a local brothel, some drunken troopers began pelting the building with stones. Texas Rangers arrived, and a black soldier was killed resisting arrest.[4]

On 27 July 1917, the army ordered 654 black enlisted men and eight white officers of the 3rd Battalion of the 24th (Companies I, K, L, and M) to Houston, Texas, as a guard force for Camp Logan, then under construction approximately three and a half miles from downtown Houston. The troops were garrisoned in a tent camp outside the city. The 24th Infantry had been formed on 1 November 1869, from two Civil War regiments, the 38th and 41st Infantry. All the enlisted soldiers were black, primarily veterans of the U.S. Colored Troops, and the regiment saw service in the southwest during the Indian wars. In 1898, during the Spanish American

War, they were deployed to Cuba as part of the U.S. Expeditionary Force and fought with distinction at the battles of Santiago and San Juan Heights. Once Cuba was secured, the 24th was sent to the Philippines to battle rebels led by Emilio Aguinaldo. They left after his capture in 1901, but they would return to the Philippines in 1905 and 1911. In 1916 the regiment was posted to New Mexico to secure the border during the Mexican Revolution, and it was part of General Pershing's Punitive Expedition against Pancho Villa from March 1916 through February 1917. Shortly after arriving back in New Mexico, the 3rd Battalion was ordered to Houston.[5]

Houston, in Harris County, had been chosen as the location for two military training bases, Camp Logan and Ellington Field. With a growing population of over 130,000, a temperate climate, and an active port, shipping lumber, cattle, petrochemicals, and cotton, Houston was thriving economically. But it was less than an ideal location for the stationing of black troops. Although Houston had the largest black population in Texas, it had a tradition of segregation that was unacceptable to many of the soldiers. Additionally, the city's 160-member police department was poorly trained and was mistrusted by whites and blacks alike. The Houston police had a reputation for beating prisoners in custody, taking bribes, and ignoring violations. The police also had a reputation among the city's blacks for being racist and abusing their authority. The chief of police, Clarence Brock, was inexperienced, exerted little control or discipline over his force, and lacked support from the city government. The police routinely referred to blacks as "niggers" to their faces, which created active hostility between the troops and the police.[6]

Additionally, the leadership of the battalion was new and inexperienced. With the war in Europe going on, experienced officers were needed to train new troops. Twenty-five officers of the 3rd Battalion, including the battalion commander, were transferred to other bases, as well as senior enlisted men, including the battalion sergeant-major and all the first sergeants. They were replaced with less capable officers who were unfamiliar to the men.

The new commanding officer, Lt. Col. William Newman, tried to establish a good working relationship with Chief Brock to ease the tension between blacks and whites, tension that increased on 2 July with news of a second race riot in East St. Louis, Illinois. In the first riot earlier that year, on 28 May, striking white workers, angry at being replaced by blacks, surged in a mob downtown, randomly beating blacks on the streets. The governor called in the Illinois National Guard, and the violence diminished.

Nothing was done to address the white workers' grievances or to correct the actions of the police, who had been noticeably ineffective during the riot. The National Guard was withdrawn on 10 June. On 2 July, violence returned to East St. Louis with a vengeance. Mobs entered black neighborhoods and set fire to homes. Men, women, and children were beaten and shot at. Mobs lynched blacks and burned their neighborhood, and police fled to their station house. Again, the Illinois National Guard was called, but this time there were reports of guardsmen joining the rioters. When the violence subsided there were between forty and 120 dead, uncounted injured, and approximately six thousand homeless. Many of the 3rd Battalion in Houston sent part of their pay to help. It was one of the bloodiest race riots in the nation's history, and there was a national outcry. Congress began an investigation that would eventually result in the indictment of several members of the East St. Louis police force.[7]

On 18 August 1917, Houston police officers John Richardson and J. W. Spaulding beat and arrested Pvt. Richard Brown and Pvt. Gerald Meims for disturbing the peace after taking offense at being called niggers. Later in the day, Pvt. Richard Griggs was beaten and verbally abused for sitting in the white section of a streetcar.

On 20 August, Lieutenant Colonel Newman was transferred out, and Capt. Kneeland Snow, the Company I commander, was promoted to major and to command of the battalion. Snow's relationship with Chief Brock wasn't as close as Newman's had been. To ease tension, twelve black noncommissioned officers (NCOs) were appointed as provost guards, or military police (MPs), to monitor the soldiers' behavior in town. Unlike in other cities, however, they weren't armed and were required to call white police to make arrests. Even though Chief Brock had ordered his officers to use the word "colored" and not "nigger" when referring to black troops and to cooperate with the MPs, he had little influence in the department, and his orders were largely ignored. The troops continued to be treated with disrespect and physical abuse, and tension grew.

On the afternoon of 23 August, two mounted officers, Lee Sparks and Rufus Daniels, broke up a dice game at the corner of Felipe and Bailey Streets in a black neighborhood, then fired at the men as they fled. Under the pretext of looking for one of the fugitives from arrest, they entered the house of Mrs. Travers, a black housewife. Failing to find him, they abused and arrested the woman and forced her, with her five children, out onto the street, partially clad, in front of neighbors. As they waited for the patrol wagon, a crowd gathered around the hysterical woman, who repeatedly begged to know why she was being arrested. A soldier in the crowd, Pvt. Alonzo Edwards of Company L, stepped forward. He asked the police why the woman was being arrested and declared that she should be allowed to dress and get her shoes. The policemen immediately set upon him, striking him with the butts of their pistols; they knocked him to the ground, kicked him, and placed him under arrest for interfering with an arrest. A witness heard Sparks say, "That's the way we do things in the South. We're running things, not the damned niggers." (Mrs. Travers was arrested for "abusive language" but was later released.)[8]

A short time later, Cpl. Charles Baltimore, a provost guard from Company I, tried to get information from Sparks and Daniels about Edwards' arrest, as was his duty, and was told by Sparks, "I don't answer to niggers." Then Sparks struck Baltimore on the head with his pistol and fired at him three times as he fled. Baltimore was subsequently arrested in a house in which he was found hiding and taken to the Fourth Ward Police Station. Word began circulating that Baltimore, a popular and respected NCO, had been shot and killed by the police. Major Snow telephoned the station to find out what happened, learned that Baltimore was in custody, and arranged to have him released and returned to camp. He also learned that Sparks had been suspended without pay.[9]

Snow met with his first sergeants, briefed them regarding Baltimore, canceled passes for the night, and increased the camp guard by three. Otherwise he seemed unconcerned, or uninformed, about the mood of the men. Captain Shekergian of the 24th met with Chief Brock that afternoon; neither believed the situation to have reached crisis level.

The following account of the riot that ensued, by Pvt. Leroy Pinkett of Company I, appeared in the 24 August 1917 edition of the *New York Times:*

> Yesterday at about 3:00 PM, we heard that Corporal Baltimore of our company had been shot by special officers. All the boys said "Let's go get the man that shot Baltimore." We stood retreat at 6:00 o'clock and then I heard Sergeant Henry of our company say "Well, don't stand around like that. If you are going to do anything, go ahead and do it." After that, I saw some boys slip over to Company K and I heard them say they had stolen the ammunition.
>
> Then Captain Snow called the men out in line. He asked what we were doing and ordered a search made for the ammunition and also ordered our rifles to be taken up. Another sergeant, I forget his name, took up our rifles from our tents. In this same talk, Captain Snow told us that Baltimore was not in the wrong, that the policeman was in the wrong.
>
> A big fella in our company named Frank Johnson then came running down the company street hollering "Get your rifles, boys. They are coming. The mob is coming to camp." We all made a rush then for the supply camp and got our rifles and we went to a large ammunition box and got our ammunition. Sergeant Henry was the leader.[10]

Although later white accounts would claim that the riot was planned and retaliatory in nature, it seems to have been spontaneous, motivated among the whites by fear and memories of recent events in East St. Louis. Gunfire was heard; evidence suggests that shots were fired into the camp. Approximately 125–150 men, primarily men from Company I, armed themselves and began a march into town.[11]

Because of the dark and confusion of the night, there is no way to create an accurate chronology of the riot, but the following events occurred, probably in this sequence. Some of the men remaining in camp, believing they were being fired on, returned an indiscriminate fire that may have accounted for some civilian casualties. Although the soldiers were armed only with military rifles, some of the wounds received by men in the vicinity of the camp were from nonmilitary firearms. A police officer, L. E. Gentry, would testify that some of the shots "didn't sound like rifles to me."[12]

It is almost certain that the target of the march was the Fourth Ward Police Station. The men wreaked havoc as they moved forward. A townsperson, E. A. Thompson, was fired on and killed as he drove west on Washington Street with his wife, sister-in-law, and friend. Another, A. R. Carstens, was shot stepping off a trolley. Charles Wright, who was visiting his parents on Wood Street, was shot as he stepped outside to investigate the disturbance, as was fifteen-year-old Fred Winkler. Winkler's friend William Drucks was shot in the arm, requiring later amputation. Fifteen-year-old Alma Reichert was shot in the abdomen as she stood in the doorway of her father's grocery; she survived. Manuel Gerardo was killed in his sleep. As townsman C. W. Hahl recalled, "They were walking and shooting, coolly and with deliberation, halting to take aim."[13]

Surprisingly, despite rumors of trouble, neither Chief Brock nor Sheriff Frank Hammond had taken any special precautions. In fact, Sheriff Hammond had left town early in the evening, and Chief Brock retired early. Major Snow and the other officers tried to restore order at the 24th's camp, which was segregated from the rest of Camp Logan. At one point, an unarmed Snow confronted thirty armed soldiers outside camp, who then had a heated discussion over whether or not to shoot him. In Snow's own words, the men "paid no attention to me whatsoever." Unable to contact Camp Logan on the telephone, Snow sent a runner there to contact Capt. L. A. Tuggle of the 5th Illinois. Tuggle, with his officers and eight hundred men, responded and rendered valuable assistance in keeping armed civilians away from the 3rd Battalion's camp and in arresting rioters along San Felipe Street.[14]

Chief Brock, awakened from his slumber, authorized a civilian posse of a thousand volunteers, who broke into hardware stores to arm themselves. Rather than confront the rioting armed mob, the men cordoned off and protected the downtown area. The result was a much lower loss of life than might have occurred had the two groups squared off. By early morning of the 24th, Texas governor James E. Ferguson had declared martial law and placed Brig. Gen. John A. Hulen of the Texas National Guard in charge of restoring order. Three companies of coast artillery from Fort Crockett at Galveston and a battalion of the 19th Infantry at Fort Sam Houston were called out.

Meanwhile, a second group of soldiers left the camp, this one made up of the camp guard—seventeen sentries with loaded weapons, under the leadership of the corporal of the guard, John Wilson. Two soldiers returned to camp almost immediately and would later testify for the prosecution. The remainder continued on, attempting to join the first group. After terrorizing a group of whites outside a restaurant, they fired at a car that refused to stop, killing the driver, E. M. Jones.

Sergeant Henry's group reached the area where Private Edwards had been beaten and found it guarded by two mounted police officers. The two fled and were fired upon by the approaching mob, wounding one of them. A car approached carrying five men, four of them police officers, including Officer Daniels. The men emerged from the vehicle and confronted black soldiers pointing weapons at them. Enraged, Daniels charged and was cut down by gunfire. The other officers fled, seeking cover, but one fired at the soldiers, and a return volley wounded one of the officers.

During this encounter, one of the soldiers, Pvt. Bryant Watson, was killed by friendly fire, and some of the men began arguing that the march should end. While the issue was being debated, the group was approached by another car, this one containing two police officers and three armed civilians. The car was stopped and the men ordered out. One of the policemen, John Richardson, was too slow to obey and was clubbed over the head with a rifle butt by Cpl. Henry Peacock. The others ran, and the mob opened fire, killing Officer Ira Raney and wounding two others.[15]

The fleeing men flagged down a police car, which accidentally drove toward the mutineers. Inside were Officer E. G. Meineke and an officer and three enlisted men of the Illinois National Guard from Camp Logan. The soldiers opened fire, killing three, including Capt. Joseph W. Mattes, an officer in Battery A, 2nd Illinois Field Artillery, and Officer Meineke. It was at this point, the men perhaps horrified that they had killed a military officer, that the mutiny fell apart. After a heated debate, the majority headed back to camp. Sergeant Henry, wounded earlier, remained and allegedly committed suicide by shooting himself in the head, at about 2:00 a.m. By dawn, Houston was calm. Fifteen whites, including four policemen, were dead. Another twelve whites were seriously injured; one later died. Four black soldiers had died: Sergeant Henry, Private Watson, and two soldiers who subsequently died from wounds.

The next day, 24 August, as the army began its investigation, the soldiers of the 24th marched to a parade ground where, flanked by a battalion of the 19th Infantry under the command of Col. Millard Waltz, the men were disarmed and placed under heavy guard. Their weapons were transported to a camp storehouse. Thirty-four rioters arrested by civil authorities and in custody at the Harris County Jail were released to the military. That action angered city residents and resulted in an investigation of the sheriff, and Harris County district attorney John H. Croker obtained indictments for murder from the local grand jury against the thirty-four soldiers who had been in custody.[16]

Maj. Gen. George Bell, Jr., arrived from San Antonio and assured the locals that "the justice meted out by army authorities will be much quicker obtained than it could be by civil procedure," reminding them that mutiny in time of war was punishable by death. He promised the citizens of Houston that "Punishment will be dealt out to those participating in the disturbance promptly and effectively."[17] The thirty-four soldiers, along with the rest of the battalion, were transported aboard two heavily guarded trains to Camp Furlong, outside Columbus, New Mexico.

Camp Logan court-martial in session, 1917 (National Archives and Records Administration).

The army investigation, conducted by Col. G. O. Cress, was hindered by that fact that no accurate list of who had left the camp during the mutiny and who had remained in camp existed. Captain Shekergian tried to produce one, but many soldiers had left the camp that night and returned without participating, while others had hid in fear of mobs and weren't counted. The "Cress Report" was issued on 13 September. The army arrested 151 soldiers, ultimately charging 118 soldiers with mutiny and murder.[18]

Maj. Gen. John Wilson Ruckman, commander of the Southern Department of the Army, ordered courts-martial convened. The first opened in the chapel at Fort Sam Houston, San Antonio, Texas, on 1 November 1917. A court of thirteen officers—three brigadier generals, seven colonels and three lieutenant colonels, eight of them graduates of West Point—was empanelled. Sixty-three men were charged with disobedience to orders of the commanding officer, mutiny, assault on civilians, and murder. Close to two hundred witnesses testified over twenty-two days. The prosecution was hindered by what its members later called a "conspiracy of silence"; most of the soldiers refused to speak to investigators. Ultimately seven soldiers testified in exchange for clemency.

Fifty-four of the sixty-three were found guilty on all charges, four were convicted of the lesser charge of disobeying orders, and five were acquitted. Of those convicted of all charges, thirteen were sentenced to death by hanging, the remaining forty-one to life imprisonment at hard labor. The four convicted of lesser charges received two-year sentences. Since the highest-ranking soldier tried was Sgt. William Nesbit, the trial became known as the "Nesbit case."[19]

Ordinarily in military courts-martial, verdicts and sentences are not announced until the mandatory review process is complete, but on this occasion thirteen soldiers were executed while the review process was still under way. The departmental judge advocate, Col. George Dunn, reviewed the record of the Nesbit case, approved the sentences, then forwarded the matter to General Ruckman on 3 December. On 9 December, the thirteen condemned prisoners (among them Corporal Baltimore) were advised of the sentence but not of the time or place. The court's recommendation of clemency for a Pvt. Thomas Hawkins was ignored by General Ruckman.

The unlucky thirteen were transferred to a guarded barracks on 10 December, and scaffolds were constructed at nearby Camp Travis. Engineers worked through the night by the light of bonfires to finish before dawn of the 11th. The prisoners were awakened and transported to the place of execution at 5:00 a.m. The thirteen were hanged simultaneously at one minute before sunrise, 7:17. The execution and subsequent burial were carried out in secret, witnessed only by several army officers and the county sheriff, John Tobin. The scaffold was disassembled and returned to Fort Sam Houston.[20]

When General Ruckman announced the verdicts and sentences and that the death sentences had already been carried out, there was outrage in a large part of the nation, especially in the black press. There had been no chance for the men to appeal the case and no independent review; the case had not yet been reviewed by Secretary of War Newton Baker and President Woodrow Wilson.

On 17 December the second court-martial was convened at Fort Sam Houston for the fifteen members of the camp guard charged with leaving their posts, threatening civilians, and murdering E. M. Jones. There was a high degree of uncertainty as to who had actually shot Jones, and again the prosecution relied on testimony from soldiers granted clemency or lighter sentences. Five of the fifteen were found guilty of shooting at Mr. Jones' car and were sentenced to hang. Three were sentenced to ten years hard labor, and the remaining seven received seven-year sentences. Learning from past mistakes, Ruckman approved the sentences and announced them on 2 January 1918 but delayed punishment pending review by the secretary of war and the president. The case became known as the "Washington case," for Cpl. John Washington.

The White House received hundreds of letters and petitions for clemency, and President Wilson met with black leaders. Meanwhile, a third court-martial was convened at San Antonio on 18 February 1918, putting forty soldiers on trial for mutiny, riot, and disobedience of orders. On 26 March twenty-three soldiers were convicted on all counts, nine for disobeying orders and riot, five for disobeying orders. Two were acquitted, and one had charges dismissed. Of the twenty-three, eleven received death sentences, and the other twelve were sentenced to life at hard labor. The lesser sentences varied in severity. This case became known as the "Tillman case," for Cpl. Robert Tillman, the senior defendant.[21]

On 31 August 1918, President Wilson commuted ten of the death sentences to life in prison, leaving the other six death sentences intact. In a public statement, Wilson characterized the investigation as "very searching and thorough" and the court-martial as having been "properly constituted" and made up of officers "of experience and sobriety of judgment." Wilson further stated that he had confirmed the six death sentences because there was "plain evidence" that the accused had "deliberately" engaged in "shocking brutality."[22]

Five death sentences were carried out at daybreak on 29 September

1918; the sixth execution took place a week later. Those not executed served their sentences at the Fort Leavenworth Federal Penitentiary in Kansas. Many of the soldiers were paroled during the 1920s following appeals by the National Association for the Advancement of Colored People (NAACP). The last prisoner was released in 1938.[23]

It was the largest murder trial in American legal history, the largest court-martial in American military history, and one of the bloodiest race riots in American history altogether. While the military and much of the American public viewed the event as nothing less than unprovoked and premeditated murder, the NAACP would later characterize the men as "Martyrs in the cause of Democracy."[24]

9

Operation Pastorious (Ex Parte Quirin)

TREASON, SABOTAGE—1942

> *I want one thing understood, Francis. I won't give them up. I won't hand them over to any United States Marshal armed with a writ of habeas corpus.*—President Franklin Roosevelt to Attorney General Francis Biddle

> *[Constitutional rights] should not be granted to belligerent enemies who, in time of war, enter this country in order to destroy it by acts of war.*—Attorney General Biddle and Judge Advocate General

On 13 November 2001, President George W. Bush signed a military order providing for the detention, treatment, and trial of suspected terrorists. Its statement that they could be tried by military tribunals rather than in the regular civilian courts raised concern among civil rights advocates. The order was modeled to a large extent on President Franklin D. Roosevelt's proclamation and military order of 1942 after the capture of eight German saboteurs.

Shortly after midnight, on the morning of 13 June 1942, Coast Guardsman John C. Cullen was patrolling the beach along Amagansett, Long Island. The United States was at war, and what he discovered along that deserted shoreline would subsequently define the president's war powers as commander in chief and the scope of military tribunals for future generations. Although World War II began in Europe on 1 September 1939, with Germany's invasion of Poland, political opposition to involvement in another "European" war kept the United States neutral until the attack on Pearl Harbor by the Japanese on 7 December 1941. The following day, 8 December, the United States declared war on Japan, and three days later, on 11 December, Germany and Italy declared war on the United States.

The major contribution of the United States in the early months of the war was the industrial production of vehicles, aircraft, munitions, equipment, and supplies, which were furnished to nations actively opposing the Nazis with armies in the field. Consequently, German military intelligence initiated a plan aimed at sabotaging and undermining America's war effort and reducing its production of war materials.[1]

The mission was code-named Operation Pastorious, by Adm. Wilhelm Canaris, chief of the German Abwehr (Military Intelligence), who named it for Francis Daniel Pastorious, the leader of the first organized settlement of Germans in America in 1683. The plan was meant to disrupt American war production through a series of acts of sabotage aimed primarily at the aluminum and magnesium industries. Other targets, chosen for their potential to disrupt the production and transportation of war materiel, included the hydroelectric plants at Niagara Falls; the Hell Gate Bridge in New York City; Aluminum Company of America factories in Illinois, Tennessee, and New York; the Philadelphia Salt Company's Cryolite plant in Philadelphia, which supplied raw material for aluminum manufacture; the locks on the Ohio River between Cincinnati and St. Louis; Horseshoe Curve, a critical railroad pass near Altoona, Pennsylvania; and Pennsylvania Station in Newark, New Jersey. Additionally, major railroad station locker rooms and Jewish-owned department stores were to be bombed to create panic and terror.[2]

The man placed in charge of recruiting agents for the effort was a thirty-seven-year-old Abwehr officer, *Leutnant* Walter Kappe, an ardent National Socialist who had lived in the United States for twelve years, from 1925 to 1937, and who had been active in the German-American Bund as publisher of the Bund newspaper in Cincinnati, *Deutscher Weckruf und Beobachter.* As an official of Germany's Ausland Institute, Kappe had organized Germans living abroad, worked to win over German-Americans to the Nazi Party, and used propaganda to recruit German immigrants. Now back in Germany, Kappe was primarily responsible for recruiting Germans in the Fatherland who had lived in the United States to go back as saboteurs.[3]

Kappe selected twelve men, all loyal members of the party, for the initial group. Four dropped out, leaving eight, whom he organized into two groups of four. They were a disparate group. Georg Johann Dasch had been born in Speyer-am-Rhein, near Frankfurt, Germany, on 7 February 1903, one of twelve children in a devout Roman Catholic family. He had entered the seminary at age thirteen but had been expelled the following year and had lied about his age to enlist in the Imperial German Army. He had served in Belgium during the final months of World War I. He had gone to the

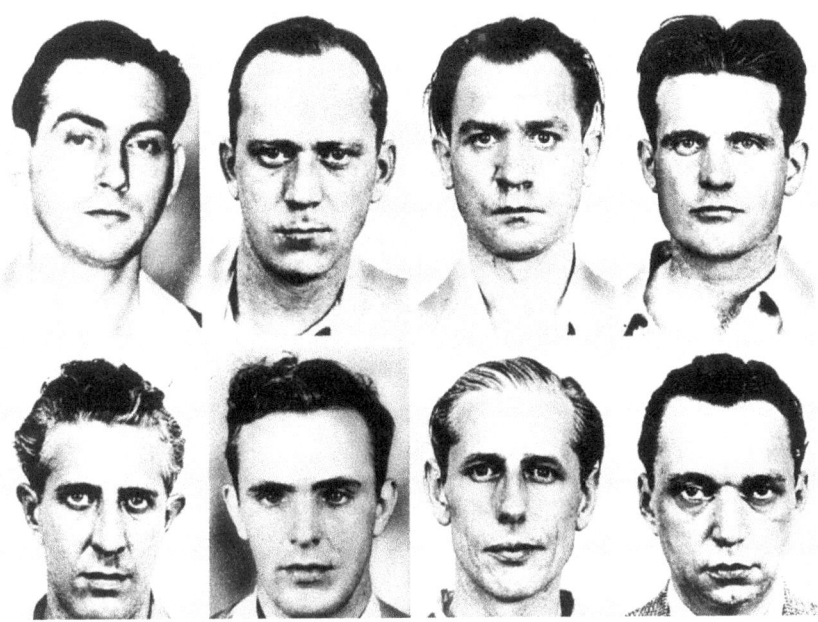

Nazi saboteurs (top row, left to right): Herman Otto Neubauer, Heinrich Harm Heinck, Werner Theil, Edward Kerling; (bottom row, left to right): Richard Quirin, Herbert Hans Haupt, George John Dasch, Ernest Peter Berger (Library of Congress).

United States as a stowaway on board the SS *Scholarie*, landing in Philadelphia in 1922. He had worked a week helping a German baker before hitchhiking to New York City. There he had lived on 145th Street with an Irish family named Callahan, worked as a waiter by day, and took classes at night to learn English.

He served in the U.S. Army Air Corps in Honolulu in 1927 and was honorably discharged the following year with a rating of "excellent." He worked as a waiter at hotels and restaurants in Miami, Los Angeles, and San Francisco, where, already fluent in French as well as his native German, he improved his English. He returned to New York and married Rose Marie Guille, a Pennsylvania-born hairdresser in September 1930. He was accepted for American citizenship in 1933 but never finalized the paperwork.

His disillusionment over his inability to make good and a looming war in Europe caused Dasch to announce to his wife on Christmas Eve 1940 his intention that they would start a new life by returning to Germany. They received their passports in January 1941, but the Neutrality Act and poor health kept his wife from accompanying him; Dasch arrived in Berlin alone on 13 May 1941. Although Dasch later would later testify that he had been opposed to National Socialism, he played the loyal party member well enough to be sought out by Kappe upon his return to Berlin. Dasch was initially hired by the Abwehr to monitor American radio broadcasts but was recruited by Kappe when the latter took over the "American" section of the sabotage school at Quentz Lake in February 1942. At thirty-nine, Dasch was the oldest of the eight and was chosen to head the first team.[4]

Ernest Peter Burger had been born in Ausberg, Germany, on 1 September 1906 and joined the Nazi party at seventeen, participating in the abortive Munich beer-hall putsch in 1923. Described as stocky and intelligent and with slicked-back hair, Burger fled had Germany for the United States in February 1927 to escape criminal charges in the Bavarian courts for brawling. He had worked as a machinist in Detroit and Milwaukee, studied English, and served in the Michigan and Wisconsin National Guards. In 1933, Burger became an American citizen.

But that same year, with the deepening of the Great Depression and Hitler's rise to power, Burger headed home, urged by letters from his parents describing Germany's new prosperity. He rejoined the Nazi Party and became a senior aide to Ernst Röhm, chief of the Nazi Sturmabteilung (storm troopers), or S.A. By sheer luck, Burger was away on assignment and escaped Hitler's bloody purge of that organization during the "Night of the Long Knives" the following year, on 30 June 1934. He took a minor post in the propaganda section of the party, attended the University of Berlin, and graduated. But an analysis he wrote at the university of German actions in Czechoslovakia and Poland that was critical of the Gestapo caused his arrest, for falsifying government documents, on 4 March 1940. He was confined in a concentration camp for seventeen months, during which time his pregnant wife was interrogated by the Gestapo and miscarried. Charges were eventually dropped, and Burger was released and sent to the army as an infantry private. He was assigned to guard Yugoslavian and British prisoners of war at a camp outside Berlin. Interviewed in February 1942 by Kappe, who hoped to redeem a man he saw as a loyal Nazi, Burger reported to Quentz Lake in April and was assigned to Dasch's team.[5]

Born in Berlin on 26 April 1908, Richard Quirin, was at thirty-four perhaps the most ardent National Socialist of the group. After attending trade schools as a machinist apprentice, he had borrowed money from an uncle and emigrated to the United States, arriving at the Port of New York on 17 October 1927. He had moved in with an uncle in Schenectady, New York, where he studied English at night school and found work in the maintenance department of General Electric. Laid off during the Depression, Quirin moved to New York City, where he worked as a housepainter and joined the German-American Bund. He openly and passionately supported Hitler and joined the National Socialist German Workers' Party (NSDAP) in 1934. In 1939, when he heard that Germany was paying the passage costs for Germans who wanted to repatriate, he and his German-born wife returned to Germany, after twelve years in America. Upon his return, Quirin was interviewed by officials of the German Labor Front. He obtained work with Volkswagen at its plant in Braunschweig, where he became friends with Heinrich Heinck. The two became the first recruited by Walter Kappe, and would be the third and fourth members of Dasch's team.[6]

Heinrich Heinck had been born in Hamburg, Germany, on 27 June 1907, and like Quirin he had attended public schools, had been trained as a machinist apprentice (in the machine shop of the Hamburg-American Line), and married a German-born wife, with whom he would return to Germany in 1939. In his case, however, in the summer of 1926, after working as a machinist aboard Hamburg-American's SS *Westphalia* and making several voyages to the United States, Heinck had jumped ship at the Port of New York. As an illegal he kept a low profile, taking work as a busboy, waiter, and handyman. He obtained employment in various German-owned machine shops in the New York area and by 1934 was a member of the German-American Bund, where he became acquainted with Kappe. Heinck and his wife returned to Germany in March 1939, the trip paid for in part by the German consulate. He obtained work in the Volkswagen plant in Braunschweig and was recruited with Quirin to return to America.[7]

The leader of the second team, Edward John Kerling, had been born in Wiesbaden, Germany, on 12 June 1909 and had been one of the earliest supporters of National Socialism, joining the Nazi party in June 1928 at the age of nineteen. He had left Germany to find work and entered the United States on 5 March 1929, under an immigrant quota visa. He obtained work in New York City as a shipping clerk. On 31 October 1931 he married German-born Marie Sichart, and the two worked for numerous affluent families in New York and Connecticut as a cook/butler-chauffeur team. Still an ardent Nazi, he joined both the German-American Bund and maintained his membership in the NSDAP back home. Unlike the other agents, he never made any effort to obtain U.S. citizenship. He returned to Germany for short visits in 1933, when Hitler assumed power, and again in 1936 for the Berlin Olympics.

Upon returning from Berlin, he separated from his wife and began several relationships with women, including a waitress in Miami, a German immigrant named Hedwig Engemann, who became his mistress. With the outbreak of war in September 1939, Kerling and several friends, including Hermann Neubauer, bought a yacht, *Lekala*, for under $2,000 and attempted to sail home to defend the fatherland. The boat was intercepted by the U.S. Coast Guard off Atlantic City and was turned back, under the provisions of the Neutrality Act. Selling the boat in Miami and leaving wife and mistress behind, Kerling sailed for Lisbon, Portugal, aboard the SS *Exochorda* in late June 1940. By August Kerling was working as a civilian employee of the German army at a listening post in Deauville, France, where he translated English broadcasts into German. He then took a position with the Ministry of Propaganda in Berlin, where he was interviewed by Kappe in April 1942 and was accepted for the mission, although he had no idea of its nature until just before reporting to Quentz Lake.[8]

Hermann Otto Neubauer had been born in Hamburg, Germany, on 6 February 1910, trained as an apprentice cook, and obtained work as a cook on the SS *Hamburg*, of the Hamburg-American Lines. In July 1931 he had jumped ship in New York City and obtained employment as a cook aboard the SS *Leviathan*, of the United States Lines. On 23 November Neubauer entered the United States and applied for permanent residence under an immigrant quota visa. In 1934 Neubauer joined both the German-American Bund and Nazi party. He remained in the United States, working as a cook in hotels and restaurants, and on board oceangoing vessels, traveling to Europe, Australia, and South America. Neubauer made a short visit to Germany in 1936. He married Alma Wolf, an American, on 10 June 1940, and returned with her and Kerling to Germany via Lisbon on board the *Exochorda*.

Drafted into the German army almost immediately upon his return in November 1940, Neubauer received military training at Magdeburg until May 1941, when his unit was sent to Poland. Three days after Germany's declaration of war on the Soviet Union on 21 June 1941, Neubauer was seriously injured by shrapnel, suffering wounds to his right eye and leg. He was decorated for his wounds and hospitalized in a military hospital at Stuttgart for six months.

While convalescing at an army medical center near Vienna, Austria, Neubauer received a letter from Kappe asking if he would be willing to go on a secret assignment. He accepted the assignment in late March 1942. Called to his company's orderly room, he was furnished a railroad ticket to Berlin, given an address, and told to report there in civilian clothes. It was not until after he had proceeded to Kappe's office that he learned the nature of his mission to the United States and that his friend Edward Kerling was also to go.[9]

Werner Thiel had been born in Dortmund on 29 March 1907 and had received the equivalent of a high school education before going to work as a machinist for the German railroads and, later, in a bicycle factory. He had gone to America on an immigrant quota visa, arriving on 26 April 1927 and seeking work as a machinist. He found work at the Ford Motor Company in Detroit as a tool-and-die maker but was laid off after the stock market crash of 1929. He sought work in Indiana, California, Pennsylvania, and Florida.

Thiel filed papers declaring his intent to become a citizen on 30 April 1927 but never followed through. He joined the Friends of New Germany in 1933 and later the German-American Bund, joining also the NSDAP, in 1939. He helped establish a chapter of the Bund in Hammond, Indiana. Thiel returned to Germany on 27 March 1941 on a German passport, assisted, like many Germans, by a German consulate. He departed San Francisco, California, on a Japanese liner, proceeding to Germany via Japan, Manchuria, and Russia on the Trans-Siberian Railroad. George Dasch was aboard the same ship, and the two became acquainted. After visiting his family upon his return to Germany, Thiel took work in a war plant until March 1942, when he was recruited at a social gathering by Kappe. Thiel had known Kappe in Chicago, and Kappe now asked about his willingness to return to the United States on an unspecified mission. Thiel left his job at the war plant on 1 April 1942 and reported to Quentz Lake two days later.[10]

The last, youngest, and most American of the saboteurs was, like Ernest Burger, an American citizen. Herbert Hans Haupt had been born in Stettin, Germany, on 21 December 1919, the son of Hans Max Haupt, a soldier in the German army during the World War I who had gone to the United States in 1923. Two years later, in March 1925, Haupt and his mother had joined his father in Chicago. Haupt became a citizen at the age of ten on 7 January 1930, when his father was naturalized. Haupt attended public schools but dropped out of high school in 1936. He too was also a member of the German-American Bund in Chicago, where he drilled and was described as a loyal Nazi.

Whether motivated by the fact that his girlfriend, Gerda Stuckmann Melind, was pregnant or by the impending requirement to register for the American draft, Haupt decided to take a "vacation" to California. On 16 June 1941, he left for Mexico City with two friends, one of whom was denied entry into Mexico. Haupt and his second friend, Wolfgang Wergin, went to the German consulate in Mexico City, where arrangements were made for their return to Germany via Japan. The consulate paid the expenses and provided German passports. The voyage to Japan was made in company with other Germans leaving Mexico. After arriving in Yokohama, Japan, they took positions as seamen on board a German freighter, which evaded the British blockade to land them at Bordeaux, France.

Haupt visited relatives, staying with his grandmother, and Wergin enlisted in the German army. Haupt, unable to obtain employment in Germany, was eventually recruited by Kappe to return to the United States on a secret mission. He reported to the sabotage school at Quentz Lake, where he was made aware of the nature of the mission. Haupt would later claim that he'd been stranded in Europe after the outbreak of war and had accepted the mission only as a means to return home.[11]

Kappe brought the eight men together in early April 1942 at Quentz Lake, located in the wooded German countryside near Brandenburg, about thirty-five miles west of Berlin. The Reich had confiscated the private estate from a Jewish family and remodeled the buildings into a training facility where between sixteen and twenty students at a time could be instructed in the art of sabotage. Already training agents for missions in Europe, the facility would provide fundamental training for the eight recruits. Classes began Monday, 13 April.

Subjects included the manufacture and use of explosives and incendiary devices, the employment of timing devices and fuses, the use of radios and codes, "secret writing," and classes in current American culture (slang, hit songs, and current events). Background histories were created, and the students conversed in English. Practical exercises in the surrounding countryside included the actual demolition, under supervision, of bridges and railroad tracks constructed on the property for the purpose. The trainees were shown maps of the United States detailing major rail junctions and the locations of principal aluminum and magnesium plants, as well as other important war industries.[12]

Following completion of their training in early May and a brief leave, the eight were taken on a three-day tour of aluminum plants, rail yards, and canal locks in and around Berlin, Bitterfeld and Aachen, during which they were shown how best to deploy explosives to disable the entire plant, terminal, etc. They returned to Quentz Lake for a graduation dinner and were issued forged identity papers, including passports, draft cards, Social Security cards, ration coupons, and driver's licenses. They departed on 22 May by express train to occupied Paris, where they spent two days enjoying the cafes, nightclubs, and women, courtesy of the Third Reich, and then traveled to the submarine base at Lorient on the French coast. There they boarded two submarines for transportation to the United States.[13]

Each team of saboteurs carried four waterproof suitcases containing a large quantity of high explosives disguised as chunks of coal, as well as fuses of various types, timers, detonators, and a considerable quantity of abrasive material to be used for disabling railroad engines and other machinery. No incendiary material was transported, as the expectation was that these materials could be purchased in-country. Each team had also been supplied with a large quantity of authentic American currency to be used for expenses and bribes. Each team leader was given $50,000, and each saboteur carried four thousand dollars in a money belt around his waist. Additionally, each carried four hundred dollars in small bills for immediate use upon landing. Almost all the money was in fifty-dollar bills. All were genuine, but they most likely would have raised suspicion or have led to detection, as many were gold-backed currency notes, which were no longer in circulation.

On the evening of Wednesday, 27 May 1942, the crew of the submarine *U-202* made preparations to get under way from the submarine base at Brest. Just hours before sailing, the *U-202*'s captain, *Kapitanleutnant* Hans Heinz Linder, opened his sealed orders. They were from Adm. Karl Donitz and were labeled "Most Secret"; they instructed him to proceed to the base at Lorient to pick up supplies and a group of saboteurs to be transported and landed on the southern coast of Long Island. The landing, the orders specified, "should be timed to coincide with the new moon night around the middle of June."[14]

The four men of the first team—Dasch, Burger, Quirin, and Heinck—came on board with four large wooden crates. They were dressed in naval fatigues, but the rumor on board that they were war correspondents was quickly dismissed, given their reserved demeanor, and new rumors circulated that they were "secret agents."

At 7:57 p.m. on 28 May, the *U-202* left the protection of the massive concrete submarine pen, built to protect the boats from Allied air raids, and sailed out to sea. The four saboteurs were invited by the captain to the bridge to view their departure and then repaired to their bunks in petty-officer quarters. They were replaced on the bridge by four lookouts, each scanning the horizon in ninety-degree quadrants, vigilant for approaching aircraft—seconds gained or lost in making an emergency dive could make the difference between life and death for the boat.[15]

The *U-202* was a Type VIIC submersible, launched by F. Krupp Germaniawerft AG at Kiel, Germany, on 10 February 1941. It was powered by two 1,160-horsepower diesel engines and was now on its sixth war patrol. In its nine patrols, the *U-202* would sink nine ships, totaling 34,615 tons, and damage four others in its career.[16] On this occasion, for most of the sixteen-day journey the boat ran on the surface, usually at night to avoid detection. Conditions were crowded, as the 145-foot interior was filled with equipment, supplies, ammunition, and men. There was little space to move around, and the roar of the diesels and close conditions made sleep difficult. On the third day out the crew was apprised of the men's special mission.

The *U-202* arrived off Amagansett, Long Island, 115 miles east of New York City, at about 8:00 p.m. on 12 June but remained submerged until after midnight. The four saboteurs were dressed in full German marine fatigue uniforms, so that if they were caught they would be treated as prisoners of war rather than spies. They boarded an inflatable boat with two armed sailors from the crew and rowed through heavy fog toward the shore.

In these early stages of America's involvement in the war, responsibility for the patrol and defense of beaches was shared by the U.S. Coast Guard and Army. In the Long Island area the Coast Guard ran a beach patrol, headquartered at the East Amagansett Coast Guard Life Saving Station. Army coastal defense was provided by the one hundred officers and men of the 113th Mobile Infantry.

Early on the morning of 13 June, Coast Guard Seaman 2nd Class John C. Cullen prepared to go out on patrol, which consisted of a three-mile walk up the coast toward Montauk to punch a time clock, then three miles back to the station. It was a dark night, and the fog was so thick that, Cullen would later recall, he couldn't see his feet. He armed himself with a flare gun and flashlight and departed the station at ten minutes after midnight, walking quickly along the sand dunes and high grass, anxious to complete the patrol and get out of the cold.

At nineteen, Cullen had less than six months' service, having enlisted after Pearl Harbor. He had entered service after Christmas and, after being given a medical exam and issued uniforms at Ellis Island, received only minimal instruction at the Short Beach Lifeboat Station and the Georgica Coast Guard Station in the East Hamptons before being sent to Amagansett in April 1942.

Dasch and his team came ashore about three hundred yards from the Coast Guard station. They began to change out of the German uniforms into civilian clothes immediately and started digging in the sand to bury their uniforms and equipment. As the men worked, Dasch moved up on a dune, from where he observed a figure approaching in the fog.[17]

Accounts on the exact sequence of events differ between Cullen,

Dasch, and official Federal Bureau of Investigation (FBI), Navy, and Coast Guard sources, but according to a Coast Guard report, events transpired essentially as follows. As Cullen came over the dune, he saw a man in civilian clothes and the outline of another man. He called out, "What's the trouble?" There was no answer. The man started toward Cullen, who again called out, "Who are you?" Again there was no answer, and the man continued to approach. Cullen reached for his flashlight; the man saw the motion and, apparently thinking the Coast Guardsman was reaching for a gun, cried out, "Wait a minute. Are you the Coast Guard?" Cullen answered, "Yes. Who are you?" The man replied, "A couple of fishermen from Southampton who have run aground." Cullen invited the men to come up to the station to await daybreak out of the cold. His suspicions were aroused when the man declined, giving the excuse that he had no papers or permit to fish.[18]

When Cullen seemed to insist, Dasch broke away and said, "Now wait a minute. You don't know what this is all about. How old are you, boy?" When Cullen answered "Nineteen," Dasch asked, "You have a father and mother, don't you boy?" When Cullen said, "Yes, I do," Dasch warned, "Well, if you ever want to see them again, please do exactly as I tell you. I wouldn't want to have to kill you."[19] Cullen many years later would recall Dasch asking about his parents, then saying, "Well, it's best that you don't know too much. You just do what we tell you and everything will be fine." At some point Burger approached the two men and asked Dasch in German if he needed any help. Dasch, angered, ordered Burger in English to return to the others. Then, returning his attention to Cullen, he extracted two fifty-dollar bills and offered them to Cullen, saying, "Forget about this and I'll give you some money and you can have a good time." When Cullen declined, Dasch upped the amount to $300, and Cullen accepted the money. As Cullen later recalled in the same interview, "I thought 'Who's going to believe this? I'd better get the money.'"[20]

As Cullen began to back away, Dasch stopped him and, asking him to shine the flashlight onto his face, said, "I want you to shine your light in my face so that you'll recognize me when I have you called to Washington. My name is George John Davis." Some historians give this as proof that Dasch, who had a distinctive grey streak in his hair, intended to abandon the mission from the beginning and wanted Cullen to remember him. That position is supported by the fact that Cullen was unarmed and that Dasch had access to two armed German sailors just over the dune and orders to dispose of any persons they might accidentally encounter. He was trying to save Cullen's life by bribing him and sending him away.[21]

Cullen left the men at about 12:25 a.m., and backed away, into the fog. Once out of sight of the other, he ran back to the Coast Guard station and reported the contact to Boatswain's Mate Second Class Carl Ross Jenette, who was in charge. The commander, Warrant Officer Oden, was off station on a liberty pass, but Jenette telephoned Chief Boatswain's Mate Warren Barnes, who lived nearby. Jenette armed Cullen and three other sailors with .30-caliber rifles, and the armed party returned to the beach at 1:05 a.m. Poor visibility rendered the search superficial at best. As Cullen later recalled, "We'd had no training as to what to do in this situation."[22]

Chief Barnes arrived at 1:12 and took charge on the beach. Several men reported smelling diesel and hearing a diesel engine in the fog, and Barnes later claimed to have seen the outline of a vessel through a rift in the fog, not more than 150 yards offshore. Fearing a landing in force, Barnes deployed his force of untrained guardsmen into defensive positions, and the noises eventually faded away. (Records from *U-202* put the boat's departure at approximately 4:15 a.m.)[23] Barnes and Cullen returned to the station, and Barnes made the first telephonic report to Coast Guard Headquarters in New York City.

The Coast Guard duty intelligence officer, Lieutenant Nirshel, warned Barnes to keep the matter secret and admit no one onto the station. He then phoned the District Intelligence Office, Third Naval District, at 1:55 a.m. and reported the contact at Amagansett. The assistant duty officer, Ensign Fitzgerald, contacted the duty officer at Headquarters, Eastern Sea Frontier (ESF) at two o'clock in the morning; he in turn contacted Coast Guard Headquarters in New York for more information and to inquire whether the army should be notified and troops sent. Eventually, an army lieutenant arrived on the scene with twenty soldiers of the 113th Mobile Infantry.[24]

In the interim, Chief Radioman McDonald at the Amagansett Naval Radio Station had heard the diesel engine offshore and, fearing that a landing party was being put ashore to destroy the station, evacuated his family into Amagansett in the middle of the night. He then contacted the Coast Guard station but was told that it was not permitted to discuss any details. He then contacted the 113th Mobile Infantry. Shortly after 2:30 a.m. the ESF duty officer made contact with the Federal Bureau of Investigation in New York City, which advised him that it was already aware of the situation, having been contacted by the army.

At dawn, the Coast Guard searched the beach and found German cigarettes and a furrow in the wet sand caused by dragging a heavy object. They followed it to where the sand showed evidence of recent digging.

Eventually, the sailors uncovered four wooden crates and an assortment of German uniforms. By 10:23 that morning all the recovered material was in the office of Capt. John Baylis, commanding officer of the New York City Coast Guard.[25]

The night before, however, once Cullen had departed, Dasch had returned to the five men. Burger had informed the others about Cullen, and there was increased tension and nervousness, Quirin complaining that their orders were to kill anyone they encountered. Dasch ordered them, either forgetfully or by intent, to bury their uniforms, despite his instructions to return the uniforms with the U-boat crewmen. He ordered the two crewmen to return to the sub and report to Captain Linder that the landing had been successful. They moved down the beach and buried the crates, moving tufts of sea grass over the site to hide the holes. Overlooked, or planted, was a shovel left upright in the sand. Dasch claimed later to have left it. Burger later claimed that he too left clues—a bottle of German brandy, German cigarettes, and a German naval rating's cap.[26]

As the men made their way in the darkness over the dunes, without the aid of a map or compass, they heard the submarine's diesel engines. *U-202*, caught on a sandbar, had been unable to free itself using its electric motor and had resorted to the louder diesel engine to get free. They came to a road and walked until they arrived at some railroad tracks, which they followed, getting to the Amagansett rail station at about 5:00 a.m. Passing themselves off to the ticket agent as city fisherman, not uncommon in the village, Dasch bought four tickets for the 6:57 train to New York City. Upon arrival Dasch and Burger took rooms at the Governor Clinton Hotel, across from Penn Station, while Heinck and Quirin registered at the Hotel Martinique. They bought new clothes, dined at fine restaurants, and disappeared into the population of the world's largest city.

Meanwhile the phone wires burned between Third Naval District headquarters in Washington, D.C., and the intelligence offices of the army, Navy, Coast Guard, and FBI. The decision was made for the FBI to assume jurisdiction in the case, and its first agents arrived at Amagansett at 10:00 p.m. on 12 June. But all they could do there was place the beach under constant surveillance and interrogate Cullen. The FBI was initiating the largest manhunt in bureau history, but there were no leads, and later, despite massive publicity to the contrary, it would not be FBI investigative prowess that broke the case.

On the morning of 14 June, only thirty some hours after landing, Dasch confided misgivings about the mission to Burger, and after some discussion the two agreed to betray the plot to the FBI. That evening, as

Burger stood beside him at a telephone booth, Dasch called the New York office of the FBI and spoke with Agent Dean F. McWhorter. Identifying himself as Frank Daniel Pastorious, recently arrived from Germany, Dasch stated that he had important information and that he would contact the Washington, D.C., office the following Thursday or Friday. When McWhorter asked the nature of this information, Dasch replied that it was so important that it could only be revealed to J. Edgar Hoover himself. He then hung up. Almost certain the caller was a crank, McWhorter nonetheless logged the call.

Unbeknownst to anyone in American intelligence, the Germans had by now accomplished a second landing of saboteurs onto American soil, this time totally undetected. Kerling and his team of Thiel, Neubauer, and Haupt had departed Lorient two days earlier than Dasch's group, on 26 May on board *U-584*, but didn't arrive off the coast of Ponte Vedra Beach, Florida, five miles southeast of Jacksonville, until the evening of 16 June. Like the other team they landed after midnight, and buried their uniforms and equipment. They made their way to Jacksonville, then took a train to Cincinnati, where they split up, Haupt and Neubauer going on to Chicago and the other pair, Kerling and Thiel, to New York City.

Meanwhile, Dasch, after waiting several days in order to, as he later explained, give the others "their own opportunity to save their skins by surrender," boarded a train to Washington on Thursday afternoon and on arrival checked into room 351 of the Mayflower Hotel. On Friday morning, 19 June, Dasch telephoned the Washington office of the FBI, made contact with Agent Duane L. Traynor, and asked to speak with Mr. Hoover. Advised that the director was not available, Dasch confided that he was the leader of a group of German saboteurs. Traynor, aware of the explosives discovered at Amagansett and the manhunt for the missing men, convinced Dasch to disclose his location. Agents quickly arrived at room 351 and took Dasch into "protective custody."[27]

Transported back to FBI headquarters and interrogated for several days, Dasch provided the names of the other saboteurs, their locations, the target objectives, and a handkerchief on which information on contacts was written in invisible ink. He also turned over $84,000 in American currency. It was only through Dasch's information that the government became aware of the second landing in Florida.

The search for the outstanding saboteurs was conducted without publicity and was accomplished without much difficulty. Burger was waiting at the hotel to be arrested; he, Heinck, and Quirin were taken into custody on 20 June. Known to be in New York City, Kerling and Thiel were quickly located and arrested, on 23 June. Kerling was transported to Ponte Vedra, where he showed the FBI where the explosives and uniforms were buried. Only Haupt and Neubauer still remained at liberty.

Haupt had traveled from Cincinnati to his home in Chicago, followed by Neubauer on a later train. Aware of his identity, the FBI located Haupt at his parent's address and kept him under surveillance. His activity consisted of movies, fine dining, and dates until he met with Neubauer at the Sheridan Plaza Hotel on 27 June. Both men were taken into custody immediately.

That same day, the story of the saboteurs, their mission, and their arrest made national headlines. Hoover issued a statement to the press revealing the two landings, details of the saboteur's plans to cripple American industry, their targets, and their arrests. Hoover kept secret the fact that Dasch had defected and turned himself in and that the others would not have been detected, much less arrested, without Dasch's assistance. Nor was any mention made of the Coast Guard's role. The FBI took all credit for the capture.

These omissions were meant in part to prevent retaliation against Dasch's and Burger's families in Germany. But more importantly, the FBI had no desire to spotlight how easily the saboteurs had landed and avoided detection. Keeping the defections secret would reinforce the bureau's reputation for omnipotence in counterintelligence and discourage further attempts to land infiltrators; also, perhaps most important to Hoover, it would enhance the prestige of the FBI.[28]

Although it was initially assumed by the FBI that the saboteurs would be arraigned in the federal courts, Dasch was encouraged to go before a judge and plead guilty on the promise of a presidential pardon. Several considerations, however, ultimately led President Roosevelt, who had been closely following events, to issue an order for a military tribunal.

For one thing, Dasch had decided to withdraw his offer to plead guilty when he was informed on 27 June that he would be indicted with the others; he now wanted the opportunity to justify his actions in open court. Perhaps more importantly, as the army judge advocate general, Maj. Gen. Myron Cramer, wrote to Secretary of War Henry L. Stimson in a letter dated 28 June 1942, in a civilian court "the maximum permissible punishment for these offenses would be less than [it] is desirable to impose."[29]

Cramer explained that given federal rules of evidence in U.S. district courts, it was highly unlikely that the men would be convicted of sabotage, since no acts had been committed. They might be convicted only of conspiracy, under Title 18, Section 88 of the U.S. Code, punishable by two years in prison, a fine of ten thousand dollars, or both. As Attorney General Francis Biddle later pointed out, buying a gun to commit a murder was not attempted murder. In contrast, a trial by military commission would not be limited by federal procedural or evidentiary rules, and there would be no limitation on any sentence that could be imposed, including death.

The following day, 29 June, Stimson met with Attorney General Biddle, and the two agreed that a military commission would best serve the needs of the government. Hoover, also at the meeting, liked the facts that a military trial would ensure complete secrecy and impose penalties up to death and that a jury of military officers would likely be less sympathetic than a civilian jury. Biddle and Stimson made their recommendation to President Roosevelt. On 30 June, both the *Washington Post* and *New York Times* broke the story that the eight saboteurs would be tried by the military. The following day they reported that a seven-member military panel would be appointed by the president, with Biddle and General Cramer serving jointly as prosecutors.[30]

On 2 July 1942, President Roosevelt issued Proclamation 2561, "Denying Certain Enemies Access to the Courts of the United States" (7 Fed. Reg. 5101 [1942]), creating a military tribunal. The initial paragraph stated that the "safety of the United States demands that all enemies who have entered upon the territory of the United States as part of an invasion or predatory incursion, or who have entered in order to commit sabotage, espionage, or other hostile or warlike acts, should be promptly tried in accordance with the law of war." The reference to "law of war" rather than "Articles of War" was significant, in that the latter would trigger undesired statutory procedures established by Congress for courts-martial.[31]

The second paragraph denied the men access to civilian courts: "such persons shall not be privileged to seek any remedy or maintain any proceeding directly or indirectly, or to have any such remedy or proceeding sought on their behalf, in the courts of the United States, or of its States, territories, and possessions, except under such regulations as the Attorney General, with the approval of the Secretary of War, may from time to time prescribe." Roosevelt claimed this authority both under the Constitution as commander in chief and as granted him by Congress.

At the same time, Roosevelt issued a military order appointing the members of the military commission, the prosecution, and the defense counsel, acting under the thirty-eighth Article of War. The commission would "have power to and shall, as occasion requires, make such rules for the conduct of the proceeding, consistent with the powers of military commissions under the Articles of War, as it shall deem necessary for a full and fair trial

9. Operation Pastorious (Ex Parte Quirin)

A special seven-man American military commission opens the third day of its proceedings in the trial of eight Nazi saboteurs in the fifth floor courtroom of the Department of Justice building, 1942. Sitting on the commission (in the far rear of the room, left to right) are Brig. Gen. John T. Lewis; Maj. Gen. Lorenzo D. Casser; Maj. Gen. Walter S. Grant; Maj. Gen. Frank R. McCoy, president of the commission; Maj. Gen. Blanton Winship; Brig. Gen. Guy V. Henry; and Brig. Gen. John T. Kennedy (Library of Congress).

of the matters before it." Essentially, this freed the tribunal from procedures enacted by Congress and the *Manual for Courts-Martial*.[32]

The members of the commission, appointed by Roosevelt, were four major generals and three brigadier generals. As president of the commission Roosevelt appointed Maj. Gen. Frank R. McCoy, whom he recalled from retirement to head the court. McCoy, a graduate of the West Point class of 1897, had had a long and distinguished career, beginning as a second lieutenant in the 8th Cavalry. He had seen service at San Juan Hill in Cuba during the Spanish-American War and in the Philippines during the Moro Rebellion, during which he had been credited with killing Moro leader Datu Ali in hand-to-hand combat. He had served as an aide to both Gen. Leonard Wood and Lt. Col. Theodore Roosevelt, whom he served again later, as a military aide, when Roosevelt was elected president.

Appointed a member of the General Staff of the American Expeditionary Forces (AEF) in Europe when America entered World War I, he commanded the 63rd Infantry Brigade and was awarded a Distinguished Service Medal. More significantly, McCoy served on the Billy Mitchell court martial in 1925 and on the Lytton Commission investigating the Japanese military invasion and occupation of Manchuria in 1932. He took part as well in the investigation in early 1942 into the attack on Pearl Harbor. Now, he'd been chosen to preside over the first military tribunal since the Civil War. The other generals selected represented a wide spectrum of military experience. All were combat veterans, and one had been awarded the Medal of Honor.

Maj. Gen. Walter S. Grant was a cavalryman who had been awarded the Distinguished Service Medal for his actions during the St. Mihiel and Argonne-Meuse offensives of World War I, when he had been recalled to active service. Retired in 1942, he was recalled again for the trial of the Germans.

Maj. Gen. Blanton Winship had graduated from the University of Georgia in 1893, enlisting in the 1st Georgia Infantry in 1898 during the Spanish-American War before accepting a commission in the regular army as a judge advocate. He had been awarded the Distinguished Service Medal and Silver Star for his service during World War I. Following the war he had returned to the Judge Advocate Corps and served as a military aide to the president and as legal adviser to the governor-general of the Philippines before being appointed judge advocate general in 1931. Appointed as military governor of Puerto Rico in 1934, he had been unpopular with Puerto Rican nationalists and was investigated by Congress for his role in the Ponce Massacre on Palm Sunday, 1937, in which nineteen civilians had been killed. He survived an assassination attempt in 1938 but was removed by the president in 1939. Recalled to active duty in 1942, he would retire for a second time in 1944 at age seventy-five, as the oldest army officer on active duty.

Maj. Gen. Lorenzo D. Gasser was primarily a staff officer who had been named assistant chief of staff of the American Expeditionary Force following the war in 1919. He was acting deputy chief of staff of the army when he retired in 1940. He was recalled to active duty in 1941.

Brig. Gen. Guy V. Henry Jr., was the son of Gen. Guy Vernon Henry, Sr., an 1861 West Point graduate who had risen to the rank of brigadier general in the regular army during the Civil War. As colonel of the all-black 10th U.S. Cavalry, Guy Henry, Sr., had received successive brevets and the Medal of Honor for gallantry during the Indian wars. Following in his father's footsteps, Guy Henry, Jr., had attended West Point, seeing service in the Spanish-American War and receiving a Silver Star. He was a member of the American riding team in the 1912 Olympics, served as commandant of cadets at West Point, and was a brigadier general during World War I. Guy Henry, Jr., attended the Army War College, graduated from the General Staff School, and held the rank of major general in 1939 when he retired. He was recalled to active duty in 1941.

Brig. Gen. John T. Lewis served in France during World War I and then remained in France following the war, as a military attaché at the U.S. embassy in Paris. He attended the Army Command and General Staff College and the Army War College. He worked at Headquarters, Office of the Chief of Coast Artillery, until he was appointed Secretary of the War Department General Staff as a Brigadier General late in 1941.

Brig. Gen. John T. Kennedy was the junior member of the court. He had graduated from West Point in 1908. During the Philippine Insurrection, on 4 July 1909, Kennedy had led several enlisted men in a frontal assault on a cave on Patian Island occupied by a "desperate enemy," taking severe wounds. For his actions Kennedy had received the Medal of Honor. Kennedy served with the AEF in France during World War I and was awarded the Distinguished Service Cross as a regimental commander during the St. Mihiel and Meuse-Argonne offensives. He was commanding Fort Bragg, North Carolina, in 1942 when he was appointed to the commission.

As mentioned, Biddle and Cramer had been named as the trial judge advocates, responsible for prosecuting the saboteurs. Biddle, an army veteran of World War I, would after the war serve as a judge in the Nuremburg war trials of Nazis. Major General Cramer had been born in Portland, Connecticut, attended Wesleyan University, and graduated Harvard Law School with an LLB in 1907. In 1910 the twenty-nine year old attorney had enlisted in the Washington National Guard as a cavalry private; the following year he had been commissioned as a second lieutenant in the 1st Washington Cavalry. He was promoted to first lieutenant in 1915, and his unit was federalized the following year for service on the Mexican border with Gen. "Black Jack" Pershing, serving until February 1917. Cramer briefly returned to the law as a prosecutor until his unit was again federalized for World War I. Cramer, now a captain, shipped overseas in January 1918 for service at the Army General Staff College in Langres, France.

Later, as chief of staff for the 1st Replacement Depot in St. Aignan, he oversaw the movement of more than 500,000 replacement troops (approximately 40,000 a month) to all parts of the AEF. His superiors rated him a "man of excellent character [who] had [displayed] an indefatigable attention to duty." In July 1919, when Cramer returned to the United States, he was a thirty-seven-year-old Officers' Reserve Corps infantry lieutenant colonel. He resumed his civilian law practice, but he had already decided that he liked the army better, and while still on active duty in France had applied

Key figures in the trial of the eight saboteurs, 1942: (1) Maj. Gen. Myron Crammer, Judge Advocate General of the Army and assistant prosecutor; (2) Attorney General Francis Biddle; (3) FBI Director J. Edgar Hoover; and (4) Col. Carl L. Ristine, a lawyer in the Army's Inspector General office appointed as a defense attorney for George Dasch only (National Archives and Records Administration).

for a regular army appointment to the Judge Advocate General's Department.

In July 1920 his application was processed, and an interview board recommended him for a commission as a major in the judge advocate corps. The Judge Advocate General's Department concurred and offered Cramer a commission as a regular army major. He had assignments with the 3rd and 4th Divisions, taught as a law professor at West Point, and in 1930 graduated from the two-year Command and General Staff College at Fort Leavenworth, Kansas. In 1934 Cramer was sent to Manila as the top army lawyer in the Philippine Department, where he served until 1937. He returned to Washington, D.C., and on 1 December 1941 was appointed the army's judge advocate general and promoted to major general. Less than a week later, America was at war. Following his retirement in 1945, he would be called back in 1946 to work at the International Military Tribunal of the Far East/Tokyo war crimes trial.

The prosecution at the trial of the Germans was aided by Col. F. Granville Munson, Col. John M. Weir, Col. Erwin M. Treusch, and Maj. William T. Thurman of the Judge Advocate General's Department, as well as by James H. Rowe Jr., assistant to the attorney general.

Two outstanding military attorneys were appointed to represent the eight defendants, although Dasch would later obtain his own separate attorney, fearing that his testimony might implicate his codefendants. The lead attorney for the defense was Col. Kenneth Claiborne Royall (1894–1971), a native of Goldsboro, North Carolina, and a graduate of the University of North Carolina in 1914, and Harvard Law School, in 1917. He had enlisted shortly after graduating and had served in France as a second lieutenant in the 317th Army Field Artillery until 1918. He had been commissioned a captain in the North Carolina National Guard in 1919 and organized a field artillery battery in 1921 before returning to the practice of law in Raleigh. He had also served in the North Carolina State Senate in 1927.

Following America's entry into World War II, Royall was commissioned a colonel and appointed chief of the Legal Section, Fiscal Division, Headquarters, Services of Supply (later Army Service Forces) in early 1942. The fact that Royall was not a career soldier would influence his defense of the Germans.

The other defense counsel appointed on 2 July was Col. Cassius M. Dowell (1880–1957), a native of Illinois and a forty-year career soldier and attorney. Born in Landers, Illinois, he had enlisted in the army as a private in 1902 but by the beginning of World War I had been a captain in the Judge Advocate General's Department, writing regulations to facilitate the drafting of men into the armed services.

Dowell served overseas in France with the 26th Division during World War I, serving as an assistant to the provost marshal general (April–September 1917), judge advocate of the 26th Division (September–January 1918), then as chief of staff for the division until April 1918, when he had taken command of the 103rd Infantry Regiment. Wounded in action, his unit had fired some of the last shots of the war on 11 November; He had finished the war as an acting lieutenant colonel and a holder of the Silver Star and Distinguished Service Medal.

Returned to the rank of major following the war, he spent the next decade teaching law and in 1925 wrote *Military Aid to the Civil Power*, a guide on administering the laws of war and a military government. He was in command of Fort Dix, New Jersey, when he was selected as defense counsel.

The defense was aided by Maj. Lauson H. Stone, son of Harlan F. Stone, chief justice of the United States, and Capt. William G. Hummell. On 7 July, Col. Carl L. Ristine was appointed to represent Dasch, the other seven continuing to be defended by Royall and Dowell. Ristine, special assistant to the attorney general since 1932, would now oppose him in court.

Roosevelt's order directed the tribunal to meet on 8 July "or as soon thereafter as it is practicable." The order stated that two-thirds of the commission needed to agree on a verdict or sentence, unlike a court-martial, which required a unanimous vote for a death sentence. The order also laid down that Roosevelt, as commander in chief, would make the final decision on the sentence, on the basis of the commission's recommendation. There would be no appeal, no review by the judge advocate general; the order vested "final reviewing authority" in the president.

On 4 July, the eight men were moved in secret from New York to Washington and incarcerated in the second floor of a wing of the District of Columbia jail, isolated from each other by empty cells on each side. Other than counsel, the men were allowed no visitors, writing material, or outside communication. A guard detail of four officers and thirty soldiers maintained constant surveillance on the men, twenty-four hours a day.

The trial was held on the fifth floor of the west wing of the Justice Department building in room 5235, a lecture hall. One of the first decisions made when the tribunal met on 7 July was to exclude the public and press: "The sessions will be closed ... due to the nature of the testimony, which involves the security of the United States." With the court's permission, Biddle and Cramer drafted a statement on the reason for secrecy: "We do not propose to tell our enemies the answers to questions which are puzzling them."

The president's proclamation having given the commission power to "make such rules ... as it shall deem necessary for a full and fair trial," it issued a three-and-a-half-page statement of rules. Along with excluding the press, these rules excluded peremptory challenges, allowed only one challenge for cause, and provided that though the commission would be governed by the Articles of War, "the commission shall determine the application of such Articles to any particular question."[33]

The trial opened the following day, 8 July. The government charged the eight Germans with four crimes. First, they were charged with violation of the law of war with two specifications: first, that "being enemies of the United States, [they] secretly and covertly passed in civilian dress ... for the purpose of committing sabotage, espionage and other hostile acts," and second, for attempting to commit acts mentioned in the first specification. The next two charges were for violation of the Articles of War, enacted by Congress, specifically the eighty-first (Sabotage) and the eighty-second (Espionage/Spying). The last charge, "Conspiracy to Commit All of the Above Acts," charged that the men "did plot, plan, and conspire with each other, with the German Reich, and with other enemies of the United States, to commit each and every one of the above enumerated charges." All eight defendants pled not guilty.

Royall rose first thing and challenged the constitutionality of the commission itself, calling it "invalid and unconstitutional" and citing the principle established in the Supreme Court case in *Ex Parte Milligan* (see chapter 3) that military tribunals had no jurisdiction over civilians in areas where the civil courts were open and operating, such as Washington, D.C. Additionally, he challenged that Roosevelt's order violated several particulars in the Articles of War.

Biddle responded that he couldn't imagine a panel of high-ranking military officers commissioned by order of the commander in chief questioning its own power and authority in the matter. If there was a question of law involved, he went on, it could be determined by the civil courts if and when the case was brought before a civil court. However, Biddle argued, this was "not a trial of offenses of law of the civil courts, but is a trial of the offenses of the law of war, which is not cognizable to the civil courts."

Then Royall argued that the articles cited in the charges applied solely to U.S. citizens caught aiding an enemy, and not to the enemies themselves. Biddle countered with the example of Maj. John André, the British officer caught out of uniform passing through American lines during the Revolution and his subsequent trial and execution. Acknowledging to himself that asserting the civil rights of the defendants might require some limited disclosure of actions by the commission and conflict with the secrecy restrictions, Royall made sure the language of the secrecy oath was adjusted so as to allow for that possibility.

On 6 July, Royall and Dowell had written to President Roosevelt about their concerns as to the validity and constitutionality of his 2 July proclamation and order. They had stated as their opinion that defense counsel should be allowed to institute "an appropriate proceeding" to test the validity and constitutionality of the proceedings. They questioned whether they, as military officers, could act contrary to the wishes of the commander in chief; if it was the president's position that they were not to institute such proceedings, they proposed that he either specifically grant them or someone else the appropriate authority. (They also requested a meeting with Roosevelt, but the request was not granted.)

Royall and Dowell were contacted by telephone by Marvin McIntyre, a White House aide, who communicated the president's desire that they "act in accordance with their own judgment." The two followed up with a second letter, dated 7 July, to Roosevelt in which they declared their conviction that they had the necessary authority, and also the duty, to "try to arrange for civil counsel to institute the proceedings necessary to determine the constitutionality and validity of the Proclamation and Order of 2 July." If those arrangements couldn't be made, they would institute those proceedings themselves at the appropriate time, unless otherwise ordered by Roosevelt. They never received a response to the letter. The trial opened the next day.

The early days of the trial concerned testimony from Cullen, who identified Dasch, and from two FBI agents. Agent Charles Lanham stated that Burger had declared that he and Dasch had never planned to follow through with the sabotage; Agent Norval Wills testified as to the promise of a presidential pardon for Dasch in return for pleading guilty. They were followed on the stand by the Germans, who testified in their own defense that it had never been their intent to carry out the sabotage.[34]

On 21 July, the twelfth day of the trial, Royall decided it was the appropriate time to advise the court that, unable to secure civilian counsel for the defendants, he'd prepared an application for a writ of habeas corpus to test the constitutionality and validity of the proclamation and order. Dowell, for his part, announced that as a soldier for over forty years he could not personally support Royall's decision, but he had nonetheless worked on the appeal to the Supreme Court. Royall began contacting the justices of the Supreme Court, and a 23 July meeting was held with Justices Hugo Black and Owen Roberts at Roberts' farm in Alexandria, Virginia, attended by Dowell, Biddle, and Cramer. After subsequent communications, it was agreed that the Supreme Court would meet in special session to hear oral arguments on 29 July. The Court had agreed to hear the case although there had been no action in a lower court. On 27 July, after sixteen days in session, the military tribunal's defense rested. All the defendants but Burger and Dasch signed a letter thanking the defense team and stating that they had been represented well and had received a fair trial.[35]

On 28 July, at 8:00 p.m., District Judge James W. Morris issued a brief statement denying the petition requesting a writ of habeas corpus for the seven defendants (Dasch, represented separately by Ristine, was not included in the motion). Morris ruled that the defendants were "subjects, citizens or residents of a nation at war with the United States" and that under Roosevelt's proclamation "are not privileged to seek any remedy or maintain any proceedings in the courts of the United States."

Nevertheless, oral arguments before the Supreme Court began at noon on 29 July, and they continued for nine hours over two days. Royall argued for the petitioners, and Biddle represented the government. In a petition for a writ of certiorari (that is, a decision by the Supreme Court to review the case), Royall and Dowell asked the court to bring up the case from appellate court, where at that time it was pending and had yet to be filed. The writ was granted. Their seventy-two page brief in support of petitions for a writ of habeas corpus addressed two fundamental questions: Could the petitioners, six of whom were enemy aliens, request a writ of habeas corpus? If so, had their liberty been unlawfully restrained?

The main points of the defense's arguments were as follows. First, Articles of War 81 and 82 in Charges II and III had not been violated by the defendants, as they had not committed any act in a zone of military operations, nor was there any proof of any attempt to obtain or transmit military information. Regarding Charge I, the defense held, the law of war was little more than a species of international law comparable to common law, concluding that "no principle is better settled than the principle that there is no common law crime against the United States Government." Crimes had to be covered by statute enacted by Congress under the Constitution; the defense thus raised the issue of constitutional separation of powers. The offenses of sabotage and espionage were statutes enacted by Congress and thus were "triable by the civil courts," as was Charge IV, conspiracy; neither was triable by a military commission.

The defense also raised *Ex Parte Milligan*'s prohibition of military trials for civilians where the civil courts are in operation, as well as the issue of the Constitution's prohibitions of ex post facto crimes (Roosevelt's proclamation increasing the penalty for sabotage to death having been issued on 2 July, after any acts had been committed) and the presidential prohibition of judicial review.[36]

Biddle and Cramer, answering the writ for certiorari, argued that as enemies of the United States the defendants had no standing to sue in any civil court and that the court had no jurisdiction to disturb the right of the provost marshal, Gen. Albert Cox, to hold the defendants in lawful custody. They submitted a longer (ninety-three-page) brief to rebut the petition for a writ of habeas corpus. They argued that the Germans were not entitled to access to civil courts and that American civil liberties had never been intended to apply to enemy invaders in time of war.

Biddle and Cramer addressed the issue of *Milligan* by pointing out that whereas Milligan had not worn the uniform of a nation at war with the United States, had continuously been a resident of Indiana, and had never crossed military lines to enter a theater of operations, the defendants had arrived in German uniforms, were residents of Germany, and crossed American lines secretly in enemy warships to commit hostile acts. They also pointed out that the nature of war had changed since the time of *Mil-*

ligan; modern warfare was fought on many fronts, including the battlefields of production, transportation, and morale. Total war of 1942 was as different from the static land warfare of 1864, Biddle argued, as a Stuka dive-bomber from a musket.[37]

Perhaps the most persuasive argument they presented was that the Fifth Amendment did not guarantee indictment by grand jury to "cases arising in the land or naval forces." U.S. soldiers charged with military crimes had no right to the protections of grand juries or access to civil courts; it was ridiculous to assert such rights for enemy invaders in time of war. As to the citizenship issue with respect to Burger and Haupt, the government asserted that by actively aiding the enemy they had changed their status from citizen to enemy of the United States.

Oral arguments were completed on 30 July. Having considered them, the Court issued a unanimous *per curiam* decision (i.e., a collective one, except that Justice Frank Murphy, a reserve colonel in the army, had taken no part), known as *Ex Parte Quirin,* on 31 July. (A full decision, explaining the legal basis, would be published only on 29 October.) The *per curiam* decision ruled that the president had the power to appoint military tribunals in time of war and that his proclamation of 2 July was constitutional, but that the decisions of those courts would be subject to review by civil courts. The defendant's petition for a writ was denied; the commission had the authority and jurisdiction it needed to proceed with the trial.

The arguments before the commission when it took up the case on 1 August centered on the issue of the death penalty. Royall held that none of the defendants had committed acts severe enough to warrant a sentence of death, while Cramer argued the merit of executing the men as a message to future potential saboteurs. As to the assistance provided by Dasch and Burger to the FBI, Biddle argued that it was a matter of clemency for the president to decide; the men were guilty and should receive the death penalty.

The commission reached a unanimous verdict on 3 August and recommended death for all eight saboteurs. The three-thousand-page trial record was flown to the president at Hyde Park, New York, and Roosevelt read it during the train ride back to Washington. Roosevelt reviewed the transcripts over the next two days and, following Biddle's recommendation, commuted Dasch's sentence to thirty years and Burger's to life in prison.[38]

The following morning, at ten o'clock, General Cramer contacted Brig. Gen. Albert L. Cox and advised him to make preparations for the execution of six of the men. Cox, the provost marshal general for the Military District of Washington, D.C., and a decorated World War I veteran, was advised to expect the president's order no earlier than Wednesday, 6 August. He was to maintain secrecy, as the verdict had yet to be announced to the public.

On the 6th, Cox ordered Maj. Thomas Rives to escort six chaplains, four executioners, and three medical officers to the District of Columbia jail and stand by there. That same day, Jack Vincent of the International News Service broke the story that the commission had arrived at a verdict of guilty. At 7:10 p.m., Cox was advised by telephone that the execution was to take place on Friday, 8 August. Cox directed Rives to stand down.[39] In response to a call from the White House the next morning, Cox met the president's naval aide, Capt. J. L. McCrea, at the south entrance of the White House at 1:00 p.m. and received the order for the executions, even as Vincent was running a follow-up story announcing the verdict of death for six of the saboteurs. Cox began making preparations for the executions, which would be by electrocution.

At the jail, the execution chamber, on the third floor of the jail, was prepared. Checks were conducted on the electric chair itself and on the electrical transformer. Helmeted troops were brought in to assist with security, and guards were posted at every phone to prevent outgoing calls. The head executioner would receive fifty dollars per execution, each of his three assistants twenty-five dollars.

At 7:00 on the morning of 8 August, the prisoners were given a breakfast of scrambled eggs and bacon. Then General Cox arrived, accompanied by several guards and six chaplains. Upon Cox fell the duty of informing the eight defendants of the verdict. The six condemned men responded with stunned silence. Burger seemed indifferent; Dasch was outraged and refused to accept the verdict. Dasch and Burger were moved to the exercise yard and the other six upstairs to death row, in holding cells about one hundred yards from the execution chamber, each with two guards and a chaplain. The twelve-by-eighteen-foot chambers each had a one-way opaque glass panel through which the prisoner could be seen. Witnesses arrived throughout the morning, including General McCoy, Director Hoover, and representatives of the War and Justice Departments.[40]

The men were to be executed in alphabetical order. Haupt entered the chamber at 12:01 p.m.; the switch was thrown at 12:03. With the words, "This man is dead," Dr. A. Magruder MacDonald pronounced Haupt deceased at 12:11. One by one, Heinck, Kerling, Neubauer, Quirin, and Thiel followed, their executions averaging about ten minutes. Thiel was pronounced dead at 1:04 p.m. At 1:24, two ambulances transported the six bodies to Walter Reed Medical Center for autopsies. About the same time,

Graves of six electrocuted Nazi saboteurs in Potter's Field at Blue Plains, D.C. (D.C. Public Library, Star Collection).

the White House issued a brief statement announcing the executions and ordered the records sealed until the end of the war.

The six men were secretly buried in the District of Columbia "Potter's Field" at Blue Plains Cemetery, under unpainted wooden-stick markers numbered 276 through 281. Burger and Dasch remained at the District of Columbia jail until being moved to federal prisons first at Danbury, Connecticut, then in Atlanta, Georgia, where they were held incommunicado. In 1948, President Truman commuted their sentences and ordered them deported to Germany, where they were considered traitors and treated with contempt and hostility. Dasch saw himself as a hero and never stopped trying to clear his name until his death in 1992. Burger lived quietly until his death in October 1975.

J. Edgar Hoover became a national hero after the trial, and the FBI gained an undeserved reputation of invincibility, so much so that the Abwehr would attempt only one other landing, in 1944. It would be detected quickly.

U-202 returned to Brest on 25 July 1942. She would be sunk at 3:00 a.m. on 2 June 1943, southeast of Cape Farewell, Greenland, by depth charges and gunfire from the British sloop HMS *Starling*, with a loss of eighteen dead. There were thirty survivors, all taken prisoner. It was her ninth patrol, and *U-202* had never previously lost a crewman.[41]

U-584 returned to Brest on 22 July 1942. She would be sunk on 31 October 1943 in the North Atlantic, at 49° 14' N, 31° 55' W, by a Fido homing torpedo from three TBF Avenger aircraft of Composite Squadron 9 operating from the U.S. escort carrier USS *Card* (CVE 11), with a loss of fifty-three dead (all hands).[42]

Cullen testified at the trial in Washington and achieved some minor celebrity at the time. He went on a war bond tour of the East Coast, then worked in a public relations assignment until the end of the war, receiving the Legion of Merit for "outstanding performance of duty" on 9 November 1943. He was honorably discharged from the Coast Guard as a boatswains mate first class on 20 June 1946. He would record his recollections in a Coast Guard oral-history interview in 2006, at age eighty-five.

Ex Parte Quirin remains a landmark case in the definition of executive power, the scope and constitutionality of military tribunals, and judicial review on their verdicts and proceedings.

10

Fort Lawton Courts-Martial
Riot, Murder—1944

William G. Jones came upstairs and said, "The Italians have knocked one of your boys out, out there. You Texas boys always talking about what you will do. All right, now let's go!"—Pvt. Jesse C. B. Sims, 650th Port Co.

In 1896, when the secretary of war was seeking a site for construction of an artillery battery to provide coastal defense for Seattle, Washington, from Spanish naval attack, businessmen of Seattle donated 703 acres of farm and timberland on a sweeping plateau north of the city overlooking Puget Sound. The installation was named Fort Lawton, after Maj. Gen. Henry Ware Lawton, a veteran of the Civil War, where his actions had earned him the Medal of Honor, and of the Indian wars—he had been the officer to whom Geronimo surrendered. As a brigadier general of regulars during the Spanish-American War, he had commanded the 2nd Division, V Corps, spearheading the invasion of Cuba at Daquiri on 22 June 1898. Sent to the Philippines in 1899, he had been killed by a Filipino sniper while directing American troops in the battle of San Mateo on 19 December 1899—the only general to be killed in battle during the conflict.

The post opened on 9 February 1900, and the first troops—Company C, 32nd Coast Artillery Corps, under the command of 1st Lt. Mervyn Buckey—arrived in July 1901. Seattle welcomed the troops and the 106th Coast Artillery Corps arrived soon after to man the coast. No coastal weapons ever arrived, however, and the fort remained an infantry post until 1921.

The presence of black troops was not unusual to either the fort or the community of Seattle. Troops of the all-black 9th Cavalry had passed through the post on their way to China during the Boxer Rebellion. On 5

October 1909, nine hundred men of the 25th Infantry Regiment, an all-black unit in the segregated U.S. Army, was transferred to Fort Lawton upon returning from the Philippines. Residents petitioned twice for their withdrawal, but President William H. Taft refused to comply, and the 25th Infantry remained until 1913, when it was transferred to Hawaii.[1]

Thus it is ironic that it was at Fort Lawton that, in perhaps the only such occurrence in American history, a group of African Americans was put on trial for lynching a white man. It would result in the largest and longest army court-martial of World War II.[2]

During World War II, Fort Lawton, which had been used by the Civilian Conservation Corps in the twenties and thirties, became part of the Port of Embarkation, Seattle, a major staging area on the West Coast. A total of 1.1 million troops passed through the installation during and after the war. It was also a major conduit for supplies and equipment headed for the Pacific theater. Port companies of the army's Transportation Corps loaded and unloaded supplies. In February 1944, the 650th and 651st Port Companies, both all-black units, arrived at Fort Lawton for basic training and were stationed in segregated barracks. Following training, they began work at the Port of Seattle.

On 21 May 1944, the 28th Italian Service Unit (ISU) arrived at Fort Lawton from the prisoner of war (POW) compound at Camp Florence, Arizona, and was assigned to quartermaster duties in and around Fort Lawton. It was formed of Italians who had surrendered on 3 September 1943. Men assigned to ISUs were technically prisoners, but they were organized

Fort Lawton court-martial in session, 1944. This was World War II's largest Army court-martial (Hearst Communications, Inc./Hearst Newspapers, LLC).

like American military companies. Their members swore allegiance to the Allies and were paid for noncombat duties but remained under guard. The lenient conditions of their confinement, as well as their popularity with local females, created friction between the Italians and American GIs, black and white alike.

On 14 August 1944, troops of the 650th and 651st Port Companies were ordered to prepare for embarkation overseas to the Pacific war zone the following day. Anxious, the soldiers packed their bags, checked their gear, wrote letters home, played cards, and read the Bible, and some went the post exchange (PX) for beers. At approximately 11:05 the night of 14 August, three members of the 28th ISU, Corporal-Major Giuseppe Belle, Pvt. Antonio Pisciottano and Sgt. Angelo Fumarola, were returning to their barracks from a day pass into Seattle when they were confronted behind the 578th Port Company mess hall by four black soldiers—Technician 5th Grade (T/5) Willie Montgomery, Cpl. Luther Larkin, Pvt. Roy Daymond, and William G. Jones. Both groups had previously consumed alcoholic beverages. Insults were exchanged, and a drunken Montgomery attempted to assault Belle, only to be knocked to the ground. Montgomery was carried unconscious by Larken, Daymond, and Jones to the steps of the 578th's Barracks 719.[3]

At about 11:15 p.m., several events occurred concurrently. A jeep carrying two military policemen (MPs), Sgt. Charles M. Robinson and Pvt. Clyde V. Lomax, arrived in the area of Barracks 719, where Montgomery lay on the ground. Lomax later testified that he "heard a whistle blown" (usually a signal for troops to fall out) and heard Corporal Larkin say, "They got one of our boys, and we are going to mob them." After spending, by their own account, fifteen to twenty minutes at Barracks 719 watching the blacks assemble but taking no action to disperse them, Lomax and Robinson transported Montgomery to Post Hospital 2, in the southeast section of the post more than a mile away, arriving five minutes later. After approximately fifteen minutes at the hospital and a three-minute ride to the guardhouse, Robinson and Lomax finally reported to SSgt. Regis Callahan.[4]

In the interim, three groups of black soldiers, allegedly led by Jones, Larkin, and Sgt. Arthur Hurks, went down into the Italian area looking for revenge. They tore apart a picket fence surrounding the mess hall to use as clubs. They also carried axes, baseball bats, golf clubs, entrenching tools, and other improvised weapons. Pvt. Samuel Snow, armed with a sharpened piece of timber, led the first wave down Lawton Road toward the Italians, only to be struck down by an Italian, which only further incited the black troops.

As one Italian later testified, he and two companions "were going to their quarters when they passed a group of Negroes and one of them expressed vulgar words which I understood. One of my fellows asked me what was said. I took several steps and turned around. I saw one of the Negroes strike a blow at [my comrade]. Then [my comrade] struck the negro and he fell down. I called and said we'd better go before there was trouble." He testified that black soldiers stormed the barracks armed with "stones, clubs and axes" and attacked the Italians, as he called in English for them to stop. He identified Private Jones as one of the attackers.[5]

By all accounts, the MPs were incredibly slow in responding, even after one of the Americans assigned to the ISU, Sgt. Grant Farr, called for assistance at 11:25 p.m., a call repeated by 1st Sgt. Robert Aubrey at 11:30. At between 11:45 and 11:50, Staff Sergeant Callahan arrived with Cpl. John M. Biscan, the first MPs on the scene, to observe that "the place was filled with colored men acting in a riotous manner, carrying clubs." He estimated the number later at near two hundred. He sent Biscan for additional MPs and, after dispersing a group from the front of the Italians' Barracks 709, went to the ISU orderly room, where he had to pull his pistol to disperse rioters. At 11:50, Sgt. Thurman Jones arrived with other MPs and began to disperse the rioters and care for the injured. At one point, Private Lomax was chased by an ax-wielding black soldier but refused to draw his weapon and instead left the area in his jeep.[6]

By 12:30 a.m. on 15 August, twenty-eight Italians and three Americans—SSgt. Fred Perata, Sgt. Grant Farr, and Pfc. Harold Gould, all attached to the ISU—were transported to the base hospital with serious injuries. Three black soldiers—Pvt. Samuel Snow, T/5 Willie Montgomery, and Pvt. Alvin Clark—were also admitted with injuries. Of the latter three, only Snow would be charged and convicted. Fort Lawton's provost marshal, Maj. William Orem, arrived at about 1:00 a.m., and with the officer of the day, Lieutenant Sistrunk and Pfc. George E. Durel, an MP, walked through the black barracks and discovered Private Snow with a head injury. White officers responded to the black area and worked to restore order, ordering lights out, as MPs searched the adjacent woods for missing Italians.

Major Orem ordered two MPs, Technician 4th Grade Carl A. Johnson and Private First Class Durel to begin an investigation. Both men had civilian police experience, Johnson as a Kansas City Police detective and Durel as a member of the Louisiana State Police. The two would subsequently search the vacated barracks of the 650th and 651st Port Companies, now preparing to board trains, eventually bound for Camp Stoneman, California, where they were to be shipped to New Guinea. Johnson and Durel collected sticks, rocks, entrenching tools, and blood-stained clothing that would be identified as belonging to Cpl. Joseph Trice. Trice was arrested and placed in the guardhouse, along with Pfc. Roy Montgomery, who admitted in the hospital having been present. Montgomery named thirteen other participants.[7] Lomax patrolled the Italian area and along the beach for the rest of his shift, accompanied by Pvt. John Pinkney, a black soldier serving as an MP. All the regularly assigned military police at Fort Lawton were white, but blacks were detailed as MPs from time to time to help maintain order. At daybreak, approximately 6:00, as they crossed near the obstacle course, they discovered the body of Pvt. Guglielmo Olivotto. It was hanging by a tent rope attached to a wire strung between two trees at the base of the obstacle course at the bottom of Magnolia Bluff. The place was approximately four hundred yards from the Italian area and accessible only by a steep path over rough terrain.[8]

At 8:30 a.m. on 15 August, Capt. John Walker, the post pathologist, performed an autopsy at Hospital 2 and concluded that Olivotto had died of strangulation and placed time of death at about midnight. There were no bruises on the body. The initial investigation must, at the most charitable, be characterized as incompetent and negligent. The assistant provost marshal, Capt. Milton Carter, later admitted in testimony that very few of his officers had any training, that in fact "fifty percent were unfit for MP duty." This assessment is supported by how the investigation was conducted.

The military police had no log of incoming calls and no explanation for their slow response. They made no attempt made to identify culprits, no arrests, and no attempt to secure the scene or gather evidence. No one monitored the black soldiers as they returned to their barracks, to uncover evidence of participation, such as injuries, torn clothing, or blood. No fingerprints were taken or lifted. No photos were taken, no plaster casts were made of the footprints found at the foot of Olivotto's body, and no evidence, such as weapons, rocks, etc., was tagged. Evidence, such as the tent rope used to hang Olivotto and some of his clothing, disappeared. The investigation, or lack of one, was grounds for the defense to move (unsuccessfully) to dismiss on several occasions.[9]

Almost immediately the post commander, Col. Harry Branson, tried to cover up the incident. On 15 August, the barracks where the brawling had occurred was repaired; it was painted, its windows fixed, and its floors and walls were cleaned of blood. Although orders were given for the obstacle course to be closed, units used the area on 15 and 16 August before it could be searched, photographs or fingerprints taken, or any evidence collected. Additionally, Branson ordered the departure of the 650th and 651st to Camp Stoneman moved up from 5:00 p.m. to 2:00 and ordered both black companies to move first eight miles south to Camp George Jordon. Col. Frederik Teague, the Seattle Port of Embarkation (SPOE) chief of staff, tried to dissuade Branson and, when unsuccessful, obtained from the War Department a seventy-two-hour delay, which was ultimately extended to 23 August. By the late afternoon of 15 August, both companies were back at Fort Lawton, confined inside a enclosed tent stockade. When the 650th and 651st finally departed on 23 August, sixty soldiers remained behind, pending further investigation. Finally, to isolate the Italians, Branson first ordered that all Italian prisoners be locked down and guarded by MPs. Following complaints by the Italian community, he arranged for the transfer of the 28th ISU to Tacoma, Washington. (Branson would be relieved of command on 28 October 1944.)[10]

Within forty-eight hours, Johnson and Durel were removed from the investigation and replaced by Maj. Robert Manchester, the SPOE officer in charge of security and intelligence. (The findings of Manchester, an experienced criminal investigator, would be absorbed into the subsequent inspector-general (IG) investigation.) Adding to the confusion, Branson also appointed a board of three officers—Lt. Col. Vincent Hewitt, Capt. Reino Panula, and Capt. Alan Christensen—to inquire into the incident. Their report, basically a summary of events meant to absolve post personnel of any responsibility, was concluded within a week.

The army at first tried to limit the release of information concerning the riot and murder, but with hundreds of military personnel and civilians working on the base, it proved impossible. An Army Bureau of Public Relations news release issued on the evening of Tuesday, 15 August tried to play down the riot, stating that it had lasted "only a few minutes." The release suggested that Olivotto's death may have been a suicide and promised an "immediate investigation," after which the "attacking soldiers" would be disciplined. It praised the positive relations between the Italians and Americans but made no mention of race. It stated that no further information would be available until after the investigation was complete.[11]

The reaction in the press was immediate and wide-ranging, with stories appearing in the *Washington Post* and all over the country. Having few released facts to use, the newspapers began printing rumors. The attacks were characterized as "premeditated," and it was reported that the riot had been the "climax of trouble that had been brewing" between American and Italian service troops. They also reported on a riot by Italian prisoners that had occurred at Fort Lawton the previous month.[12]

At the Pentagon, Maj. Gen. Archer Lerch, responsible as provost marshal general for all military police and POWs, was receiving phone calls from the State Department and reporters. He understood as well as anyone the international implications of mistreatment of prisoners by American military authorities. Reports of the riot were printed in the *International Herald-Tribune,* available in all the capitals of western Europe, and the story was beginning to create political and diplomatic problems.

Finally, the army's inspector general's office ordered an independent and classified investigation into the circumstances surrounding the riot and murder, as well as the army's response. The purpose was to investigate allegations of gross negligence on the part of Fort Lawton's commanders, not to prosecute those guilty of crimes, a task that would be handled by the army's judge advocate general. Appointed to conduct the investigation was Brig. Gen. Elliott D. Cooke, who as head of the IG's Overseas Inspection Division had jurisdiction over SPOE.

Cooke's background was unique. Born the son of a prosperous New York stockbroker on 15 August 1891, fifty-one years to the day before Olivotto's murder, Cooke had dropped out of school and ran away to Honduras with a friend when he was fourteen. Hired as armed muscle for the United Fruit Company to prevent "anti–American" activity, he had returned to the United States after being injured. He boxed in Nevada before being hired into a sheriff's militia to intimidate striking miners. After a stint as a mercenary in Mexico during the Mexican Revolution and service with the Foreign Legion in Nicaragua, Cooke had been in Panama when war broke out in Europe in 1914.[13]

He enlisted in the U.S. Army as a private on 16 November 1914 and by September 1917 was in France, a first lieutenant in command of a company of Marines. Cooke's actions on 18 July 1918, in the battle of Vierzy, east of Paris, commanding his Marines in combat against the Germans earned him the Croix de Guerre with palm, bronze star, and *fourragère.* Cooke was the only U.S. Army officer to earn all three distinctions during World War I. Now a general and an investigator for the IG, he was responsible for pursuing corruption, malfeasance, and incompetence.[14]

Cooke was preceded at Fort Lawton by his deputy, Lt. Col. Curtis Williams, who arrived on 2 September and began hearing testimony from 164 witnesses. He would be joined later in the month by General Cooke. The inquiry was completed on 5 October. Cooke returned to Washington, D.C., to write his report, which was issued on 28 October.

The findings were highly critical of the initial investigation and of the various commanders at Fort Lawton. They cited lax conditions at the base and inept leadership in the response to the incident. It concluded that the event had been a "fistfight," not a race riot, and that there was no evidence of animosity as reported in the newspapers. Most importantly, the report documented numerous ways in which the crime scene and the investigation had been compromised, inadequate, or incomplete, including lack of identification of suspects, the absence of photographic or fingerprint evidence, conflicting testimony, and destruction or contamination of the crime scene. Although this classified report was available to the prosecution, the findings were initially unavailable to the officers conducting the defense. After defense objections, the report would be made available on a very limited and narrow basis.[15]

In view of the international ramifications regarding the treatment of enemy POWs, there was pressure to proceed with a prosecution, and the army sent one of its brightest prosecutors, Lt. Col. Leon Jaworski, to conduct a two-month investigation into the incident. He was assisted by Capt. Robert Branand III.

Jaworski, who later became one of the most prominent attorneys of the twentieth century, would serve as a war-crimes prosecutor in Germany after the war, prosecuting Nazis for crimes at the Dachau concentration camp. In 1962 U.S. attorney general Robert Kennedy would appoint Jaworski as a special prosecutor when Mississippi governor Ross Barnett was cited for contempt for defying a federal order to allow James Meredith to become the first black student admitted to the University of Mississippi. He would also serve on the Warren Commission, investigating the assassination of President John F. Kennedy, and as a special prosecutor investigating President Nixon during the Watergate scandal.

At Fort Lawton, Jaworski offered immunity from prosecution to several black soldiers in exchange for testifying, and five accepted the offer. Although a lineup had been conducted at Camp Jordon on 21 August at which fifty suspects had been identified, most Italian prisoners of war were unable to identify a single black soldier, citing the darkness and confusion. Two Italians, however, claimed to be confident in their identifications of dozens of the Americans, and those two became witnesses for the prosecution.

On 27 October 1944, criminal charges were filed against forty-three black soldiers for rioting. Three of those—Sgt. Arthur Hurks, Cpl. Luther Larkin, and Pvt. William O. Jones—were charged with the murder of Private Olivotto.[16] Brig. Gen. Eley P. Denson, commanding officer of SPOE, ordered a court-martial convened, and it opened on 16 November. Appointed to defend the forty-three soldiers were Maj. William T. Beeks and Capt.

Howard Noyd. Both would later join Jaworski in Germany prosecuting war crimes. One of Beeks' first motions was a request for a continuance, arguing that nine days was insufficient time to prepare a defense for forty-three defendants, three of them charged with a capital offense. The motion was granted.

The jury panel was headed by Col. Wilmar W. Dewitt, the base director of supply and transportation, who acted as president of the court. He was a combat veteran who had risen from private to second lieutenant during World War I. Lt. Col. Gerald O' Conner, a New York attorney and another combat veteran of World War I who had risen from the ranks, was named the law member. O'Conner had studied law between the wars and flown missions in B-29s with the Twentieth Air Force before becoming a judge advocate. Other members included Lt. Col. Anthony F. Stecher, Maj. George N. Crocker, Maj. Milton S. Kimball, Maj. Hector J. Carpenter, Maj. Samuel MacLennan, Capt. George N. Atkinson, and Capt. Ken A. Weller.[17]

The trial was kept in session six days a week, including Thanksgiving Day, and lasted until 18 December, becoming the longest army court-martial of World War II, lasting twenty-one days and calling eighty-nine witnesses. Numerous reporters, monitors from the National Association for the Advancement of Colored People, and two family members—Sadie Hughes, mother of Pvt. Robert Sanders, and Jeanne Barber, wife of Pvt. Richard Barber—attended all the court sessions.[18]

The forty-three accused soldiers were housed in tents and shacks near the Duwamish River, surrounded by barbed-wire fences and guarded by armed MPs. About twenty had been called back from overseas. They were kept busy picking up trash, cleaning latrines, and other menial tasks. They were trucked to court every morning and returned after each day's session.[19]

The prosecution presented its case primarily through the testimony of the Italians, of the white soldiers assigned as cadre to the ISU and who had been present during the attack, and the five black soldiers who had agreed to testify in exchange for immunity. Since no evidence existed linking any of the defendants to the murder, Jaworski's strategy was to prove that the lynching had been part of the riot, which was a felony. That link would make all the men, especially the leaders, guilty of the murder without having to prove they had actually committed the murder.

Corporal-Major Belle, the Italian who had decked Montgomery, was first up; he testified about the attack and the Italians' withdrawal under a deluge of rocks. Pvt. Dan Daymond testified that he had been one of the men who carried away the unconscious Montgomery, declared that he had

Accused Army soldiers proceeding into court (Hearst Communications, Inc./Hearst Newspapers, LLC).

observed Larkin blow the whistle, and named several other black soldiers he saw chasing Italians or carrying weapons. T/5 Willie Ellis named several men he saw chasing Italians, and Pvt. Alvin Clarke also testified to seeing Larkin blow the whistle, as did Pvt. Jesse Simms, who also testified to hearing Jones recruit others to join the attack and to having witnessed Hurks lead a group down into the Italian area. Pvt. Thomas Battle testified that he had seen Willie Curry ramming a tent with a jeep.[20]

Through Jaworski's questioning, Major Beeks became aware that Jaworski was using transcripts of testimony submitted in Cooke's IG report. It was at this point that Beeks requested access based on discovery. His request was initially denied but, as noted above, but later he was granted access to the reports.

On 4 December, the prosecution rested, and the defense was granted a three-day recess. The defense was hampered by the fact that twenty-five defendants had waived their right to testify on their own behalf, possibly because their testimony might incriminate others.

Accused Army soldiers listening to court proceedings (Hearst Communications Inc./Hearst Newspapers, LLC).

Beeks began the defense by attacking the credibility of the prosecution's witnesses, stating that in the darkness and confusion it would have been impossible to identify anyone and pointing out that the MPs had failed to identify any suspects. Additionally, Beeks challenged the prosecution's assertion that mere presence in the area was de facto proof of rioting. Beeks entered into the record all the errors in the investigation—the destruction of the crime scene, lack of fingerprints or photos, absence of chain of custody with regards to missing evidence, etc. Beeks called witnesses to rebut the testimony of prosecution witnesses. (Had Beeks had full access to Cooke's reports, the discrepancies between their IG testimony and court-martial testimony would have made it easy to impeach several critical prosecution witnesses.)

With regard to Olivotto's death, Beeks reiterated the lack of any physical evidence linking any of the men to it. As to the hanging itself, he suggested that Olivotto, a psychiatric patient, might have committed suicide, though lack of processing and documentation of the scene had made that determination impossible. Concurrently, he also suggested that Olivotto

Flanked by Maj. William Beeks, right, and Capt. Howard D.E. Noyd, counsel for the defense, Pvt. Jesse C.B. Simms, in foreground, who identified black soldier-comrades charged with rioting, is subjected to lengthy cross-examination at the Fort Lawton court-martial trial. Published 23 November 1944. Sketch by Henry Roth for *Seattle Post-Intelligencer* (Hearst Communications, Inc./Hearst Newspapers, LLC).

might have been murdered by white MPs, noting previous tension at the PX between the Italians and white troops (a comment that was stricken from the record) and that during the morning MPs had gone through the entire area where the body was. The defense rested on 13 December.

On 16 December both sides made their closing arguments, and the case went to the jury. The court deliberated fourteen hours before reaching a verdict. Two-thirds of the court was needed to convict on the charge of riot. The charge of murder required a unanimous verdict, and sentences of more than ten years required the concurrence of three-fourths of the court. Charges had been dismissed against thirteen soldiers. At 7:00 on the evening of 17 December, Colonel Dewitt announced the verdict: all the remaining twenty-eight soldiers were found guilty of rioting; two of the three charged with murder were convicted of the lesser charge of manslaughter. The court would hear evidence on the military history of the convicted before sentencing.[21]

The following day, the court announced the sentences, which ranged from six months to twenty-five years, with those reportedly involved in the assault on the orderly room, and NCOs, receiving the harsher sentences. Larkin and Jones, both convicted on the charge of manslaughter, received twenty-five and fifteen years hard labor, respectively. Hurks, acquitted on the manslaughter charge, received twelve years at hard labor for rioting. Most sentences varied between four and ten years, over two hundred years in the aggregate. All the defendants were reduced in rank to private, dishonorably discharged from the army, and all of them forfeited all pay and benefits. The response from the African American community was immediate. Edgar G. Brown, director of the National Negro Council, called for a "Second Emancipation Proclamation" and urged the nation's thirteen million African Americans to "end discrimination against members of their race."[22]

On 4 January 1945, MPs Robinson and Lomax were brought before a court-martial, charged with two violations of the ninety-sixth Article of War: neglect, in not having given information of a threatening disturbance to proper authority without delay, and failure to use reasonable force to prevent destruction of government property. Both men were acquitted on both charges, but Lomax was additionally charged with failure to use reasonable force to quell a riot (failure to draw his pistol) and on that charge he was convicted and discharged from the army.

On 19 April 1945, the sentences of the Fort Lawton defendants were found to be "legally sufficient" by the Army Board of Review and were upheld. However, on 28 July 1946 the clemency board reduced the sentences of all seventeen defendants who had been given terms exceeding five years; the terms of most, including Hurks, were reduced to three years. Larkin and Jones had their sentences reduced to five years. In December 1946, President Harry S. Truman issued a "Christmas clemency" to thousands of imprisoned serviceman with less than three years remaining on their sentences. As a result, only three Fort Lawton defendants remained in custody after 1946. On 1 June 1947, Larkin was paroled for good behavior, but Barber and William Jones, convicted of additional crimes while incarcerated, remained behind bars until 1948.[23]

10. Fort Lawton Courts-Martial

The Fort Lawton courts-martial must have influenced President Truman's decision to end segregation in the armed forces. On 26 July 1948, Truman signed Executive Order 9981: "It is hereby declared to be the policy of the President that there shall be equality of treatment and opportunity for all persons in the armed services without regard to race, color, religion, or national origin." The action also established the President's Committee on Equality of Treatment and Opportunity in the Armed Services.[24]

Some of the defendants, like Arthur Hurks, John Hamilton, Lee Stewart, Willie Prevost, and Roy Hamilton, reentered the army after their release and earned honorable discharges. Over the years, several petitioned the Army Board for Correction of Military Records (ABCMR) for reviews of their conviction and honorable discharges. The petitioners included Samuel Snow in 1949, Robert Sanders in 1950, Willie Curry in 1951, and Frank Hughes in 1975. The petitions were rejected.

Two books about the courts-martial—*Riot at Ft. Lawton: 1944*, by Dominic W. Moreo, in 2004, and *On American Soil*, by Jack Hamann, in 2005—renewed interest in the case. On 1 July 2005, Rep. Jim McDermott (D.-Wash.) introduced House Resolution 3174 asking the secretary of the army to reevaluate the Fort Lawton convictions. The bill was supported by Duncan Hunter (R.-Calif.), chairman of the House Armed Services Committee, and twenty-four cosponsors. On 8 June 2006, the army announced that it would review the convictions in the Fort Lawton courts-martial if the surviving soldiers or their families appealed the original decision. Aided by McDermott and Hunter, one defendant, Samuel Snow, and the families of three others—Luther Larkin, Booker Townsell, and William Jones—petitioned for a review.[25] In her petition, the daughter of Booker Townsell alleged her father had been denied due process; that he had been a victim of racial discrimination; that he'd had inadequate counsel, in that there had been only two lawyers representing forty-three defendants, and that the lawyers had had conflicting interests; that the investigation had been flawed, inadequate, and negligent; and that exonerating evidence in Cooke's report had been withheld from the defense and illegally suppressed.

On 26 October 2007, after fourteen months of evaluating the records, the ABCMR reversed the sixty-three-year-old verdict and overturned the convictions. Citing "egregious error" by Jaworski in withholding crucial, exculpatory evidence and holding that the resulting trial had been "fundamentally unfair," the board granted the petitioners honorable discharges and gave them "due pay and allowances" dating to 6 March 1946. That decision was later extended to all twenty-eight defendants.[26]

As part of a three-day tribute at Seattle's Discovery Park, site of Fort

Lawton, Assistant Secretary of the Army Ronald James publically apologized on 26 July 2008, the fortieth anniversary of Truman's desegregation order, to the families of the twenty-eight soldiers convicted in the Fort Lawton court-martial. Only two of the defendants were still alive; Roy Montgomery chose not to attend, and Sam Snow had been hospitalized just prior to the event for problems with his pacemaker.[27] James, whose ancestors had escaped slavery in Missouri to fight in the Civil War, called the convictions a "grievous wrong" and said the men "deserve the applause of angels."

11

Port Chicago Court-Martial
Mutiny—1944

I didn't talk to nobody. I didn't conspire with nobody. I just made up my mind I was tired of it. I wanted to be a sailor.—Seaman Martin Bordenave

On 17 July 1944, at about 10:19 p.m., a loud boom echoed over the waters adjacent to the Port Chicago Naval Magazine, and a brilliant flash of light lit up the moonless night on the eastern end of San Francisco Bay. Three to six seconds later, a second, massive explosion encompassed the area, sending a huge fireball 12,000 feet into the sky and obliterating the pier, two ammunition ships, and most of the town of Port Chicago a mile distant. The explosion, heard as far away as Nevada, was the worst home-front disaster and largest military loss of life within the continental United States during World War II. Events of that night would lead to the largest mass court-martial for mutiny in the history of the U.S. Navy.[1]

Early in the war, the facilities at the Naval Ammunition Depot at Mare Island, on San Francisco Bay, had expanded to maximum capacity, and the demand for ammunition in the Pacific theater necessitated the construction of additional munitions-handling facilities. Port Chicago had deep tidal water along the northern boundary, was serviced by two transcontinental railroads, and had room to expand.[2]

The facility at Port Chicago was formally established by order of the secretary of the navy on 27 June 1942. Located in a sparsely settled area remote from industrial activities, the site was on Suisun Bay, in the estuary of the Sacramento and San Joaquin Rivers. It had connections by water to San Francisco Bay and the Pacific Ocean. It was formally commissioned on 30 November 1942, and the first ship was loaded there on 8 December.[3]

Port Chicago Naval Ammunition Depot disaster (U.S. Navy).

The Naval Magazine, Port Chicago was designed to receive munitions by rail and transfer them onto seagoing vessels or barges. The ship-loading pier was built especially for handling explosives, and it was upgraded as experience dictated. By May 1944 the pier could handle two ships simultaneously. A second pier was under construction and a third was being planned at the time of the explosion. The facility was intended solely as a transfer point; there were no facilities for the storage of munitions.[4]

A variety of munitions passed through Port Chicago, including aerial bombs, artillery shells, naval mines, depth charges, torpedoes, grenades, and small-arms ammunition. The materiel arrived by rail at a loading platform at the end of the pier, opposite the hold of the ship to be loaded. The cars were unloaded, and the munitions were placed under the ship's booms. They were then hoisted on board and stored in the holds. So great was the need for ammunition that three shifts worked around the clock to meet demand.

Originally it had been planned that work at the magazine would be carried out by a civilian workforce, but an adequate number of commercial stevedores wasn't available, due in part to the remoteness of the site. The decision was made to utilize enlisted naval personnel to load and unload the munitions. A minimum number of buildings was constructed to house and feed the men (barracks, mess halls, etc.), but few provisions were made for laundry, transportation, recreation, or other amenities. Morale suffered.

The United States in 1942 was a country where racial discrimination was widely practiced in employment and government; "separate but equal" was the law of the land, upheld by the Supreme Court. At the outbreak of World War II, the military, like many parts of the country, was strictly segregated. There were only five African American officers in the army, none in the navy, and there were no black Marines, commissioned or enlisted.

Even with war looming in Europe, the War Department was opposed to integrating the military, on the grounds that it would undermine the morale of white soldiers. Even with wartime manpower shortages, military leaders were reluctant to utilize blacks as officers or in combat roles. Accordingly, blacks were disproportionately represented in certain service branches of the army, like the Quartermaster Corps, Engineer Corps, and Transportation Corps. The navy didn't accept black volunteers or conscripts until forced to by Roosevelt's Executive Order 9279, issued in December 1942, which ended such restrictions. Still, 93 percent of blacks enlisted or drafted into the navy served as messmen, laborers, or stewards. Black women were not allowed to serve in the navy until the end of 1944.[5]

The enlisted men selected to work as loaders in the ordnance battalion at Port Chicago were all African Americans, commanded by white officers. All of the men had been trained in naval ratings while at the Naval Station Great Lakes, but few men had received any instruction in handling cargo, and none had received any training in the handling of munitions or explosives. Men operating the winches that transported the loads from pier to hatch were given one week's training on a training winch before starting work on ships' winches.[6]

Further, in reference to their training, the subsequent board of inquiry found:

> Because of the level of intelligence and education of the enlisted personnel, it was impracticable to train them by any method other than by actual demonstration. Many of the men were incapable of reading and understanding the simplest directions. Division officers were responsible for the actual training of the men and they carried out their duties by personally instructing and demonstrating with the materiel being handled, the proper methods of procedure. The division officers attempted to impress on the men the need for care and safety, and the highly dangerous nature of materiel being handled.[7]

The black petty officers and the majority of sailors assigned as laborers scored in the lower 60 percent of the navy's General Classification Test, with scores averaging 31, the lowest twelfth of the navy. According to the board of inquiry's later characterization of the men, "These enlisted personnel were unreliable, emotional, lacked capacity to understand or remember orders or instructions, were particularly susceptible to mass psychology and moods, lacked mechanical aptitude, were suspicious of strange officers, disliked receiving orders of any kind, particularly from white officers or petty officers, and were inclined to look for and make an issue of discrimination. For the most part, they were quite young and of limited education."[8]

Nor were the officers selected to command the black sailors any more familiar with their duties. As with everything else in wartime, there was a shortage of qualified officers, and the best and brightest were generally selected for service with the fleet. The officers assigned to Port Chicago had no training or experience in commanding enlisted personnel, and while they had observed ship-loading operations at Mare Island, few had any practical experience in handling cargo and none had any experience loading munitions. As with the enlisted men, most of what they learned was through actual experience. Even the commanding officer of Port Chicago, Capt. Merrill T. Kinne, had no training in handling munitions and very little experience in loading them.[9]

The ordnance battalions were divided into eight divisions of about one hundred men, each comprising five platoons. Each platoon worked one hatch. The platoons were further divided into two squads, one squad, under the command of a petty officer, on the pier to remove the materiel from the car and put it into the hoist, and the other squad, also under a petty officer, in the hold to receive the materiel and stow the munitions. Each division provided its checkers, winch men, hatch tenders, and carpenter's mates. No unnecessary personnel were permitted on the pier.

On 13 July 1944, at 8:15 in the morning, the SS *E.A. Bryan*, a Liberty ship, was moored at Port Chicago to take on munitions. Owned by the War Shipping Administration, it was a fairly new vessel, having gone into service the previous February. It had one prior voyage to the Pacific, had undergone repairs at sea, and had been inspected for readiness for loading prior to arrival at Port Chicago by the operators, port director, and captain of the port. No defects had been noted. It was fully fueled, with 5,292 barrels (841,360 liters) of heavy fuel oil.

Loading began at 10:00 a.m. the day of arrival and continued around the clock. No variation from the routine was noted, with the exception of some minor repairs to the winches. By the evening of 17 July the ship was loaded to about 40 percent capacity, with 4,606 tons of cargo, including 1,780 tons of high explosives and 199 tons of smokeless powder.

At about 6:15 p.m., the SS *Quinault Victory*, a second Liberty ship, moored across the pier from the *E. A. Bryan*. The ship was less than a week old, having entered service at Portland, Oregon, on 11 July. It too had passed inspection with no defects noted. The ship was scheduled to commence loading at midnight. The night was clear and cool, and the wind was blowing from the southwest. The fire barge was moored at the end of the pier. Sixteen loaded railcars were spotted along the pier—five cars, containing bombs and antiaircraft projectiles (253 tons), for the *Quinault Victory* and seven cars for the *E. A. Bryan*, containing cluster bombs and ammunition (176 tons). Of the 429 tons of cargo on the pier, 146 tons were high explosives.[10]

Present on the pier that night were ninety-eight enlisted men of the Third Division, about half on the dock and half on board the *E. A. Bryan*, and 102 sailors of the Sixth Division rigging the *Quinault Victory* for loading. Also present were two division officers, two assistant division officers, and two junior officers under instruction, as well as the assistant loading officer and the dock and transportation officer. The assistant planning officer was also present, conducting an inspection.

Sixty-seven officers and crew members were at their stations on board the two ships, as well as one officer and twenty-nine enlisted men of the vessels' armed guard details. A Coast Guard crew of five enlisted men was on board the fire barge. A train crew of three civil service employees was working the dock, and a Marine sentry stood guard at Post 5. The pier was well lighted, and an inspection by the officer in charge, loading officer, and assistant loading officer noted that operations running routinely thirty minutes prior to the explosion. The sergeant of the guard reported the pier sentry alert and conditions normal at about the same time. No one on the pier survived the night.

The cause of the explosion cannot, and will not ever, be determined with certainty. As the court of inquiry explained, "Because of the magnitude and intensity of the explosion, all persons who were in a position to observe the act or acts actually causing the initiation of the explosion were lost. All material evidence which might indicate the chain of circumstances in the initiating explosion was lost."

Surviving eyewitnesses reported that the massive first explosion was subsequently followed by an even larger second detonation that sent a boiling, billowing mass of burning gasses skyward, changing from brilliant white, to yellow, and to reddish-orange. The *E. A. Bryan* detonated in a huge fireball and disappeared. The *Quinault Victory* was literally blown out of the water and torn into sections; the stern landed upside down in the water some five hundred feet away. Coast Guard fire barge *CG-60014-F* was thrown six hundred feet upriver, where it sank. The pier, along with the locomotive, boxcars, rails, cargo, and men were blown to pieces. Chunks of glowing hot metal and burning ordnance were flung 12,000 feet. Nearby boxcars, staged at revetments and waiting to be unloaded, were bent inward and knocked from their tracks by the force of the explosion.

On the base, buildings were knocked from their foundations, and fences, power and water systems, telephone lines, storage tanks, automobiles, trucks, and other equipment, as well as roads and rail lines, were heavily damaged or destroyed. The nearby town of Port Chicago sustained extensive damage. Flying debris, metal, and glass caused numerous injuries to civilians and military personnel, but there were no fatalities outside the area of the pier itself. Seismographs at the University of California, Berkeley, recorded two shock waves measuring 3.4 on the Richter scale. In total, over five thousand tons of munitions detonated, resulting in over an estimated $10 million (in 1994 dollars) in property damage.[11]

Almost immediately following the blast, firefighting and rescue operations began. The Martinez, Mt. Diablo, Rio Vista, Crockett, and Berkeley Fire Departments all responded, as did troops from the army's Camp

The cost of the explosions in human life was horrendous. Of the 320 killed, only 51 bodies could be identified; the others were listed as missing. Two hundred two of the dead were black sailors. An additional 390 persons were injured, including 233 black sailors. The explosions accounted for 15 percent of all African American servicemen killed during World War II (U.S. Navy).

A U.S. Navy sailor views his wrecked car following the Port Chicago explosions (U.S. Navy).

Stoneman, and the Mare Island Navy Yard and Ammunition Depot. The Red Cross, Salvation Army, and United Service Organizations also worked to assist the survivors. Every building on the post suffered damage from the blast, except the sentry-dog kennels.[12]

Once the fires were extinguished and the 245 injured Marines and Naval personnel had been transported to medical facilities, the work of recovering bodies and parts of bodies, clearing debris, rerouting ammunition, rebuilding the facilities, and transferring personnel to nearby facilities began.

The commandant of the Twelfth Naval District, Rear Adm. Carleton H. Wright, appointed a court of inquiry to investigate all the facts surrounding the explosion. Three senior officers—Capt. Albert G. Cook, Capt. John S. Crenshaw, Capt. and William B. Holden—made up the board. They were assisted by a judge advocate, Lt. Cdr. Keith Ferguson. They convened at Port Chicago on 10:00 a.m. on 21 July, heard testimony for thirty-nine days, and issued their findings on 30 October 1944.

The court heard testimony from ordnance experts, inspectors, eyewitnesses to the explosion, survivors injured in the blast, and other base personnel, a total of 125 witnesses in all. It investigated the possibility of sabotage, defects in the ordnance itself, rough handling of the munitions, winch failure, problems with equipment, or accidental ignition of the vessel's fuel system. No mention was made of the men's lack of training in handling explosives.

During the hearing it was disclosed that there had been a competition between the officers of the different divisions to see which could load the most munitions fastest and that officers bet on the results. On a prominent chalkboard, Captain Kinne had tallied each crew's average tonnage per hour. Although most would see that this might not be the wisest of courses when dealing with high explosives, it was explained away as "healthy competition." The report cleared all officers in charge of any "fault negligence or inefficiency" in connection with the explosion.

The court of inquiry was unable to determine the cause of the explosion, but among its sixty-three opinions it asserted "that the loading procedures and gear used at Port Chicago were safe and in accordance with standard naval practice" (Opinion 26) and "that a loading rate of ten tons per hatch per hour with the personnel available was high but a goal that could be attained with *proper training and supervision*" (Opinion 40). But it also held that "the enlisted personnel comprising the ordnance battalions at Port Chicago were poor material for training in the handling and loading of munitions, and required an unusual amount of close supervision while actually engaged in this work" (Opinion 14) and that, further, the officers were required to put out great effort "because of the poor quality of personnel with which they had to work" (Opinion 13).[13]

What is revealing is that the board was able to reach these conclusions after interviewing only five black sailors, none of whom subsequently refused to load ammunition. The court listed the most likely causes as, in order of probability, "supersensitive elements" that detonated during handling, "rough handling" of the munitions, and "failure of handling gear" (winches, booms, hooks, etc.).

The Third and Sixth Divisions had been almost entirely lost in the explosions. The Second Division was divided into two groups, with half remaining at Port Chicago to assist in the cleanup. The other half, along with the Fourth and Eighth Divisions, was transferred to Camp Shoemaker, thirty miles south, where it was assigned barracks duty until the end of the month. Divisions One, Five, and Seven were reassigned other duties and shipped out.

Meanwhile, the men of the Second Division were anxious about the future and were unaware that the navy was holding a court of inquiry. In early August, the Second Division was reunited, and with Divisions Four and Eight it was transferred to the Ryder Street Naval Barracks in Vallejo, across the Napa River from the Mare Island Navy Yard and Ammunition Depot. They were assigned no ship-loading duties. Most of the men were nervous and jumpy, some in shock after spending days recovering their shipmates' remains. No psychological counseling was offered, and requests for "survivors leave"—a thirty-day leave granted to survivors of serious incidents where death occurred—were denied, even to injured sailors, although they were granted to the white officers. This created resentment in the ranks. The eventual return to ship-loading duties was on everyone's minds and had been the subject of numerous discussions, some declaring that they would refuse to resume loading munitions without proper training and equipment.

On 8 August 1944, the USS *Sangay* (AE 10) arrived at Mare Island to be loaded with munitions. The Second, Fourth, and Eighth Divisions were scheduled to load it. After chow on the morning of 9 August, the Fourth Division was ordered to form up in ranks and was marched off. The men had heard rumors but were uncertain as to their destination as they marched toward the end of the street. A right turn would take them to the parade grounds; a left turn would take them to a ferry that crossed over to Mare Island. The Fourth Division officer, Lt. Ernest Delucchi, gave the command "Column, left!" The men stopped as one, dead in their tracks. "Forward, march! Column, left!," Delucchi ordered. Nobody moved.

Delucchi approached one sailor, whose name was Richardson, and told him that "if he wasn't going to obey orders, to fall out." With that, Richardson, and almost the entire division with him, broke ranks. Astonished and nonplussed, Delucchi ordered the division leader, Coxswain Elmer Boyer, to get the names of those sailors willing to work.

Delucchi made his way to the Administration Building to report the matter to the commanding officer, Cdr. Joseph R. Tobin. The base chaplain, Lt. Cdr. Jefferson Flowers, tried to persuade the men to return to work voluntarily, appealing to their sense of duty, patriotism, and racial pride; he even offered to go to the docks with the men. He was unsuccessful. The men expressed their willingness to obey every order except handling ammunition, admitting that they were afraid to do so.

Meanwhile, Tobin had ordered Delucchi to have his men stand fast on the parade ground, and Delucchi returned to his men. Once the chaplain was finished, he marched the division to the parade ground to await Tobin's arrival. While there, he attempted to persuade the men to return to work, pointing out that they, like he, had taken an oath to obey lawful orders and appealing to their pride and reminding them of the importance to the war effort of the work they were doing.

With Tobin's arrival, the Fourth Division was ordered to the recreation building to be interviewed individually regarding their unwillingness to return to work. Tobin spoke to only six or seven sailors before being interrupted by a telephone call reporting that the officers of the Second and Eighth Divisions had found themselves in similar situations. Tobin directed Lt. James E. Tobin (no relation), who was the Second Division officer, and Lt. Carleton Morehouse, of the Eighth Division, to order their men to work. It is unclear whether these divisions were ever given direct orders to return to work or were merely asked about their willingness to return to work. This point would be brought up later in the court-martial.

Delucchi also spoke individually to some of the men and ordered seventeen of them back to work. Among these was Seaman 1st Class Joseph Randolph "Joe" Small, a twenty-three-year-old high school dropout from New Jersey, a winch operator in the Fourth Division who was well liked and a natural leader. When asked why he wouldn't return to work, Small, like the others, answered that he was afraid. Seen by the men as a "spokesman," Small would be perceived by the navy as a "ringleader."

Of the 328 men in the three divisions, 258 refused to return to work loading ammunition and were confined on board a barge, densely packed into the hold, where they remained for three days. Civilian contract stevedores were brought in to load the *Sangay*.[14] There was a lot of tension among the confined men, some urging unity, others arguing that they should return to work. Additionally, there were tensions between some of the sailors and their guards. These led to a fight in the chow hall between a prisoner and a guard on 10 August.

A meeting was called that evening among the prisoners. Small spoke, urging the men to "knock off the horseplay" and advising them that conflicts with black shore patrolmen would only result in their replacement by white Marines. What is in dispute is whether at this meeting Small said, "We've got the officers by the balls—they can do nothing to us if we don't do anything to them. If we stick together, they can't do anything to us." At the court-martial, some sailors would testify hearing Small make those statements, or variants of them, while others would deny hearing them. Small would deny under oath ever making any such statement.[15] Besides urging unity and encouraging the men to avoid confrontations, Small also organized the men in preparing and serving meals and cleaning the chow hall. He and three others were charged by the officers with maintaining order on board the barge.

The following day, 11 August, the 258 men were marched from the barge to a baseball diamond and formed into ranks on three sides of a square. Admiral Wright arrived by jeep and addressed the men,

> Just in case you don't know who I am, my name is Admiral Wright and I am the commandant of the Twelfth Naval District. They tell me that some of you

men want to go to sea. I believe that's a goddamn lie! I don't believe any of you have enough guts to go to sea. I handled ammunition for approximately thirty years and I'm still here. I have a healthy respect for ammunition; anybody who doesn't is crazy. But I want to remind you men that mutinous conduct in time of war carries the death sentence, and the hazards of facing a firing squad are far greater than the hazards of handling ammunition.[16]

The admiral told the men that the ammunition they were to load was desperately needed on Saipan. Then he plainly stated that the choice between returning to work or continuing to refuse to load ammunition was a choice between obeying lawful orders and mutiny, ultimately a choice between possible death and certain death. The men were stunned; for most this was the first time that they had considered that their actions could be defined as mutiny. Seaman Small spoke for many when he explained later, "As far as we were concerned, mutiny could only be committed on the high seas. I, for one, didn't consider refusing to go to work mutiny. We didn't try to take over anything. We didn't try to take command of the base. We didn't try to replace any officers. We didn't try to assume an officer's position. How could they call it mutiny?"

After the admiral departed, the men were ordered to form into two groups, one those willing to obey all orders, the other those who still refused to obey orders to load ammunition. All of Division Eight chose to obey orders, while Divisions Two and Four were split. Small and forty-three others formed the group still unwilling to load ammunition, and it was escorted to the brig, with the remaining 214 ordered to return to their barracks. The next day, 12 August, six men of the Second and Fourth Division failed to report for work and soon joined the others in confinement, bringing to fifty the number of seamen that would be charged with mutiny. Of the fifty men confined to the brig, only Small was kept in solitary confinement.

Throughout August, the fifty men were taken to Camp Shoemaker, where they were questioned about who had said what to whom, in an attempt to identify the leaders of the work stoppage. The men, some barely literate, were told to sign statements summarizing the interviews, statements that they later disputed in court. Some refused to sign. Some refused to make statements. Officers interviewed the men separately, frequently with armed guards present, and threatened the men with serious consequences. All of the men were questioned without benefit of counsel.

Once the interviews were complete, 208 men, those who had agreed to return to work, were convicted by summary court-martial of disobeying orders under Article 4 of the *Articles for the Government of the United States*

Navy (known as "Rocks and Shoals"), sentenced to the loss of three months pay, and shipped out to the Pacific. There they were employed in menial labor, except for a small number who agreed to testify at the court-martial. All were given bad-conduct discharges upon completing active duty.[17]

The remaining fifty men came to be known as the "Port Chicago 50." In early September, Admiral Wright, as convening authority, formally charged the men with conspiring to make a mutiny with "a deliberate purpose and intent to override superior military authority." He appointed a seven-member court to hear evidence and decide the verdict, naming Rear Adm. Hugo W. Osterhaus as president of the court. Osterhaus, the son of an admiral, was a forty-year career officer brought out of retirement to lead the panel. He had been awarded the Navy Cross during World War I for actions against German U-boats while in command of the USS *Wilson* in May 1918.[18]

The judge advocate selected was Lt. Cdr. James F. Coakley, who prior to the war had served as a deputy chief prosecutor under Alameda County district attorney Earl Warren, future chief justice of the United States. Coakley would gain notoriety in the 1960s prosecuting antiwar activists and Black Panthers like Huey Newton and Eldridge Cleaver. On this occasion Coakley was assisted by Lt. (jg) John T. Keenan.

The defense comprised a team of five lawyers, one for every ten men, headed by Lt. Gerald E. Veltmann, a Texas attorney in civilian life. He was assisted by Lt. Harley Carswell, and Lieutenants (junior grade) Irving Hayutin, Daniel F. Hanley, and Philip J. Hermann. As his team interviewed their clients, Veltmann learned that two of the men charged with mutiny had never loaded munitions before. They had been assigned as cooks because they were physically unsuited to load ammunition. Another sailor who had refused had done so because he had a broken wrist in a sling.

In a pretrial motion, Veltmann moved to have the formal charges of mutiny dismissed. Citing *Winthrop's Military Law and Precedents*, which defined mutiny as an attempt to "usurp, subvert or override superior military authority," he argued that nothing in the formal charges alleged that any of the men conspired together to accomplish any of those things and that a more proper charge would be failure to obey an order. Coakley opposed the motion, arguing that under military law, a persistent refusal to work by two or more men was sufficient to establish a conspiracy to override superior military authority. The court agreed with Coakley and dismissed the motion.

The court-martial convened in a vacant Marine barracks, converted into a courtroom, on Treasure Island in the San Francisco Bay, on 14 September 1944. It was the first mutiny trial of World War II. There was nationwide interest, and the case was given extensive coverage in the black press and by the NAACP. The First Lady, Eleanor Roosevelt, in a letter to Secretary of the Navy James V. Forrestal, expressed the hope that "special care will be taken." The trial was open to the public, openness facilitated by the navy in part to counter charges of racial discrimination, in part to serve as an example for other sailors considering similar actions. The trial opened with pleas by all fifty defendants of not guilty.

The prosecution's aim was to show that a conspiracy had taken place. It first called Commander Tobin and the three division officers, Delucchi, Morehouse. and Lieutenant Tobin; all testified that they had ordered men to load munitions. Tobin testified that he had given orders only to seven sailors and couldn't verify that the others actually received orders to load ammunition. He also admitted that the men had been neither aggressive nor disrespectful. Delucchi admitted under cross-examination by Veltmann that he had personally given orders to only four men and that the reason they had given for refusing was that they were afraid. Both Morehouse and Lieutenant Tobin both related that they had ordered their men to load munitions and that the majority refused until Admiral Wright's speech implying firing squads. There was also testimony from black sailors already court-martialed for refusing to obey orders who testified against Small and the others accused of mutiny. Coakley gave the prosecution's summation on 22 September.[19]

The following day, 23 September, the defense opened, and for three weeks each of the accused took the stand to speak in his own defense. Much of their testimony contradicted that of the prosecution's witnesses.

Seaman Ollie E. Green, a truck driver in the Fourth Division who had broken his wrist one day prior to 9 August, testified that although he had been named in an officer's testimony as having refused a direct order, he'd only been asked how his wrist was, to which he had answered, "Not good." Green told the court that he was afraid to load munitions because "them officers [had been] racing each division to see who put on the most tonnage, and I knowed the way they was handling ammunition it was liable to go off again. If we didn't want to work fast at that time, they wanted to put us in the brig, and when the exec [executive officer, second in command of the depot] came down on the docks, they wanted us to slow up.... That is my reason for not wanting to go down there."[20] This was the first time the press had heard of allegations of speed and tonnage competitions between divisions. The story broke on front pages across the country the following morning, causing the navy to issue a statement denying Green's allegations.

Seaman Alphonso McPherson testified that the judge advocate, Coakley, had threatened to have him shot if he refused to answer questions during his interrogation, stating, "I am going to give you another chance, but if you don't come clean this time I am going to see that you get shot." McPherson didn't change his testimony even under cross-examination by Coakley, who denied threatening anyone. Many testified that they were afraid to load munitions and that they had come to their decisions not to obey orders independently and there had been no conspiracy. Most testified that they had never received a direct order to return to work.

On 9 October, Thurgood Marshall, chief counsel of the NAACP, arrived and sat in on the proceedings, by permission of the secretary of the navy. Marshall spoke with the fifty defendants and conferred with Veltmann and the other lawyers on the team. The next day he called a press conference at which he accused Coakley of racial prejudice in the handling of a case that should be tried as one individual insubordination, not mass mutiny. Many agreed. A week earlier, fifty Bay Area black churches had sent a petition to President Roosevelt asking for justice.

On 17 October, Marshall called another press conference at which he put the navy on trial, calling for a formal investigation by the government into the circumstances leading to the refusal to load ammunition by black sailors. Marshall wanted answers:

> I want to know why the Navy disregarded official warnings by the San Francisco waterfront unions—before the Port Chicago disaster—that the explosion was inevitable if they persisted in using untrained seamen in the loading of ammunition. I want to know why the Navy disregarded an offer by these same unions to send experienced men to train Navy personnel in the safe handling of explosives.... I want to know why the commissioned officers at Port Chicago were allowed to race their men. I want to know why bets ranging from $5 up were made between division officers as to whose crew would load more ammunition.[21]

Marshall also wanted to know why, when sailors of the First Division refused to work, they had been quietly shipped out and not court-martialed.

The two final witnesses for the defense were a navy psychiatrist, Richard H. Pembroke, who testified that experiencing a huge explosion could generate fear, and Coxswain Boyer, chief petty officer of the Fourth Division. Boyer testified that there had been no mention of unloading duties prior to 9 August, that he never heard any derogatory remarks from the men, that the men's breaking ranks was a surprise to everyone, and that at no time had he heard Lieutenant Delucchi give any man a direct order to load ammunition. Boyer's credibility was enhanced by the fact that he was not among the men who had refused to work.

In Coakley's rebuttal, it came out that officers had edited the official statements made by the accused, leaving in what they thought was important, which didn't include the men's fear of another explosion, that they hadn't been advised of their right not to make a statement, and that many had not been disabused of their notion that mutinies could only occur on vessels. The last day of testimony was Thursday, 19 October.

In his summation, Coakley laid out a chronology of events that he argued had led to a conspiracy by the men to refuse to load ammunition. He defined "collective insubordination, collective disobedience of lawful orders of a superior officer," as mutiny. The men had persisted after due warning from a superior officer.

Veltmann made an impressive closing argument, denying that the men had entered into a conspiracy to mutiny. The discussions on board the barge had expressed not defiance of authority but frustration that no attempt or effort was being made to address their legitimate concerns regarding workplace safety. Since there was no mention of conspiracy in the charges, Veltmann reasoned, only charges of "making a mutiny," the men could not be tried for conspiracy, nor had any of the men openly plotted mutiny. The men had received no direct orders to load ammunition; it would be impossible for them to override orders that they never received, and hence there could have been no intent to override lawful authority, "intent" being critical to the charge of mutiny. Mutiny, he stated, had not been openly declared in word or implied by deed, in the conduct of the defendants. There was no evidence that the men had conspired. What had occurred was at best disobedience to orders, but not mutiny. It was brilliant legal reasoning. But it was spectacularly unpersuasive with members of the court, who sided with Coakley.

On 24 October, the court issued its verdict of guilty on one specification of mutiny for all fifty of the Port Chicago defendants. It had deliberated for eighty minutes, making it clear that its members had given little consideration to the individual circumstances of the men. There were no sentences of death, but all of the men were uniformly sentenced to reduction in rank to seaman apprentice and fifteen years at hard labor, followed by dishonorable discharges from the navy. At the end of November, the fifty men were transported to the Terminal Island Disciplinary Barracks at San Pedro, California, south of Los Angeles.

On 15 November, Admiral Wright, as part of his review as the convening authority, mitigated the sentences of forty of the fifty defendants; twenty-four sentences were reduced to twelve years, eleven sentences to ten years, and five sentences to eight years. The dishonorable discharges remained in place. The fifteen-year sentences of ten men were allowed to stand, including those of Small, McPherson, and Green.[22]

There was an outcry against the verdict, and the men's supporters included Eleanor Roosevelt. The NAACP Legal Defense Fund obtained written permission from all fifty defendants to represent them, and Marshall began drafting an appeal. Petitions were circulated and editorials published.

On 3 April 1945, Marshall appeared in Washington, D.C., to present his appeal directly to the judge advocate of the navy. He stated that most of the men had never received direct orders, that Coakley had deliberately misled the jury as to the definition of mutiny, that disobeying orders is not mutiny, and that the mass of evidence introduced had been hearsay and thus inadmissible. He requested a complete reversal of the findings in the interest of justice. The office of the secretary of the navy ordered Admiral Wright to reconvene the court-martial, with instructions to disregard the hearsay testimony.

Admiral Osterhaus reconvened the court, and on 12 June 1945 it confirmed the verdict and sentences. Admiral Wright reaffirmed the reduction in sentences. With the surrender of Japan and the end of the war, however, the need to set an example was reduced, and in September 1945 the navy reduced all fifty mutiny sentences by one year. In October, Capt. Harold Stassen recommended to the secretary of the navy that the sentences be further reduced to two years for men with good conduct records and three years for the others, with credit for time served. (Stassen would later become famous as a perennial candidate for president, seeking the Republican nomination twelve times—in 1944, 1948, 1952, 1964, 1968, 1976, 1980, 1984, 1988, 1992, 1996, and 2000.)

On 12 January 1946, the navy informed Lester B. Granger, executive secretary of the National Urban League and special adviser to James Forrestal, now secretary of defense, that it was voiding the sentences of the fifty Port Chicago sailors, as well as those of thirty-six black sailors charged with "rout" (riot) on Guam in December 1944.[23] Forty-seven of the fifty men were released on probation to active duty overseas in the South Pacific, primarily on cleanup duties, to serve until they earned sufficient points for discharge. The character of the discharges would be "General—Under Honorable Conditions" if their records proved satisfactory. Two defendants remained in the hospital, and one was refused release because of bad conduct. For most, confinement had lasted fourteen months or less.[24]

In 1955, the navy began efforts to buy the town of Port Chicago, eventually forcing the last resident out in 1969 to create a buffer zone for the

Concord Naval Weapons Station. It razed the town in 1970, and all that now remains are a few overgrown roads.

In 1977, Martin Bordenave, with the assistance of the NAACP, requested that his case be reopened; however, his attempt was unsuccessful. In 1989, a book by Robert L. Allen on the explosion and court-martial, using recently declassified government reports, created a renewed interest in the trial and caught the attention of Rep. George Miller (D.-Calif.), the congressman for the Seventh District, which included the site of Port Chicago. In 1990 Miller, along with twenty-four other members of Congress, asked Secretary of the Navy H. Lawrence Garrett to review the case to "ameliorate an unsavory chapter in the history of the segregated Navy" and set aside the convictions if they seemed unwarranted. When action was not forthcoming, Miller sponsored a bill (which ultimately passed) to amend the 1992 Department of Defense Authorization Act to require that the navy review the Port Chicago verdicts and direct the secretary of the navy to "correct the individual military records as necessary to rectify an error or injustice."[25]

On 6 January 1994, the navy acknowledged that the Port Chicago seamen had been victims of racial prejudice in having been put in segregated units and assigned to manual labor. They had also had a "reasonable basis of fear" in their refusal to load live ammunition after the explosion, but no evidence of racial prejudice could be found in the court-martial proceeding. Accordingly, the navy rejected the request that it overturn the World War II courts-martial of the 258 Port Chicago black sailors.[26] "The Secretary of the Navy concluded that neither racial prejudice nor other improper factors tainted the original investigations and trials," the navy said.[27] "Sailors are required to obey the orders of their superiors, even if those orders subject them to life-threatening danger," William J. Perry, the secretary of defense at the time, said in a 1994 letter to Congress.

Former Seaman Small, not surprisingly, disagreed with these conclusions. "I think that the trial and convictions were unfair and illegal," said Small, who had served sixteen months in a military prison, in a 1990 interview. "Our manual said mutiny is an attempt to usurp authority and take command. We did not in any way try to take command. If we had been given proper training and safety conditions, we would have gone back to work."[28]

Another perspective was offered by former chief petty officer Gordon Koller, who along with other sailors continued to load ships after the blast. He believed it was they, not those convicted of mutiny, who should be receiving special attention. "They didn't need to shoot the captain or something to meet the definition of mutiny," said Koller. "The loading of ammunition and bombs was an important part of that war. We were doing a necessary job, which was sending ammo to be used to defeat our enemy."[29]

In May 1999, almost fifty-five years after the explosion, lawyers for former Seaman Freddie Meeks, then seventy-nine, petitioned the White House for a presidential pardon, arguing that Mr. Meeks and the others had had no intent to mutiny but were simply afraid that they too would become victims of a careless navy that used only black sailors to load munitions but gave them no training. Meeks' lawyers said that they had been able to find only one other survivor among the court-martialed sailors—Jack P. Crittenden of Montgomery, Alabama, who wanted no part of a pardon application. "I know they did me wrong," he said. "I don't need them to say that." The power to pardon is given to the president by the Constitution. No hearing is permitted, and there is no appeal. The president has the power to grant a pardon, deny it, or close a case without action.[30]

On 23 December 1999, President Bill Clinton granted Meeks a presidential pardon, one of thirty-seven Christmastime pardons that year. "The lesson is we stood up for our rights," Meeks said. "We stood up to get the same rights the whites had. We all should have been treated the same, because we were all in the Navy and were going to fight for the same purpose. But they thought we should do the dirty work." But he added, "It makes a big difference to know the president gave us a pardon. We've been waiting a long time."[31]

Interest in the other Port Chicago 50 and efforts to exonerate them continue at this writing. Meanwhile, an often-overlooked event gives clarity to the significance of the "mutiny" and subsequent court-martial. Shortly after the explosion and refusal to load by the sailors, Forrestal, in a memo to Roosevelt, endorsed the idea of assigning more whites to munitions-handling duties to "avoid any semblance of discrimination against negroes." By the end of the year, both blacks and whites were loading munitions at Port Chicago, albeit in segregated shifts.

12

Freeman Field Mutiny
DISOBEDIENCE OF ORDERS—1945

> *This is the benefit of being a nation of laws. They sometimes catch up to you if you're right.*—Former lieutenant Roger "Bill" Terry in 1995, upon learning his forty-year-old court-martial conviction had been overturned

The phrases "civil rights protests" and "civil disobedience" might bring to mind the image of Rosa Parks being arrested in 1955 after refusing to move to the back of the bus in Montgomery, Alabama, and the resulting bus boycott led by Martin Luther King, Jr., or black students sitting down at a Woolworth's lunch counter in Greensboro, North Carolina. But a decade earlier, in April 1945, on an U.S. Army Air Forces (USAAF) base outside Seymour, Indiana, 162 black officers stood up against military authority, defied orders, and were arrested to protest discriminatory practices, clearly in violation of Army Regulations, at a segregated officer's club.

Unlike the conflicts at Fort Lawton or Port Chicago, where racial discrimination was an issue among larger questions like the treatment of prisoners, due process and fair trials, and safe working conditions, the confrontations at Freeman Field centered exclusively on the issues of segregation, racial discrimination, and equality under the law. The men involved were all black aviators, officers of the famed "Tuskegee Airmen." The "Tuskegee Airmen," as they are known, were African American fliers who trained to fly at Alabama's Tuskegee Institute, a sixty-year-old institution where both Booker T. Washington and George Washington Carver had taught.

The military was officially segregated in the late 1930s, but as war loomed on the horizon in Europe and the Pacific, American military authorities began to consider the idea of black military pilots. The idea was argued against in some quarters because of segregation, as well as the fact that these pilots would be officers. In May 1939, with the assistance of Sen. Harry S. Truman of Missouri, legislation was passed allowing the admittance of blacks into Civilian Pilot Training, a program under the Civil Aeronautics Authority to provide a pool of pilots in case of war. Six black colleges were allowed to enroll in the program.[1]

The year 1940 was an election year, and President Franklin Roosevelt was pulled between two constituencies: the large black vote and a threatened march on Washington, D.C., on one hand, and the southern Democratic opposition in Congress on the other. In December 1940, the Army Air Corps, at the direction of President Roosevelt, submitted a plan to the War Department to create an all-black fighter squadron on an "experimental basis," and on 16 January 1941, the 99th Pursuit (Fighter) Squadron was formed at Tuskegee Army Air Field.[2]

From the start, there was resistance to the idea of black pilots. "A secret 1924 War College Report concluded: 'Blacks [are] unfit for leadership roles and incapable of aviation.' One senior Army commander had no hesitation in saying outright what the War College Report was claiming in private. 'The Negro type has not the proper reflexes to make a first-class fighter pilot,' he proclaimed."[3]

The 99th Pursuit Squadron would consist of between thirty-three and thirty-five pilots supported by three hundred ground personnel. It would be led by white officers until African American officers could be trained to take over command of the squadron. Tuskegee Army Airfield went operational on 19 July 1941, with Class 42-C its first class, thirteen cadets.

It was a rigorous course of instruction, and the dropout rate was 50–60 percent, approximately the same as for white cadets. Tuskegee Institute provided fifteen weeks of preflight training, including ground school and classes in navigation, meteorology, mathematics, engineering, and principles of flight. This phase was followed by secondary training at Tuskegee Army Air Field. Their first commanding officer, Col. Frederick von Kimble, enforced strict segregation of base facilities and personnel.[4] Over ten thousand black men and women served at Tuskegee in support missions, such as crew chiefs, flight chiefs, armorers, dispatchers, parachute riggers and repairmen, clerks, cooks, welders, machinists, painters, and electricians.

On 7 March 1942, five of the original thirteen cadets—Capt. Benjamin O. Davis Jr., and four lieutenants, George S. Roberts, Charles Debow, Mac Ross, and Lemuel R. Curtis—completed their training. In all, sixty-five classes would graduate, filling three more fighter squadrons—the 100th, 301st, and 302nd Fighter Squadrons. On 24 August 1942, Davis took command of the 99th, and on 1 March 1943, he was promoted from captain to lieutenant colonel. On 2 April 1943, four hundred pilots and crewman of the 99th departed for North Africa on board the SS *Mariposa*.

Stationed in French Morocco, then Tunisia, the 99th flew missions over Sicily and Italy, transitioning from the Curtis P-40 Warhawk to the P-47 Thunderbolt. In October 1943, Davis returned to the United States to assume command of the newly activated 332nd Fighter Group, composed of the 100th, 301st, and 302nd Fighter Squadrons, then returned to Europe and added the 99th, forming the only four-squadron fighter group. The group transitioned to P-51 Mustangs in the summer of 1944 and spent the remainder of the war escorting bombers over Germany. In two hundred missions the 332nd never lost a single bomber, an achievement unmatched by any other fighter group.[5]

To the Germans, they became known as *Der Schwartze Vogelmenchen* (black birdmen), but to Allied bomber crews they were the "red-tailed angels" (the tails of all aircraft of the fighter group being painted bright red). Their statistics were impressive. Four hundred fifty pilots flew over 1,500 missions and destroyed 111 enemy aircraft in the air, another 150 aircraft on the ground, fifty-seven railroad locomotives, and a destroyer escort.[6]

With the success of the 99th Fighter Squadron itself, black leaders, newspapers, unions, and civic organizations had begun calling for the creation of a black bombardment group to achieve "full participation" in army aviation. There was as yet no opportunity for blacks to be trained or serve as multiengine pilots, navigators, bombardiers, radiomen, or gunners in the segregated Army Air Forces. As a result of political pressure on, and subsequently from, the Roosevelt administration, the War Department reluctantly agreed on 1 June 1943 to form an all-black bomber group, designated the 477th Bombardment Group (Medium).

There was an extended startup period, as there was no pool of experienced crews from which to draw. There being no blacks with bomber experience, all commanders and instructors were initially white, and the unit existed for a while only on paper as volunteers were sought from among black fighter pilots to be trained in multiengine aircraft. Candidates for other positions began the selection process and preliminary flight training. The 477th was activated at Selfridge Army Air Field, outside Detroit, Michigan, as part of the First Air Force (FAF) on 15 January 1944. It consisted of the 616th, 617th, 618th, and 619th Bomber Squadrons. Its authorized strength was sixty B-25J Mitchell twin-engine medium bombers and 1,200 officers and men.[7]

The commanding general of the Army Air Forces, Gen. Henry "Hap"

Arnold, had resisted its formation and tried to kill the project, believing that black officers would create an "impossible social problem" when placed in command of white enlisted personnel[8]; support was lacking generally at the higher levels of command. It is possible, therefore, to question the USAAF's commitment to the success of the 477th, especially in view of the men chosen to command it, men who seemed willing to sacrifice training and combat readiness in order to maintain racial segregation. The man assigned to command the 477th was Col. Robert R. Selway of Wyoming, a 1924 graduate of West Point and former commanding officer of the 332nd Fighter Group; his position on integration was made clear by his statement, "There will be no assimilation except over my dead body."[9]

The commander of the FAF, Maj. Gen. Frank O'Driscoll "Monk" Hunter, shared similar views. Shortly after their arrival at Selfridge Field, he assembled all the black officers together in the base theater and gave the following welcoming speech:

> The War Department is not ready to recognize blacks on the level of social equal to white men. This is not the time for blacks to fight for equal rights or personal advantages. They should prove themselves in combat first. Anyone who protests will be classed as an agitator[,] sought out[,] and dealt with accordingly. This is my base, and as long as I am in command, there will be no social mixing of the white and colored officers. The single officers' club on base will be used solely by white officers. You colored officers will have to wait until an Officers' Club is built for your use. Are there any questions? If there are, I will deal with them personally.[10]

The base commander at Selfridge Field, Col. William Boyd, enthusiastically carried out General Hunter's orders regarding the mixing of races in social settings. He closed the officers' club to black officers, an action contrary to Army Regulations and one that eventually earned Boyd an official reprimand, stating in part that "denying to colored officers the right to use the officers' club [was] in violation of Army Regulations and explicit War Department instructions."[11]

Meanwhile, manning continued to be a problem for the 477th. Since the USAAF was segregated, the training of black bombardiers, navigators, and crewmen required either the construction of new training facilities or the use of existing schools on a segregated basis. Air Force commanders chose the latter, and training continued throughout 1944 to bring the group numbers up to those required for combat readiness.

On 5 May 1944, possibly out of concern over racial issues in nearby Detroit that had resulted in race riots the previous summer, the 477th was moved to Godman Field, Kentucky, one of numerous relocations the group endured. The official reason given was "better atmospheric conditions for flying," but that is unlikely.[12] There was four times more hangar space at Selfridge than at Godman and longer, better-maintained runways. Selfridge had seven times the acreage and five times the gasoline-storage capacity of Godman, and the weather was better. Godman had insufficient hangar space to house the 477th's aircraft and little available apron space; its runways were not designed to accommodate heavy aircraft. Nor was there an air-to-ground gunnery range. Even worse, it was located in the South, where the local population openly practiced racial discrimination, refusing to serve black airmen or their families. Hunter believed that the move would isolate the men from "outside agitators."[13]

When the 477th moved to Godman Field there were only 175 of the authorized 290 officers in place, but the group grew as blacks completed their training. In October 1944 there were still only twenty-three of the authorized 128 navigators and eighty-eight pilots assigned, and the squadrons were restricted to routine proficiency training flights. However, between mid–October and mid–January 1945, eighty-four bombardiers and sixty pilots arrived, and the group finally began combat crew training.[14]

Godman's only officers' club was open to black officers, but most white officers used the officers' club at the main base, Fort Knox, on "guest" memberships thereby creating de facto segregation. Morale was further diminished by the fact that combat veterans of the 332nd were not being advanced into command positions in the 477th. With the group reaching its full combat strength, the decision was made to move the group to Freeman Army Air Field, outside Seymour, Indiana. Located halfway between Indianapolis, Indiana, and Louisville, Kentucky, Freeman was fully suited for B-25 operations, with four 5,580-foot runways, each 150 feet wide and sufficient hangar and apron space.

Built on land occupied by twenty-seven farms in nine months (May 1942–February 1943), Freeman Army Air Field had been designated an advanced training base for multiengine pilots. Freeman Field had been named in honor of Capt. Richard S. Freeman, a 1930 West Point graduate and pioneer of the Army Mail Service who was killed in the 1941 crash of his B-17 in Nevada while testing the top-secret Norden bombsight.[15] At its peak, over five thousand troops were stationed there including Women's Army Corps and Women's Airforce Service Pilots ferry pilots and the first army helicopter training facility. Future astronaut Gus Grissom would train as a cadet at Freeman in February 1944. And on 1 March 1945, the first black officers of the 477th began the move to Freeman by train.

Once again, as at Selfridge Field, a major concern for the group's commanders seems to have been the accommodations at the base officers' club.

Since there was no adjacent officers' club like at Fort Knox, and being aware from prior events at Selfridge that segregation by race was contrary to Army Regulations, Hunter and Selway attempted to segregate the races through a legal fiction. Before the move, Colonel Selway advised the black officers that at Freeman Field there would be two officers' clubs—one for supervisors and trainers and one for trainees. This was not, he said, an exclusion based on race, despite the fact that all the supervisors and trainers were white and all the "trainees" black, including the unit's medical officer and chaplain. Selway would defend himself in a subsequent inspector general investigation by stating that it was "standard operating procedure in the Army Air Forces to separate instructors and trainees in officers' clubs," although he was unable to cite any other base where that policy had been in effect.[16]

The base officers' club, designated Club 2, was reserved for permanent party, permanent party supervisors, and instructors while the base noncommissioned officers' club, redesignated Club 1, was reserved for the Overseas Training Unit (OTU) and Combat Crew Training Squadron (CCTS). Little better than a shack, Club 1 was referred to as "Uncle Tom's Cabin" by the officers of the 477th, and it wasn't used. Disturbed by what they perceived as racism, the officers spoke among themselves regarding the best way to resist this illegal segregation. Of course, their actions had to be carefully "unplanned," because to concert any action together could constitute a conspiracy, prosecutable under the sixty-sixth Article of War.

On 10 March 1945, two groups of black officers, fourteen in all, entered Club 2 and ordered drinks and cigarettes. They were refused service. They left without incident, but the event did not go unnoticed by Selway.

Although Army Regulation 210–10, paragraph 19, prohibited the use of any public building on a military installation "for the accommodation of any self-constituted special or exclusive group," thereby requiring officers' clubs be open to all officers, the regulation's intent was to prevent visiting officers from being discriminated against, and it had been written when there were few black officers—the advent of large numbers of black officers had been unforeseen. The regulation was routinely ignored by base commanders, and officers' clubs routinely excluded black officers. Nonetheless, the 477th officers interpreted the regulation to prohibit exclusion based on race and were willing to risk arrest to challenge Selway's actions.[17]

On 1 April, Selway issued an unsigned order designating Club 2 as reserved for supervisory and instructor personnel and restricting "trainees" to Club 1. Uncertain about the legality of the order, he conferred by telephone with General Hunter, who assured him that the order was legal, since it didn't mention color, creed, or race. He stated, "I'd be delighted for them to commit enough actions so I can court-martial some of them."[18]

On 3 April, Lt. William "Wild Bill" Ellis, who had been identified by Selway as an "agitator," was kicked out of Freeman and returned to Godman, where he informed the last remaining officers of the 477th still there about conditions at Freeman. In a meeting the evening he arrived, they agreed to resist this de facto segregation and fight, by nonviolent protest, for equal and fair treatment. Since they had not been at Freeman when the order was issued, senior officers would presume that they were unaware of it.

They were guided by 2nd Lt. Coleman A. Young, who took a leadership role during the meeting. Lieutenant Young, who had been a labor organizer for the United Auto Workers in Detroit before the war, had enlisted and graduated from the Infantry Officers School at Fort Benning before volunteering for assignment as a bombardier. He had been instrumental in leading a protest earlier at the Midland Army Air Field in Texas that resulted in the desegregation of the base officers' club. Young was a natural leader and would later be elected as the mayor of Detroit (1973–94). Others in the group included Lt. William Coleman, Jr., later secretary of transportation (1975–77), and Lt. Daniel "Chappie" James, who would become the first black four-star general.[19]

The officers' plan was to check in at Freeman and then, in small groups of no more than five, proceed to Club 2 at close enough intervals to be supportive but not so close as to suggest a mass demonstration. It was anticipated that their actions would be opposed and that countermeasures would follow, including the high probability of arrest. If arrested, they resolved, they would leave quietly and not physically resist, but comport themselves "by the book."

The remaining officers at Godman arrived at Freeman by train at about 4:45 p.m. and went to check in. At 7:00 p.m., Maj. Joseph A. Murphy, commanding officer of C Squadron, 118th USAAF Base Unit, received a telephone call, which he believed to be from a black officer, warning that the arriving officers from Godman planned some sort of demonstration to enter Club 2. Murphy called Selway, who in turn phoned the post provost marshal, Maj. G. F. Baumgardner, and ordered him to place the assistant provost marshal at the door of Club 2 to enforce the order of 1 April 1945. He also telephoned Maj. Andrew M. White, the officer in charge of Club 2, and ordered him to lock all doors but the front.

The first three officers to arrive—2nd Lt. Robert Payton, 2nd Lt. Clifford Garrett, and Flight Officer (F/O) (i.e., a cadet who had passed air qualification training, an approximate warrant-officer equivalent) Marcus Clarkson—were met by White and refused entrance. When Payton asked to know the reason why, White responded, "I might as well be frank about it. I have orders not to admit any colored personnel in the club." The three left without being arrested but rejoined a larger group headed for the club.[20]

By the time the larger group arrived, the officer of the day, 1st Lt. J. D. Rogers, stood in the doorway, in full uniform and wearing an "OOD" brassard and holstered .45. The first officer to attempt entry was Second Lieutenant Marsden A. Thompson who was told by Rogers, "This club isn't for you fellows." When Thompson asked, "Why isn't it for us fellows?," Rogers had him step outside, then answered, "It is a base Officers' Club and is for the use of base officers only." Second Lt. Shirley Clinton then spoke up: "I'm a base officer. Why am I not allowed go in the club?" Rogers answered, "I can't answer that." At this point, Thompson turned and entered the club, and Rogers tried to physically restrain him, pushing him to the side. Thompson said, "Get your hands off me, lieutenant," or words to that effect. Something similar occurred with Clinton as the others entered and spread out throughout the club. Thompson went to use the phone. Some ordered beer, others played pinball.[21]

Lieutenant Young would later testify that he ordered a beer and the bartender explained he had instructions not to serve nonmembers. When Young asked him how he knew that Young was not a member, the bartender replied, "No colored men belong to the club." Major White appeared, called the men together at the entrance of the bar, and told them, "If you men refuse to leave, I will have to place you under arrest." Thompson responded, "Sir we are not refusing to leave, but would like to know why we must leave." White responded only, "I have orders." When they still didn't leave, White took their names and placed them under arrest in quarters, after which they all peacefully left the club and returned to their quarters. Nineteen officers were arrested in this way.

Shortly thereafter, another group, of fourteen officers, entered the club, were confronted, refused to leave, were placed under arrest, and peacefully returned to quarters. Three more officers—2nd Lt. James V. Kennedy, 2nd Lt. Roger C. Terry, and F/O Oliver Goodall—tried to enter. Rogers physically restrained Terry, later claiming that Terry shoved him aside to enter the club. Like the others, they were placed under arrest in quarters. By this time, Major Baumgardner had arrived, denying entrance to, but not arresting, an additional three officers. White then closed down the club for the night. In total, thirty-six black officers had been arrested.

The next day, 6 April, between 3:15 and 3:45 p.m., another twenty-five black officers in three groups, entered, were refused service, and were arrested, bringing the total arrested to sixty-one, and again causing Club 2 to be closed. That same day, members of the 477th sent a communication to the inspector general in Washington with the subject, "Discrimination Based on Color against Army Officers in Violation of Army Regulations and War Department Policies." It alleged that the orders given were illegal, contrary to Army Regulations, and could not be reconciled "with the worldwide struggle for freedom for which we asked and are willing to lay down our lives."[22]

Present on base on 5 April was Lowell Trice, a reporter from the *Indianapolis Recorder*, a black newspaper, and head of the Indianapolis NAACP. He spoke with many of the officers and was instrumental in getting the story out. Soon telephones were ringing between Freeman Field, First Air Force headquarters, and Washington, D.C. As Selway considered under which articles to court-martial the officers, Col. Torgils G. Wold and Maj. Harry V. Osborne from the Judge Advocate's Office, First Air Force, arrived on base to investigate matters. Although they believed the officers technically guilty, they advised releasing all of them except the three charged with "jostling" Lieutenant Rogers—Lieutenants Thompson, Clinton, and Terry. After consulting with General Hunter, Selway released fifty-eight men from arrest on 8 April.

Wold and Osborne also recommended issuing a more detailed order, in the form of a base regulation, covering the assignment and use of facilities, written so as to eliminate any chance of it being misunderstood. It would reserve some buildings for the use of trainees, others exclusively for members of the permanent party.

The resulting Base Regulation 85-2, "Assignment of Housing Messing and Recreational Facilities for Officers, Flight Officers and Warrant Officers," dated 9 April 1945, explicitly listed buildings to be used by trainees/permanent party and clearly detailed which personnel were trainees (477th, OTU and CCTS, and C and E Squadrons), not "designated as assigned for Command and Supervisory or Instructor purposes." After consultation with Hunter, it was agreed that each officer would be given a copy, for which he would sign. Additionally, each officer would be required to sign underneath the statement, "I certify that I that I have read and fully understand the above order." The weakness of the order would be demonstrated later, when the First Air Force inspector general reported that "there is a group of approximately twenty Negro officers at Freeman Field who are not assigned to the 477th Bombardment Group or the 'Combat Crews Training Squadron' and hence are not trainees per se."[23]

On 12 April, all the officers in the group, black and white, were ordered to report to the base theater at 3:00 p.m. To the front and left of the stage was a long table, behind which sat Lt. Col. John B. Pattison, the deputy commander of the 477th, and two other officers. Each officer was given a copy of the order, while Pattison read it aloud, explaining each paragraph in detail. Pattison then directed each officer to sign the acknowledgement. All 292 white officers signed. No black officer signed, because signing the order would indicate an intention to obey it. Pattison asked if there were questions, but none were volunteered, and an uncomfortable silence ensued. The meeting was abruptly dismissed. Efforts by Capt. Anthony A. Chiappe, commander of E Squadron, to persuade black officers to sign the endorsement yielded only three signatures.

Upon consultation with the FAF inspector general and the Judge Advocate's Office, Selway convened a special board consisting of two black officers (Lt. Frank Rogers and Capt. James Pughsley), two white officers (Lieutenant Colonel Pattison and Lt. Col. Thomas Keach), and the base legal officer, Capt. Theodore B. Ochs, as well as each officer's (white) squadron commander.

On 11 April, each officer was called individually to the base legal office; there they were interviewed, then quarantined to prevent knowledge spreading of who had signed and who hadn't, making mass resistance more difficult. At the interviews the officers were again directed to read the order, offered an opportunity to ask questions, then given a direct order to sign a certification that they had read Regulation 85–2. They had the option to (a), sign the certification; (b), amend and sign their own certification; or (c), face arrest under the sixty-fourth Article of War–disobeying a direct order of a superior in time of war, an offense punishable by death. Still, 101 of 422 black officers refused to sign and were placed under arrest.[24]

Many felt like F/O Hiram Little, of central Georgia and a graduate of Morehouse College. He had enlisted in the Army Air Corps to avoid the draft. He thought the instructor/trainee distinction "a lie everybody saw through." He had no desire to socialize with white officers, had never set foot in the clubs, but perceived the regulation as an effort to keep blacks in their place. "Before I went in there, I knew I wasn't going to sign that order. I didn't talk to anyone about it, but I knew I wasn't going to sign that order that I was going to willingly lie down to segregation, because I'd been doing that all my life, and I was sick of it."[25]

As preparations were made to court-martial the three officers who had "jostled" Lieutenant Rogers, the 101 nonsigners were transported by

In April 1945, on an Army Air Forces base outside of Seymour, Indiana, 162 black officers stood up against military authority, defied orders and were arrested while protesting discriminatory practices at a segregated officer's club clearly in violation of Army regulations. In this photograph is Capt. "Chappie" James, his back to the camera, checking his officers off—Capt. James gave a direct order for his officers to affix their signatures to Base Regulation 85.2, which 82 officers refused to sign. James, a fighter pilot, flew 101 combat missions in Korea (P-51 Mustangs/F-80 aircraft) and 78 combat missions in North Vietnam (in F-4C Phantom fighter jets). "Chappie" James became the first black American to reach the rank of four-star general, in 1975 (Library of Congress).

six C-47 aircraft back to Godman Field under heavy guard as Selway considered the option of charging them with mutiny. At Godman, they would be closer to a larger force of white military police than at Freeman Field. The officers were met at Godman by seventy-five MPs armed with submachine guns in a large, flood-lit area, no doubt to the amusement of German and Italian POWs walking by free and unescorted. Placed in barracks under guard, they had nothing to do as the machine of military justice slowly completed the administrative steps necessary to court-martial over one hundred officers. Terry, Thompson, and Clinton were also later moved to Godman, but they were kept separated from the others.

On 16 April, a team of officers and legal clerks from FAF and Freeman Field arrived at Godman. The next day, the officers were ordered released from confinement pending the outcome of an IG investigation. On the 18th a team of officers led by Lt. Col. Smith W. Brookhart Jr., arrived from the Inspector General's Office, Headquarters USAAF, in Washington, D.C., to begin a high-level investigation into events surrounding the arrests of 162 officers of the Army Air Forces. The team began by interviewing the officers who had been arrested.

Selway had ordered the officers not to attempt to communicate with the outside world, but as F/O Warren recalled, "We were able to get messages out to the press and other important persons." On 28 April 1945, the *Pittsburgh Courier* featured a photograph on its front page of the officers lined up under guard along the tarmac, under the headline "These 477th Bombardment Officers Bombard Jim Crow." Selway had forbidden photographs; it had been taken covertly by a black enlisted man with a camera inside a shoebox. Shortly after publication, the War Department was flooded with over fifty thousand telegrams protesting the arrest. Congress and the White House also received thousands of letters. Walter White, secretary of the NAACP, sent a telegram to President Roosevelt, and Congressman Adam Clayton Powell telegraphed Secretary of War Henry Stimson urging "an immediate investigation of the entire situation at Freeman and Godman Field." The telegram included the names of dozens of senators and representatives.[26]

Meanwhile, guided by Lt. William Coleman, who had been a Philadelphia law student, each officer drafted a letter requesting representation by individual counsel. The case had by now generated a great deal of interest in the press and put the USAAF high command on the spot. Transcripts of telephone conversations between Hunter, Col. Malcolm Stewart (the FAF chief of training), Lt. Gen Barney Giles (the deputy commander of the USAAF), and Gen. William Welsh (Chief of Staff for Training, USAAF), declassified in 1973, suggest that some commanders hoped to keep the 477th out of combat. In one conversation between Stewart and Welsh anticipating their eventual failure in the face of Army Regulation 210–10, Welsh stated, "It's a foregone conclusion that an adverse decision will be given [by the IG investigation]. If we can stave it off in some way for a period of time, and present a staff study based on the requirements for additional training, maybe we can eliminate the program gradually and accomplish our end."[27]

The service's high command claimed that the issue was obedience to orders, not race. A written opinion by the Judge Advocate's Office endorsed by General Arnold stated, "A reasonable division of club facilities where circumstances make such division necessary or desirable from a practical, disciplinary or morale standpoint" might be allowable under 210–10.[28] On 16 April, Selway gave a fourteen-page deposition to Lieutenant Brookhart of the Inspector General's Office: "No orders based on any race segregation have been issued by me assigning the use of facilities within this program."

The separations of facilities was "based on our customs of the Air Force and in accord with the policy of the commanding general of the First Air Force, that personnel undergoing OTU ... use different facilities."

But the black officers had supporters too, like Eleanor Roosevelt and Truman Gibson, an African American attorney who served as an adviser to Presidents Roosevelt and Truman. Gibson called the charges "a fabric of subterfuge and deception." The matter was referred to a Committee on Special Troop Policies, under Secretary of War John McCloy. The committee eventually recommended the dropping of charges against all the arrested officers except the three charged with "jostling," finding that Selway and Hunter's actions were not in conformity with Army Regulations. As Col. R. E. Kunkel, chief of the Military Justice Division of the USAAF, wrote, "Long range public interest does not appear to warrant a trial by court-martial on charges growing out of the incident described." On 20 April, General Giles, with the concurrence of Gen. George Marshall, ordered the 101 men released. The following day Hunter did so—and placed in each officer's 201 (Personnel) file an administrative reprimand that accused him of "displaying a stubborn and uncooperative attitude toward the reasonable efforts of constituted authority to disseminate ... information concerning necessary and proper measures in the administration of the Officers' Clubs of that station." This letter would negatively impact the later careers of officers who chose to remain in the service.[29]

Training had come to a halt for the 477th on 12 April. On 26 April, the remainder of the 477th, still at Freeman Field, was ordered back to Godman Field, with its inadequate facilities. That sent a signal to the black officers that the USAAF had given up on sending the 477th into combat. James Warren would remain convinced that "Hunter was far more dedicated to seeing his racist policies enforced than he was in combat-readiness."[30]

On 20 June, as the three officers continued to be held in confinement, and preparations continued for their general courts-martial, plans were made to replace all the white officers in the 477th Bombardment Group and the base squadron at Godman with black officers. On 21 June 1945, Col. B. O. Davis Jr. relieved Colonel Selway and assumed command of the 477th; a formal change-of-command ceremony was held on 1 July. Davis was also named base commander, which made Godman Field the first base commanded by a black officer in U.S. military history. One of Davis' first acts as commander, carried out the day after taking over in order to get his command combat-ready, was to deactivate two squadrons (616th and 619th) and add the 99th Fighter Group, creating the 477th Composite Group. Training was scheduled to be completed and the group combat-ready by 31 August.

On 26 June, the War Department ordered the trials to be "expedited" and decided to try Terry, a member of the 477th, separately from Thompson and Clinton, who could claim the status of base officers and thus not "trainees."[31] General Hunter convened the first court-martial, of Thompson and Clinton, on 2 July 1945. He named ten officers to the panel (Col. B. O. Davis Jr., Capt. Charles R. Stanton, Capt. George L. Knox, Capt. James T. Wiley, Capt. John H. Duren, Capt. Fitzroy Newsum, Capt. William T. Yates, Capt. Elmore M. Kennedy, and 1st Lt. James Y. Carter, with 1st Lt. William R. Ming as the law member). What was unprecedented was that all of these officers were black. Davis was removed by a peremptory challenge from the defense (saving him from the awkwardness of having to preside), and Captain Stanton was removed by a peremptory challenge from the prosecution, making Captain Knox, as senior captain, president of the court.

Capt. James W. Redden and 1st Lt. Charles R. Hall were named trial judge advocates. The defense was represented by 1st Lt. William C. Coleman (later chief defense counsel of the NAACP) as military counsel and civilian attorney Theodore M. Berry (future mayor of Cincinnati, Ohio) as lead defense counsel. Berry was assisted by Harold Tyler, a Chicago lawyer.[32]

Thompson and Clinton were charged with violating three specifications of the sixty-fourth and one specification of the sixty-eighth Articles of War (willful disobedience of a direct order, to include offering violence, and involvement in a disorder). The prosecution took the position that orders from superior officers must be obeyed. The defense argued that obedience to orders was justified only if those orders were lawful and that the orders in question had not been lawful, because Army Regulation 210–10 prohibited racial discrimination.

The prosecution called Lieutenant Rogers, who testified that while acting as assistant provost marshal he had given direct orders to the men not to enter the club and that he had had orders to keep trainees out. He also testified that Thompson had pushed him aside, as had Clinton, and entered the club. Major White, the club manager, testified that he had ordered the men to leave, that they had politely refused, and that he had ordered them under arrest, after which they had left quietly. Under cross-examination, he denied remarking that the club was closed to colored officers. Colonel Selway proved an extremely hostile and evasive witness, saluting the flag but refusing to render a salute to the court, a traditional military courtesy, until reminded to do so by the court.

The defense outlined a plan by the former commanding officer (Selway) to exclude black officers from certain facilities in violation of Army Regulations and War Department directives and held that his orders were illegal. The defense called several officers, including Lieutenants Payton, Young, Clifford Jarrett, and F/O Harold Storey, to testify to events. The accused, Lieutenants Clinton and Thompson, testified that they had been confined for eighty-nine days and hadn't met with counsel until 25 June. They also denied shoving Lieutenant Rogers or receiving orders not to enter the club. No closing arguments were made by either side. After a short deliberation, the court found that the "prosecution was unable to present sufficiently compelling evidence to convict" and issued verdicts of not guilty on all charges.[33]

The Terry court-martial began the next morning, 3 July, with the same court, prosecutors, and defense counsel in place. Terry pled not guilty to two specifications of the sixty-fourth Article of War, in that he had disobeyed the order of a superior officer and offered violence to a superior officer when given an order. The defense motion to dismiss Specification 1, based on the fact that the order was illegal under 210–10, was denied.[34]

The arguments were much the same as in Thompson and Clinton's court-martial, and Selway was again called to testify, this time objecting to defense counsel's questions as "irrelevant and immaterial" until cautioned by the law member that witnesses had no right to object to questions. Terry was acquitted on the charge of disobedience of orders but found guilty of offering violence to a superior officer (a charge punishable by death) and was fined fifty dollars a month for three months. Livid, Hunter endorsed the court's decision, "The sentence, although grossly inadequate, is approved."

Japan's surrender on 14 August 1945 meant that the 477th never got its chance to prove itself in combat. That was a victory for racist and segregationist elements in the USAAF, but the victory would be short-lived. In 1948, President Truman issued Executive Order 9981, officially desegregating the armed services.

On 2 August 1995, the army overturned the sole court-martial conviction and refunded Terry $150. On 12 August of that year, at the Tuskegee Airmen Annual National Convention in Atlanta, Assistant Secretary of the Air Force Rodney Coleman announced that the reprimands were being removed from their records, and Air Force chief of staff, Gen. Ronald

Fogelman, presented Terry with his cleared official records. In 1998, President Clinton signed a law directing the National Park Service to create a national historic site at Moton Field in Tuskegee, Alabama, to honor the first African American aviators.[35]

The significance of the Freeman Field mutiny is that it forced the War Department, for the first time, to declare racial segregation a discriminatory act by definition, thereby beginning the movement toward full integration.

13

The Court-Martial of Pvt. Eddie Slovik

Desertion—1945

> *The accused is a habitual criminal. He has never seen combat, has run away twice when he believed himself approaching it and avows his intent to run again.*—Lt. Col. Henry J. Sommer, 28th Division Judge Advocate in review of court-martial findings

From 1 January 1942 through 30 June 1948, only 2,864 of the estimated forty thousand–plus soldiers who deserted or "bugged out" were tried by general court-martial for desertion. Of these, forty-nine received the death sentence, but only one soldier was executed, in the first and only execution since the Civil War, despite a desertion rate of 6.3 percent of the American armed forces in 1944 alone.[1]

By July 1944, pressure was mounting worldwide on the Axis powers. On the Eastern Front, the Soviets had recaptured Minsk and Brest-Litovsk. In the Pacific, the Japanese had been defeated on Saipan, and U.S. forces had landed on Guam. In Europe, the Allies began the breakout from Normandy, Operation Cobra, even as German generals mounted an unsuccessful assassination attempt on Adolf Hitler. Despite all this, World War II was far from over.

The Atlantic Ocean was host to countless convoys sailing east, carrying U.S. troops en route to France to replace the mounting numbers of casualties, replacements vital to the effort for the final push east into Germany.

On 7 August 1944, the RMS *Aquitania* departed the Port of New York carrying soldiers from nearby Camp Kilmer to Plymouth, England. Camp Kilmer—named for Joyce Kilmer, the poet-soldier of the World War I—was the largest staging area for troops bound overseas, eventually processing over 2.5 million soldiers during the war. On that same day in France, the

U.S. Army's 28th Division, especially its 109th Infantry Regiment, was locked in some of the fiercest fighting of the war, at Gathemo, taking heavy casualties.[2]

The *Aquitania,* a Cunard ocean liner, was already a seasoned veteran of the war. Requisitioned as a troop carrier in November 1939, she'd been refitted and armed with six-inch guns and had carried American and Canadian troops in both the Pacific and Atlantic theaters. Among the seven thousand young soldiers aboard on this voyage was a twenty-four-year-old private from Michigan.

Private Slovik was no one's idea of a soldier. Small and thin at five feet, six inches and 138 pounds, he was nervous and physically weak, had poor vision, and was afraid of loud noises and firearms. Initially, the army agreed, classifying him 4-F because of a criminal record, but manpower demands for replacements for the anticipated invasion of Europe resulted in his reclassification on 7 November 1943. On 22 December a notice arrived from Local Board 3, Wayne County, Michigan, with the official "Order to Report for Induction," directing him to report for examination and induction on 3 January 1944.

Edward Donald "Eddie" Slovik was born in Detroit, Michigan, on 18 February 1920, one of five children of Josef Slowikowski, a punch-press operator who would lose his job during the Depression. With his father often drunk and abusive, Slovik spent much of his time on the streets. He grew up in trouble with the law and was first arrested in 1932, at age twelve, for breaking into and entering a brass foundry with several pals. He was placed on probation.

He quit Pulaski School in the eighth grade, when he was fifteen. After several arrests for other break-ins and petty crimes, he was working at Cunningham Drug Store when he confessed to having pocketed change and taken candy, gum, and cigarettes without paying over a six-month period. For this embezzlement of $59.60, Slovik was sentenced on 1 October 1937 to a term of six months to ten years at the Michigan State Reformatory at Ionia.

Harry Dimmick, a supervisor at Ionia, would later describe him as a good guy, gentle, easygoing, not a troublemaker. He was granted a good-behavior parole on 9 September 1938. For four months he worked and reported to his parole officer, but on 19 January he got drunk on beer with two friends, and they stole a car to go joyriding. They lost control on icy roads and crashed the vehicle. Slovik ran away from the scene but turned himself in to the police later that night. The next day in Recorder's Court, Slovik pled guilty to unlawfully driving a vehicle and violation of parole;

he was sentenced to two and a half to seven and a half years. Initially sent to Jackson State Prison, he was transferred back to Ionia in March 1939, where he remained until he was again paroled in April 1942.

U.S. involvement in the war was in its beginning stages when Slovik was released, and there were many opportunities, especially for someone exempt from the draft. From a disaster area during the Depression, Detroit had transformed itself into the "Arsenal of Democracy," and for the first time in his life Slovik experienced prosperity. He got a good-paying job as a plumber's helper at the Montella Plumbing Company in Dearborn. Slovik's sister, Margaret, who worked as Mr. Montella's housekeeper, had persuaded him to write the parole board offering Slovik the job. Upon starting his new job, Slovik first met Antoinette Wisniewski, a twenty-seven-year-old Polish girl who worked as the company bookkeeper.

By most accounts, Slovik began to pull his life together after prison. He dated, then married Antoinette on 7 November 1942, and the two rented a two-room basement apartment. A year later, on his first anniversary, with his wife pregnant, Slovik received a notice of his reclassification to 1-A. By 24 January 1944 he was on his way to Fort Sheridan, Illinois, thereafter to Camp Wolters, near Mineral Wells, Texas, for basic infantry training. Slovik lamented, "Eighteen months ago, when I got out of jail and had nothing, they [the army] wanted no part of me. Now, when I'm a married man with a pregnant wife, and all this, now they want me to go in the Army."[3]

He arrived at Camp Wolters on 31 January 1944—a year to the day before his execution—and was assigned to Company D, 59th Infantry Training Battalion, where he spent seventeen weeks learning the infantryman's trade. With a pregnant wife suffering from epilepsy and unable to work, he spent most of his free time petitioning higher authority for a hardship discharge and writing letters to his wife. In the 372 days of his service, Slovik wrote Antoinette 376 letters. He even considered violating his parole, preferring jail to the army.

Despite his physical weakness and frailty, Slovik graduated from basic training on 27 May, but he was kept at Camp Wolters for eight weeks, while the army considered his case. He pulled guard duty and cut grass while his buddies were sent overseas without him. Like his supervisors at Ionia, his officers and the men he trained with considered Slovik a "good guy."

After a furlough from 12 to 23 July, Slovik was ordered to proceed to Fort Meade, Maryland, and report to the Ground Forces Replacement Depot. After a week on maneuvers, he was sent to Camp Kilmer, New Jersey, on 1 August 1944. From there he was shipped to Edinburgh, Scotland,

and on arrival there, on 14 August, Slovik was sent by train to Plymouth, England. There he underwent two days of training in hedgerow fighting, then was shipped out to Omaha Beach, landing in France on 20 August. Slovik and other replacement soldiers remained in the vicinity of Omaha Beach, living in tents, while they were processed through the 3rd Replacement Depot at Montain. He was assigned as a replacement rifleman to Company G, 109th Infantry Regiment, 28th Infantry Division.

The 28th Infantry Division, part of the Pennsylvania National Guard, had a long history that extended to before the American Revolution, when Benjamin Franklin had organized three companies to serve in the Continental Army. The oldest division-sized unit in the armed forces, its men had served as part of George Washington's bodyguard, stopped Pickett's charge at Gettysburg, stemmed the German offensive in July 1918 at St. Agnan, and served in every war in which Americans had been engaged. Nicknamed the Keystone Division, it was given the additional nickname of the "Bloody Bucket Division" by German troops. This was the unit Slovik was slated to join, but as a new replacement he knew nothing of its history.[4]

On 25 August, Slovik and a group of replacements departed for the front on foot. After walking about five miles, they were issued ammunition and put on trucks. Among the twelve GIs who mounted Slovik's truck with him was Pvt. John F. Tankey, a fellow Polish-American from Detroit who'd become his buddy at Camp Kilmer. They journeyed toward Elbeuf to join Company G.

Tankey later recalled,

> As we got close to Elbeuf, we heard a lot of firing. We got off the trucks at the edge of the city, and as it got dark, we began making our way into town, looking for our outfit. A lot of shells were going over, and we were fired on two or three times. Close to midnight, we got to this open lot and [a] noncom said to dig in. I dug a good deep hole and so did Eddie.... There was a lot of heavy shelling. Then after awhile, it let up [and] got quiet. Then some tanks came in. We thought it was the krauts, but Eddie yelled "Thank God, it's Canadians." We didn't know where our outfit was, and the Canadians said we might as well join up with them, so we did.[5]

The others had already moved out during the night, with only Tankey and Slovik remaining behind. Tankey posted a letter to the regiment advising it that they were lost. "We never thought of it as deserting," Tankey recalled.

The Canadian unit Tankey and Slovik joined was the 13th Provost Corps, eighteen military policemen led by a sergeant-major, which followed the combat troops posting notices in various towns instructing the residents on the provisions of martial law. For the next forty-five days the two remained with the Canadians, cooking, doing odd jobs, and making themselves useful. During this period, Slovik never spoke to Tankey of deserting.

On 5 October the two reported to 28th Division headquarters at Elsenborn, Belgium, and were sent to the 109th Regiment's headquarters at Rocherath on 7 October. They went on to Company G the following day. That afternoon, at the company headquarters in a farmhouse outside Rocherath, Slovik and Tankey reported to Capt. Ralph O. Grotte. Slovik told the captain he was "too nervous and scared" to serve in a rifle company and requested assignment to the rear area. Grotte answered there was nothing he could do and assigned Slovik to the 4th Platoon. Forbidden to leave the company area, he was turned over to his new platoon leader, who escorted him to the platoon and introduced him to his squad leader.

Sometime later that day, Slovik returned to Grotte and inquired whether he could be charged for being absent without leave. Grotte said he'd look into it, placed Slovik under arrest, and ordered him to return to his platoon. An hour later Slovik was back, asking Grotte, "If I leave now, will it be desertion?" Grotte replied in the affirmative.

As Tankey remembers it, "After awhile, Eddie came out without his gun, walking fast. The officer came out and said to me, 'Soldier, you better stop your friend. He is getting himself into serious trouble.'" Tankey chased after Slovik, caught him, and said, "Eddie, you don't want to do this," but Slovik replied, "I know what I'm doing" and walked away. Tankey never saw him again and assumed he'd been reassigned to another unit.[6]

After spending the night away from his unit, Slovik showed up in Rocherath at 8:30 the next morning, entered the mess hall of the Military Government Detachment, 112th Infantry, and handed the cook, Pvt. William C. Schmidt, a green piece of paper. The paper, a U.S. Army Post Exchange flower-order form, contained Slovik's hand-printed confession:

> I, Pvt. Eddie D. Slovik, 36896415, confess to the desertion of the United States Army. At the time of my desertion, we were at Albuff, in France. I came to Albuff as a replacement. They were shilling the town and we were told to dig in for the night. The following morning, they were shilling us again. I was so scared nerves and trembling that at the time the other replacements moved out I couldn't move. I stayed their in my fox hole till it was quite and I was able to move. I then walked in town. Not seeing any of our troops so I stayed overnight in a French hospital. The next morning I turned myself over to the Canadian Provost Corp. After being with them six weeks I was turned over to the Ameri-

can MP. They turned me lose. I told my commanding officer my story. I said that if I had to go out their again Id run away. He said their was nothing he could do for me so I ran away again AND ILL RUN AWAY AGAIN IF I HAVE TO GO OUT THEIR.
Signed Pvt. Eddie D. Slovik
A.S.N. 36896415.[7]

Private Schmidt notified his officer, Lt. Thomas F. Griffin, who telephoned the 109th Infantry to send someone to pick Slovik up. An MP arrived, transported him to regimental headquarters, and handed the confession to an MP officer, 1st Lt. Wayne L. Hurd, who in turn gave it to Lt. Col. Ross C. Henbest, the 2nd Battalion commander.

Henbest, a combat veteran who had received the Bronze Star leading his troops across France, read the confession, then looked at Slovik. He explained that the written confession could be extremely damaging and suggested that Slovik take it back and destroy it. When Slovik refused, Henbest wrote a statement on the back that read, "I have been told that this statement can be held against me and that I made it of my own free will and that I do not have to make it." Henbest then had Slovik sign it, after which he and Hurd witnessed his signature. Slovik was then confined in the regimental stockade.[8]

To Slovik, it must have appeared that he had accomplished what he wanted. He wouldn't be going to the front, and jail didn't scare him. He would do some time until the end of the war, then return home to his Antoinette. But on 19 October Captain Grotte preferred charges against Slovik for violation of the fifty-eighth Article of War, desertion to avoid hazardous duty. Five days later, on 24 October, the army began an investigation into the charges.

On 23 October Slovik wrote what would be his last letter to his wife, lamenting his fate. "I'm in a little trouble.... I'm only worried about what they are going to do to me.... Everything happens to me. I've never had a streak of luck in my life. The only luck I had in my life was when I married you. I knew it wouldn't last because I was too happy. I knew they would not let me be happy."[9]

Still, on 26 October, when Lt. Col. Henry P. Sommer, a former district attorney and the 28th Division judge advocate general (JAG) officer, had Slovik brought to his office and offered him a deal, Slovik stubbornly refused. As Sommer recalled,

> It was late afternoon, and two MPs had him in the back seat of a jeep, handcuffed. I walked out on the road to talk to him.... Slovik, I said, you're in trouble and I'd like to help you get out of it. We don't like to court-martial anyone;

we do that only as a final resort. If you will go back to your outfit and soldier, I'll ask the general if he will suspend action on your court-martial. I'll even try to get you a transfer to another regiment where nobody will know what you have done.[10]

Slovik insisted he wouldn't go back up in the line but offered to serve behind the lines as a quartermaster or something else. Sommer explained that they couldn't transfer everyone who didn't want to serve in a rifle company, reminded him that desertion in wartime was a capital offense, again suggested he was making a mistake, and recommended that he return to his unit and at least try to serve as a rifleman. Slovik said, "No, I've made up my mind. I'll take my court-martial." Sommer ordered Slovik returned to the stockade. Years later, Sommer recalled, "I wasn't particularly surprised at his attitude. I had heard too many like him say 'I'll take my court-martial.'" That same day, Slovik was transferred to the division stockade at Rott, Germany, to await his court-martial.[11]

In the period preceding his trial, Slovik met with his defense counsel, Capt. Edward P. Woods, and Capt. Arthur L. Burks, the division psychiatrist. Woods, although not an attorney, had served as defense counsel in previous courts-martial. "There wasn't much I could do," he later remembered, "Slovik's mind was made up." Burks interviewed Slovik on 26 October and concluded that he "showed no evidence of mental disease," was "sane and responsible for his actions," and that there was "no evidence that he was other than sane and responsible for his actions at the time of the alleged offenses." On 29 October Slovik's case was referred for trial.[12]

Slovik's timing wasn't good. The U.S. Army had been involved since 19 September in the battle for the Hürtgen Forest, a fifty-mile-square area east of the German–Belgian border. The goal was to keep German forces in the area pinned down to prevent their reinforcing their forces farther north. The battle would eventually cost the U.S. First Army over 33,000 casualties.[13]

The 28th Infantry Division relieved the battered 9th Infantry Division on 16 October 1944 and went into the battle on 2 November, just as its staff was preparing Slovik's court-martial. The 109th Infantry Regiment was impeded by an unexpected minefield after advancing three hundred yards, where it was pinned down by mortar and artillery fire and harassed by local counterattacks. After two days and a gain of only one mile of terrain, the 109th dug in and endured heavy casualties. The 28th Division took the heaviest casualties in what was one of the deadliest engagements of World War II.[14]

This must have played on the minds of the members of the court as they convened Slovik's court-martial on 11 November 1944, Armistice Day. The trial was held on the second floor of a public building in Roetgen, Germany, approximately twenty miles south of Aachen, in the Hürtgen Forest. The court was composed of nine officers, none of whom had seen combat. Most courts-martial in combat areas were made up of staff officers, since combat officers weren't pulled from the line for such duty.[15]

Col. Guy M. Williams, the division finance officer, was the presiding officer of the panel, joined by Maj. Orland F. Leighty, a dentist; Maj. Robert D. Montondo, an officer from special services; Maj. Herbert D. White, the division assistant adjutant general; Capt. Stanley H. French, of the Medical Corps; Capt. Benedict B. Kimmelman, dentist; Capt. Arthur V. Patterson, on the staff of the inspector general; Capt. Clarence W. Welch, headquarters staff; and 1st Lt. Bernard Altman, the only attorney, who served as the law officer. The trial counsel (prosecutor) was Capt. John L. Green, and defense counsel was Captain Wood.

The prosecution opened its case at 10 a.m. and called five witnesses. Private Thompson, one of the twelve men with Slovik at Elbeuf, testified first, followed by Lieutenant Hurd, the MP officer who had accepted Slovik's confession, which was entered into evidence without objection. Next was Captain Grotte, Slovik's company commander, who testified regarding the conversation of 8 October and the subsequent desertion, followed by Private Schmidt, the cook, and Lieutenant Griffen, the mess officer. There was little or no cross-examination of the witnesses, nor did any members of the court have any questions. The prosecution rested at 10:50 a.m., after which followed a ten-minute recess. When proceedings resumed at 11:00, Captain Wood rose and stated that Slovik understood his rights but had elected to remain silent. He requested that the law officer advise the accused of his rights, including his right to testify in his own behalf, call witnesses, make an unsworn statement, either written or oral, or remain silent with no inference of guilt attached.

After briefly conferring with his counsel, Slovik chose to remain silent, and the defense rested. The prosecution made a closing argument, and, the defense making no closing argument, the panel retired to deliberate. Colonel Williams later recalled, "I remember I insisted on three ballots. As soon as the court was closed, we took a ballot. Unanimous; death. I then suggested that we smoke a cigarette and take a second ballot. Same result! Then, just as we were about to open the court again, I said 'Well gentlemen, this is serious. We've got to live with this for the rest of our lives. Let's take a third ballot.'" The third ballot was unanimous too—death.[16] Under Article 43, a sentence of death required "the concurrence of all the members of the court-martial." There was a brief disagreement as to whether the sentence of death should be carried out by hanging or firing squad; the consensus was for a firing squad, as the less dishonorable. (The other ninety-five soldiers executed during World War II, all for rape or murder, were put to death by hanging.)

Upon reopening, the court sentenced Slovik "to be dishonorably discharged from the service, to forfeit all pay and allowances due or to become due, and to be shot to death with musketry." The trial lasted less than two hours, from 10:00 a.m. until 11:40.

It is almost certain that Slovik was surprised by the sentence. While confined in the division stockade, he'd spoken with other deserters who'd been sentenced to twenty years. They expected to be released two or three years after the end of the war. Sgt. Edward Needles, a guard, recalled, "I remember the day Slovik returned after his court. He wasn't so happy.... Of course, it never occurred to him or any other prisoner, even after he got his sentence, that he'd actually be shot." And why should it have? Despite several wars and countless desertions, no service member had been executed for desertion since the end of the Civil War. Colonel Williams agreed: "I think that every member of the court thought that Slovik deserved to be shot, and we were convinced that for the good of the division, he ought to be shot. But in honesty, I don't think a single member of the court actually believed that Slovik would ever be shot.... I know I didn't believe it.... I knew what the practice had been.... I thought the sentence would be cut down, if not by General Cota, then by Theater Command."[17]

On 14 November Slovik was moved to the stockade in Paris to await execution of his sentence. Under the Articles of War, the appointing authority—in this case the division commander, Maj. Gen. Norman Daniel "Dutch" Cota, the 28th Division's commander—had either to approve or disapprove the sentence, rather than simply decline to intervene. General Cota deliberated between 11 and 27 November, then approved the sentence of death by musketry. In his order of 27 November there was no mention of a dishonorable discharge or forfeiture of pay. There is a question of whether this omission was intentional or not, and it remains a controversy to this day.

Cota stated to the author William Bradford Huie in 1953 that he'd always assumed the next of kin received the insurance and accumulated pay. As to the sentence of death, he felt it was his duty. "I thought it was my duty to this country to approve that sentence. If I hadn't approved it, if I'd let Slovik accomplish his purpose, then I don't know how I could have gone up to the line and looked a good soldier in the face."[18]

On 9 December Slovik wrote a letter to Gen. Dwight D. Eisenhower pleading for clemency, but there is no evidence that Eisenhower ever read it. On 16 December the Germans began their counteroffensive in the Ardennes, the Battle of the Bulge, and Eisenhower certainly had other, more pressing, concerns. Considering the large number of desertions occurring at this time, it is unlikely that Eisenhower was inclined toward clemency in any case. On 23 December, most likely on the advice of Brig. Gen. Ed C. Betts, the theater judge advocate, Eisenhower confirmed the sentence.

Article of War 50.5 required a month's delay in the execution of sentence while the Judge Advocate General's Office reviewed the trial record to ensure that it could legally support the sentence. The case was reviewed by Maj. Frederick Bertolet, the assistant staff JAG for the European Theater of Operations, and the branch office of the judge advocate general, but no recommendation for clemency was made. The elements of the crime had been proven and established beyond a reasonable doubt, the accused had received every legal protection and a fair trial, and due process had been followed. Having satisfied the last administrative requirement, Eisenhower ordered the sentence to be carried out on 31 January 1945.[19]

The 28th Division was given responsibility for carrying out the sentence of the court-martial, and the division provost marshal, Maj. William Fellman, was tasked with making arrangements for the execution itself. The assistant division engineer, Capt. Robert Hummel, was responsible for the construction of a back wall to absorb the expended rounds, a post to secure the prisoner, a collapse board, should the need arise to carry the prisoner to the execution site, and other physical accommodations.

The location for the execution was St. Maries aux Mines, a small mountain village bordered by woods in eastern France. A three-story chateau with a garden enclosed by a seven-foot high masonry wall on the edge of the village, 86 Rue de General Dourgeois, was chosen as the site, since it was on the outskirts of the town and afforded privacy. The standard operating procedures (SOP) governing such events detailed the presence of three doctors; Maj. Robert E. Rougelot, Capt. Marion B. Davis Jr., and Capt. Charles Galt were assigned the duty. Father Carl Patrick Cummings, the Catholic chaplain of the 109th, was present, as was the official recorder, Lieutenant Colonel Sommer. The SOP also required a representative of the corps or army to which the division belonged.

The firing squad, under the command of Lt. Zygmont Koziak, with Sgt. Albert H. Bruns under him, was made up of twelve riflemen representing all three battalions of the 109th and selected as the best marksmen in the regiment. Slovik departed the Paris stockade on the morning of 30 January in the custody of four MPs in a weapons carrier. Scheduled to arrive that evening, they were delayed by heavy snowstorms and didn't arrive until 7:30 a.m. on 31 January.

As Father Cummings took Slovik's confession and granted absolution, Lieutenant Koziak loaded eleven M-1 rifles with one live round of ammunition each and the twelfth with a blank round. This was done according to a tradition that doing this would allow each member the firing squad to doubt that he had personally killed the prisoner. But it was in reality a myth. While it might possibly have been true for muskets, any soldier who had ever fired an M-1 would immediately be able to distinguish the substantial recoil with a live round from that of a blank cartridge. Additionally, M-1 rifles eject the casings from expended live rounds, but not from blanks.

By all accounts, Slovik calmly endured his last hours with a courage that belied the charges of cowardice, and he asked the chaplain to inform the firing squad that he didn't hold it against them. He was described as "exceptionally calm and resigned."[20]

At 9:56 a.m. the order "Attention!" was given, and the execution procession began, led by Major Fellmen and Father Cummings walking side by side, directly in front of Slovik, who was followed by two MPs and the chaplain's assistant carrying the collapse board. The morning was cold, overcast, and gray as the execution party slogged through the deep snow into the silent courtyard, the only sound that of crunching snow.

The order for his execution was read, and a blanket-draped Slovik, dressed in a plain uniform without any insignia, declining to make any last statement, was bound to the post. Just before a black hood was placed over his head, Father Cummings told Slovik, "Eddie, when you get up there, say a little prayer for me." Slovik replied, "OK, Father, I'll pray you don't follow me too soon." These were his last words.

At 10:01 a.m. the firing squad filed into the courtyard and took up positions about twenty yards from the condemned. Present besides those involved in the execution were twenty-five officer and thirty-three enlisted witnesses, drawn from all units in the regiment. Included in the group was Lt. Col William H. Ellsworth, the 3rd Division provost marshal, who was in charge of a similar pending case in the 3rd Division.

At 10:04 a.m. Major Fellman gave the order: "Squad, ... ready ... aim ... fire!" After the volley of twelve rifles and eleven bullets, the only sound was Dr. Rougelot's footsteps as he moved forward to Slovik's slumped body. MP sergeant Frank McKendrick recalled, "Slovik was slumped forward, and he may have been unconscious, but he wasn't dead. Every man in the courtyard saw him struggle up at least twice."[21]

Incredibly, although all eleven rounds had struck Slovik in the neck, left shoulder, and chest, none of the wounds were fatal. As Maj. Fellman gave the order to reload, Father Cummings spun and snapped, "Give him a second volley if you like it so much!" Dr. Rougelot stated, "The second volley won't be necessary. Private Slovik is dead."[22]

General Cota would characterize the execution as "the roughest fifteen minutes of my life," while Father Cummings would call Slovik "the bravest man in the garden that morning." Even Pvt. Aaron Morrison, of Headquarters Company, 1st Battalion, 109th Infantry, one of the members of the firing squad, remarked, "Slovik had nerve. I can't understand why a man who had the guts to face a firing squad like that wouldn't stay in the line with the rest of us."[23]

At 10:30 a.m. a secret high-priority TWX (teletype message) was sent to Eisenhower's headquarters in Paris: "Private Eddie D. Slovik, 36896415, formerly Company G. 109th Infantry, was shot to death by a firing squad at 1005 hours, 31 January 1945 at St. Marie aux Mines, France." Slovik's body was interred in an unmarked grave, Row 3, Grave-65, alongside ninety-five other American soldiers executed for the crimes of rape or murder in Plot E of the Oise-Aisne Cemetery at Fère-en-Tardenois, France. Elsewhere in the same cemetery, in a more honored section, the poet Joyce Kilmer also rests.

There Slovik remained for forty-two years until a Polish-American army veteran, Bernard Calka, paid $3,500 to have his remains reinterred beside those of his deceased wife at the Woodmere Cemetery in Detroit on 11 July 1987. Almost characteristically, Slovik's remains were temporarily misplaced when his casket was shipped to San Francisco by mistake.[24]

The question remains: Why, of all the thousands of deserters during World War II, was Slovik the only one executed? His supporters claim that he never really deserted in the face of the enemy. He never saw the enemy! What he did was refuse to serve in the front lines. Lieutenant Colonel Sommer, the judge advocate, stated, "I never expected Slovik to be shot. Given the common practice up to that time, there was no reason for any of us to think that the Theater Commander would ever actually execute a deserter."

As Slovik was waiting to be marched into the courtyard, one of the MPs guarding him, Sergeant McKendrick, told him, "Try to take it easy, Eddie. Try to make it easy on yourself ... and on us." To which Slovik replied, "Don't worry about me. I'm OK. They're not shooting me for deserting the U.S. Army. Thousands of guys have done that. They're shooting me for the bread I stole when I was twelve years old."

There is some truth that Slovik's record, his "criminal" past, played a part in dissuading the review board from recommending clemency. Certainly a written confession and his refusal to put on a defense at his court-martial also played their parts. But the government's reasoning is perhaps most clearly defined in the "Review by Staff Judge Advocate," written by Major Bertolet, not recommending clemency:

> There can be no doubt that he [Slovik] deliberately sought the safety and comparative comfort of the guardhouse. To him, and to those soldiers who may follow his example, if he achieves his end, confinement is neither deterrent nor punishment. He has directly challenged the authority of the government and future discipline depends on a resolute reply to this challenge. If the death penalty is ever to be imposed for desertion, it should be imposed in this case, not as a punitive matter, nor as retribution, but to maintain that discipline upon which alone an army can succeed against the enemy.[25]

There was a universal assumption among Slovik, his fellow prisoners, his court-martial panel, the review board, and the common GI that the sentence would not be carried out. And it was that assumption that was so dangerous in the winter of 1944–45, as desertions mounted to record levels. Slovik gave Eisenhower the opportunity to end that assumption.

Did Slovik's execution have the desired effect? Consider the words of Private Morrison, who returned to his unit: "I think General Eisenhower's plan worked. It helped stiffen a few backbones. When the report of the execution was read to my company, the effect was good.... I'm just sorry the general didn't follow through and shoot the rest of the deserters."[26]

SIDEBAR

Toth v. Quarles 350 U.S. 11—1955

On 13 May 1953, Robert W. Toth was reporting to work at his job at the Jones and Laughlin Steel Company in Pittsburgh, Pennsylvania, when he was approached by two U.S. Air Force military police officers who, after confirming his identity, placed him under arrest for murder and conspiracy to commit murder. Two days later, Toth was flown to South Korea to stand trial by court-martial. Upon arrival, he was placed in confinement and provided two military lawyers. Most unusually, Toth was a civilian. His case would eventually rise to the chambers of the U.S. Supreme Court, and its verdict would significantly alter U.S. military law.

On 27 September 1952, the United States had been at war in Korea, and Sgt. Robert Toth had been assigned as sergeant of a guard assigned to protect an ammunition depot on an air base at Taegu, South Korea.[1] While on patrol with Airman Thomas Kinder, he came across a Korean civilian, Bang Soon Kil, who was drunk and in a restricted area. The two placed him under arrest and transported him back to headquarters. En route, Bang Soon made a grab for Toth's sidearm, and Toth pistol-whipped him.

Upon arriving at headquarters they met with their commanding officer, Lt. George Schreiber, who upon seeing Bang Soon bloody and beaten allegedly ordered Kinder to prop the man on sandbags and shoot him. Kinder did as he was ordered, but later, overcome by guilt, he told his mother, who reported the story to air force commanders. By the time military authorities became aware of the murder, Toth was out of the air force, having been honorably discharged on 8 December 1952.[2]

The 1950 Uniform Code of Military Justice (UCMJ), Article 3(a), provided that "anyone who leaves the service remains liable to prosecution if the alleged offense exceeds five years and the case cannot be tried in civilian courts." Toth was charged with the murder on 8 April 1953 and arrested on 13 May.

His sister, Audrey M. Toth, immediately filed for a writ of habeas corpus in the federal district court for the District of Columbia. The court granted the writ and released Toth, holding that the military had no power to apprehend (arrest) a civilian and hold him for trial. Toth was returned to the United States and released on bail.[3]

The government appealed the decision, and on 25 March 1954 the U.S. Court of Appeals reversed the lower court. In a unanimous decision, the three-judge appellate court ruled that the provision in the UCMJ giving the armed forces authority to try former service members on charges of serious crimes was constitutional. Toth was returned to air force custody but was freed under bond while the case was appealed to the Supreme Court. The case was argued before the court on 13 October 1955. The issue was whether the air force could seize an honorably discharged veteran and, without a civil hearing, try him for a crime that occurred while he was in the service.[4]

On 7 November 1955, the Supreme Court overturned the Court of Appeals. In a six-to-three decision written by Justice Hugo Black, the Court found that Article 3 (a) of the UCMJ was unconstitutional, that Toth's relationship with the military had ended by the time of his arrest, and that nothing in the U.S. Constitution gives the military jurisdiction over civilians.[5]

Stating that "there are dangers lurking in military trials which were sought to be avoided by the Bill of Rights and Article III of the Constitution," the Court suggested that the military lacked certain legal safeguards guaranteed to civilians, like indictment by grand jury and independent appellate judges. Further, to find for the government would have placed millions of American veterans within the reach of military courts.[6] The court suggested that to correct this gap in jurisdiction Congress enact legislation to create special federal courts to try civilians for crimes committed in the military, but it rejected as unconstitutional the idea of civilians being tried by military court-martial.

Schreiber and Kinder were both court-martialed. Schreiber was found guilty of ordering the murder and sentenced to life imprisonment, and Kinder was sentenced to life in prison for carrying out the murder. Air force secretary Harold E. Talbott reduced the sentences of both men. Schreiber's sentence was reduced to five years, of which he served twenty months before being dismissed from the service. Kinder, partly in recognition of his cooperation, had his sentence reduced to two years and a dishonorable discharge but was returned to active duty when his dishonorable discharge was suspended. Toth, who always maintained that he hadn't been present when the murder took place, was never tried on the murder charge.[7]

14

Sgt. Charles Robert Jenkins
Desertion and Aiding the Enemy—1965

You are now under the control of the U.S. Army.—Lt. Col. Paul Nigara, provost marshal at Camp Zama, Japan, upon receiving Sgt. Charles Jenkins into custody

On 11 September 2004, an elderly man with thinning hair and dressed in a double-breasted gray suit stood before Lt. Col. Paul Nigara, the provost marshal of Camp Zama, Japan. Rendering a stiff salute, the man said, "Sir, I am Sgt. Charles Robert Jenkins and I am reporting for duty." Thus ended the arduous journey of an army man who had deserted to North Korea and had been held captive for forty years.[1]

Jenkins had been born in Rich Square, North Carolina (a town in Northhampton County—population 931 in the year 2000), on 18 February 1940. Rich Square was a poor town with one stoplight and one fire truck. During World War II, town folks would stand watches searching for German bombers. Jenkins's father worked at the town ice plant, having been deferred from service because, as the town doctor stated, "The town's gotta have ice." Eventually the job killed him. While fixing a large broken ammonia pipe he inhaled a copious amount of toxic fumes and died, leaving a wife and seven children. His mother later remarried, and another child was added to the family.[2]

Jenkins had little interest in schoolwork, knowing that he wouldn't graduate from high school, but he persevered as best he could. At the age of fifteen he joined the North Carolina National Guard. One had to be eighteen to join, but since he had no birth certificate and his mother could approve his entry by signing induction papers, he soon became a member of D Company of the 119th Infantry Regiment. He spent three years in the Guard, at the end of which he joined the army. After receiving training at Fort Jackson and Fort Dix, Jenkins was ordered to Fort Hood, where he became a member of the 1st Armored Division. He was assigned to tend shooting ranges, building frames and making paper targets. He made private first class, but further promotion looked doubtful. He heard rumors that his best chance for promotion was overseas duty, especially Korea. Making friends with several men in the reassignments unit, he eventually landed in South Korea as a member of the 7th Division at Camp Kaiser in September 1960. In February 1961 he made corporal, and the following June he was promoted to sergeant. After completing his Korean tour he was ordered to Germany, where he spent three enjoyable years. When his hitch was up he put in his three choices for reassignment and returned to South Korea, his top choice. He had so enjoyed his first tour there that he was delighted to return; good things seemed to happen to him in Korea. However dark days lay just ahead.

Arriving in South Korea in September 1964, Jenkins was assigned to C, or "Charlie," Company, 1st Battalion, 8th Cavalry Regiment, 1st Cavalry Division. Charlie Company was billeted in a few isolated Quonset huts east of the treaty village of Panmunjom, at the edge of the Demilitarized Zone (DMZ). The eighty-man company went on patrol day and night, manned night lookout posts watching the North Korean side of the DMZ, attended classes, and participated in drills. One week a month they would go on night ambush patrols hoping to catch any Koreans attempting to breach the thirty-eighth parallel. Eventually Jenkins was asked to lead what were called "hunter-killer team" patrols, which were both aggressive and dangerous. Often the patrols drew fire from the North Koreans, since they moved in closer than ordinary patrols and were more easily detected. Jenkins was not comfortable with such provocative missions. Though he was asked consistently to lead these patrols, he declined, since he personally believed that they were not in keeping with the unit's mission. However, in time he sensed that the requests would become an order that as a soldier he couldn't disobey.

Around Christmas he heard that his division was scheduled to

Sgt. Charles R. Jenkins (U.S. Army).

go to Vietnam. Already worried and depressed about the hunter-killer patrol situation, he began to fear that even though the United States was not as yet involved in Vietnam, it would be soon be an even more dangerous, potential war zone. Jenkins began to think of a way out. Feeling increasingly depressed, he began to drink heavily. Tired and scared, he just wanted out. Within a few weeks he had decided to desert—but which way? He heard stories that those who tried to desert southward were easily caught. The only other way was to go north. In a quandary as to what to do, he finally decided to go absent without official leave and cross the DMZ into North Korea, where he assumed that he would be handed over to the Russians, who through a prisoner exchange would in turn release him to American authorities.

He carried out his plan to desert on a dawn patrol on 4 January 1965, when he led his men toward the DMZ. Once in an ambush position in the freezing cold he told his men to stay in position as he went ahead to ensure that the road ahead was clear. Using a handheld compass he proceeded north. At dawn he saw a North Korean soldier at a guard post behind a ten-foot-high barbed-wire fence. The guard had his back to Jenkins, as wintery winds were blowing from the south. Turning and seeing the approaching American, he sounded an alarm, and a dozen North Korean soldiers came racing out of a small building. Opening a gate they quickly surrounded Jenkins with rifles in hand.

Jenkins was taken to a building adjacent to the guard post and put in a small room. They gave him food and rice-pot water. In the early afternoon he was blindfolded and with his hands tied behind his back was placed in a Russian jeep and driven to the North Korean base at Kaesong. After a brief interrogation he was taken to a senior officer's private home and further questioned about his unit, other U.S. outposts, and why he had decided to cross the DMZ. The interrogation lasted for around four hours, after which he was taken by train to Pyongyang, the capital of North Korea, and placed in a house in the center of the city. More interrogations followed, and after two weeks he was taken to a small brick house where he joined three other American deserters, Pfc. Larry Allen Abshier, Pvt. James Joseph Dresnok, and Spec. Jerry Wayne Parrish. All four were young, dumb soldiers from poor backgrounds. While their reasons for deserting varied, most were running away from trouble in the army, the law, or family problems. During the series of interrogations, Jenkins was careful not to reveal information that would prove harmful to American soldiers. The information he did provide proved of little value to North Korean intelligence.[3]

Like all other North Korean households they were assigned a Korean leader. The leader was responsible for keeping an eye on all members of the household, and in the case of the Americans, he was to ensure that they behaved properly and lived according to "correct ideology." However, within a short time they all realized that they were trapped in a country that really had no idea of what to do with them or any intention of allowing them back out. For decades they would endure the hardships of average Korean citizens.

Isolated, they lived in a house surrounded by a barbed-wire fence with a guard posted in a tower at the top of a telephone pole. There followed endless hours of forced study and memorization of the teachings of Kim Il-sung, the leader of North Korea. Additionally they underwent weekly self-criticism sessions. All studies and sessions were closely monitored by the leader. Initially the Americans were housemates struggling to just stay alive. At times they became enemies, then the best of friends. As the decades came and went they started families of their own and formed a strange, insular little community best described as a foreign society. During their early years of captivity they received monthly rations consisting of a tube of toothpaste, a bar of body soap, a bar of clothing soap, a pair of socks, two bottles of beer, and forty packs of cigarettes (stuffed with corn husks rather than tobacco). They were also were paid five *won* per month (about fifty U.S. cents) for purchasing small items at such stores as the Pyongyang Shop and the Foreigners' Store. Every Sunday they were taken into town for a bath and a haircut.

For much of the forty years Jenkins enjoyed freedom to roam about the capital city, though always under the watchful eye of the Korean masters. The Americans were fed and kept healthy looking, since their images were often used in propaganda pamphlets and films. But they still suffered from the cold, hunger, beatings, and mental torture. If one got out of line or broke a rule, the leader would order another American to punish his countryman, often brutally. One of the deserters actually enjoyed being the bully. On one occasion the group made their way to the Russian embassy, hoping somehow to seek asylum in Russia. They were turned away and told never to come back.

In January 1968 they learned of the capture of the USS *Pueblo*. None of the four ever laid eyes on the *Pueblo* captives. Throughout the year the capture of the American ship exhilarated the Korean public. The incident became a favorite part of North Korean history. In fact, a 1992 North Korean movie was made about the incident, and Jenkins played the captain of the aircraft carrier USS *Enterprise,* which had been as sent into the region at the height of the crisis. In Jenkins's later book *The Reluctant Com-*

munist: My Desertion, Court Martial and Forty-Year Imprisonment in North Korea, there is a photo of him in a U.S. naval officer's uniform (he is shown wearing an admiral's braid) standing on a mockup bridge of the ship.[4]

In 1971 Korean officials began alluding to the possibility that if the Americans kept up their studies they could someday become North Korean citizens. The Americans were told additionally that as a further reward they would each get separate houses with two "four-mat" rooms and a kitchen (like all other houses in the country, these featured unreliable electricity, no hot running water, coal-burning floor heating systems and no indoor bathroom), real jobs, and the opportunity to visit with women. None of the men were interested in citizenship, but what had been offered seemed worth working for.

Their study sessions were increased in late 1971 and early 1972, and the four were given a booklet of about a hundred pages of Korean propaganda readings to memorize word for word. The group bore down on their task. In March 1972 a North Korean official visited them, laid down fifty pages, each containing one question, face down on a table, and asked Jenkins and the others to pick three pages each. The four men gave their answers to each question, and on 30 June another official visited them and announced that they had all passed the tests. Thanks to the benevolence of Kim Il-sung, he said, they had been granted North Korean citizenship. Jenkins considered rejecting citizenship but thought better of it, since not complying might get him executed or banished to Kumok-ri, a remote area that was legendary as one giant prison.

To their surprise the men were split into pairs and were moved to their two new houses, with a North Korean female cook for each man. Dresnok was paired with Jenkins. From the beginning, neither got along with their cooks. One day the cooks simply disappeared.

In May 1973 the four were informed that they were going to teach English at a military school called Am Ran Gong on the eastern district of Pyongyang. Kim Il-sung had noticed a lack of foreign English teachers during a visit to the school, and soon afterward the four American dropouts were college instructors. Though by now all the Americans could speak Korean, they spoke in both languages in their classrooms as they stumbled through the prepared curriculum. However, most of the time they would discuss the daily news that the cadets heard over the school loudspeakers each morning. Even though it had been many years since the American instructors had known what was occurring in the world, they paid only enough attention to the newscasts to conduct their classes.

During the summer the instructors wore short-sleeved shirts. Jenkins' shirt revealed a tattoo on his left forearm, two crossed rifles above the words "U.S. Army." Before he knew what was happening he was escorted to the school's clinic where a doctor carved the tattoo from his arm without anesthesia. In August 1976, the school was closed without notice, soon after two American army officers were killed by North Korean border guards in the DMZ.[5] Over the next few years Jenkins was tasked with translating English-language radio broadcasts from Voice of America, Armed Forces Network, Japan, and NHK's English broadcasts into Korean for the military officials.

With the native cooks gone, the Koreans set about finding foreign wives for the Americans. Three were provided abducted Lebanese women, two of whom were found to be from elite society in Lebanon. The Koreans quickly sent them home. The third woman was found by an investigator who had been hired by her mother in Italy, and she was transported back home. When her mother found out that her daughter was pregnant, she sent her right back to Pyongyang, where she eventually became Parrish's wife. Dresnok ended up with a Romanian wife. Abshier married a Thai woman who had been abducted from Macau by two men who had forced her into a boat and taken her against her will to North Korea. During the years that Jenkins spent in North Korea, he was convinced that many women from various countries had been abducted, brought to North Korea, and held there against their will.

Jenkins, not interested in a foreign wife, was provided with a new North Korean cook who suffered from seizures and insane-seeming behavior. After a short period she was taken in 1980 to a textile mill where the Koreans stashed the insane, retarded, and the socially unfit. Jenkins was informed that another woman would be provided, an Asian woman who would not be a cook but whom he was to teach English. She was Japanese, though she was called by a Korean name, Min-Hae-gyum. On 30 June the woman (Japanese name, Hitomi Soga), was escorted by a Korean leader and a driver into Jenkins' house and given to Jenkins.

Hitomi Soga had been told that she was being taken to live with another Japanese woman. Jenkins and Hitomi knew that the Koreans wanted them to get married but didn't force the issue. Jenkins figured he would have to earn her trust and could understand if this twenty-one-year-old beauty didn't want to end up with a forty-year-old man. So he was very kind to her in all respects, did the cooking, and respected her privacy. Gradually they got to know each other, playing cards and smoking cigarettes (ninety in the first month). He told her one evening that he had heard that a number of Japanese had been kidnapped and brought to North Korea against their will. Without saying a word, she pointed to her nose to indicate: "I am one of them."[6]

After a few weeks together, Jenkins started to teach Hitomi English. Out of loneliness and a shared concern for each other's welfare, they grew closer. She was shy and in the beginning found it difficult to be with him because of what people would think—a young, beautiful Japanese woman in company with a Western man. She had never seen one except on television or in the movies. Though the Asian women they encountered were mystified by her attraction to Jenkins, she in time ignored their stares and would say later that she was more comfortable with him than with anyone else.

On 17 September 2002 Japanese Prime Minister Junichiro Koizumi visited Pyongyang to meet with Kim Jong-il, by this time the North Korean dictator, to improve relations between the two countries. During the discussions Kim surprisingly admitted that North Korea had abducted Japanese citizens during the past two decades and forced them to teach the Japanese language and customs at Korean spy schools; However, Kim admitted to having stolen only thirteen Japanese men and women, of whom five were still living. (The abductions had long been suspected by the Japanese, who still think that more than seventy were kidnapped and that other survivors remain in North Korea against their will.) Two Japanese male abductees, Kim said, were married to two Japanese women abductees, and the remaining woman abductee, Hitomi Soga, was married to an American army deserter, Charles Jenkins.

It was agreed upon by both governments that the five could return to Japan but would later return to North Korea. Once back in Japan, however, they decided on their own volition not to return to North Korea. While much was made in Japan about the abductions of Japanese citizens, the Western media concentrated their attention on Jenkins and his ultimate fate.

Once the abductions became known to the outside world, Hitomi told Jenkins her story of her abduction. On 12 August 1978, Hitomi had been kidnapped near her home in the town of Mano, on Sado Island, Japan. Her mother had been with her, and Hitomi doesn't know to this day what happened to her—no doubt somewhere in North Korea. Taken by boat, she was landed in Chongjin, North Korea. Hitomi was placed in Pyongyang with Megumi Yokota, another Japanese abductee, who had been kidnapped by North Koreans as she made her way home from badminton practice in Niigata in 1977. Megumi Yokota was just thirteen years old. Today she remains the strongest symbol for those in Japan who seek more information regarding Japanese citizens still missing. The North Koreans sent her remains back to Japan in 2004, reporting that she had killed herself in the early nineties. Rumors persist that she is still alive in North Korea.[7]

The two girls (Hitomi and Megumi) became close friends and lived together for eighteen months learning the Korean language. Later, like most Japanese abductees, Megumi was tasked with teaching the Japanese language to spies. Hitomi saw Megumi a few times in the years to follow, often at shops around Pyongyang. In time Megumi disappeared from their life.

Jenkins repeatedly asked Hitomi to marry him, but her answer was always no. In frustration, Jenkins told her that as it was she could suddenly be taken from him; if they were a married couple, she would be safe with him. After thinking their situation over, Hitomi said yes, and they were married on 8 August 1980. Their leader, chief of staff, the political commissioner, his aide, and their driver all attended their wedding dinner. Within a few months Hitomi became pregnant. Jenkins was cast in a movie called *Nameless Heroes*, in which he played a villainous American warmonger and capitalist based in South Korea. He was joined in the movie by the other three deserters, who played similar roles. They had all been given Korean names and were often recognized by average citizens, who treated them as celebrities. In May 1981, Hitomi gave birth prematurely, and the baby died. The parents were both devastated. However, they did go on to have two daughters, Mika and Brinda.

In 1981, Jenkins returned to his old school, which had been reopened as the Mi Dang-hi University. In addition to teaching English the four American deserters were tasked with creating a military dictionary. The typewriter used by the Americans was often proudly identified by the Koreans as a "*Pueblo*" prize. They also were involved in translating the sound tracks of Hollywood movies (Jenkins remembered translating *Kramer vs. Kramer* and *Mary Poppins*). The four instructors purposely became sloppy in their teaching until finally the Koreans discovered that their teaching was actually hurting the students' English capability and relieved them of their teaching assignments. The Koreans decided in November 1984 to move the four Americans and their families into one building, where the group lived for the next eighteen years. But in 2002 Jenkins' world turned upside down when Hitomi was identified as one of the living abductees.

When the list of the names of the suspected abductees was submitted by the Japanese to the North Koreans, Hitomi's name was not on the list. However, the names of the Japanese abductees on the Korean roster of the five still alive included her name. The Japanese government knew nothing about her, but by the following day media reporters had soon pieced together the details of her kidnapping and broadcast them worldwide. Jenkins was convinced that someone in the North Korean government had missed the fact that she was married to an American army deserter; had that been known the Koreans would have not revealed her name, because the situation was complicated.

The next day North Korean cadres picked up Jenkins and Hitomi to go shopping in Pyongyang. While en route they stopped at the Foreigners' Hospital, where Hitomi visited with the North Korean Red Cross. She was informed that because she had been a model citizen, she might be sent back to Japan. She was also told to inform her husband that she might be away for a short time. The family was next taken to a guest house in Pyongyang; later that same afternoon Hitomi met with a Japanese government delegation at the Koryo Hotel. There she was told the entire story of the meeting between the leaders of the two countries and about the abductions.

The Japanese took a blood sample from Hitomi to extract DNA and told her that the Japanese government was trying to finds ways for the abductees and their families to come to Japan. In early October Jenkins and his family were told that Hitomi would be allowed to go to Japan for a ten-day visit. Jenkins realized that once Hitomi left she wouldn't return and that he and his children would remain in North Korea.

On 15 October 2002, Hitomi and the other four abductees climbed on board a Japanese 767 for Japan, leaving Jenkins and his daughters behind. However, before she left several members of the Japanese delegation asked him if he might like to live in Japan. Jenkins was careful in his answers, since there were many North Korean officials within hearing distance and he didn't want to get her and his family in trouble.

After ten or more days, Jenkins was told by the Koreans that the Japanese would not allow the abductees to return to North Korea. Jenkins was devastated and started to drink heavily, finally suffering a nervous breakdown. At the end of a fifteen-day stay in the Foreigners' Hospital he gave an interview to Japanese newsmen blasting their government for not living up to the agreement to send Hitomi back to North Korea.

Hitomi's visit lengthened to eighteen months and then became open-ended. During this time she and Jenkins wrote each other at least thirty times, but only seven or eight letters got through. Hitomi was desperate to reunite her family. Through the Japanese government she appealed to the U.S. government to grant her husband a pardon so that her family could join her in Japan. By March 2003, with his daughters living in dorms at college and convinced that he had lost his wife forever, Jenkins became almost a hopeless drunk. By the spring of that year, Hitomi and the other abductees held a press conference to announce their decision not to return to North Korea. However, Hitomi held out the hope that diplomacy, patience, and pressure at the right time would bring them all back together. However, when the North Korean leader told Jenkins of the press conference, he lied about what was said, telling Jenkins that Hitomi and the others had condemned the Japanese government for not allowing them to return to North Korea.

By the spring of 2004 Jenkins ceased his drinking binge, due to a severe prostate problem. He was rushed to a hospital and underwent an operation. While recovering in the hospital he heard that Prime Minister Koizumi was returning to North Korea. Still enraged by what he thought Japan had done to prevent Hitomi's return, he demanded to see Koizumi. On 22 May Jenkins and his daughters went to a house outside Pyongyang, where Jenkins was subjected to a series of rants by North Korean officials. They told him what would happen if he and his daughters left the country with Koizumi—that he would spend the rest of his life in an American jail and that his daughters would live in shame and discrimination, be harassed and even harmed. Their message was clear—he and his daughters were not to leave the country with the Japanese prime minister.

Then Prime Minister Koizumi arrived with his entourage, and Jenkins and his daughters met him in a conference room. Koizumi quietly handed Jenkins a letter from his wife. Jenkins did not open her letter immediately. With only Koizumi and a few Japanese diplomats in the room, a heated debate began between Jenkins, his daughters, and the prime minister. At the time Jenkins and his children had been told by the Koreans that Hitomi was being held against her will. Koizumi told them that it was untrue, that she wanted to stay in Japan and, while his daughters argued with the prime minister, Jenkins read his wife's letter. In it she asked that he come to Japan with Koizumi. At the end of the conversation the prime minister stated that he would do his best to see that Jenkins received humane treatment by the U.S. military authorities and that Kim Jong-il had approved in writing his leaving the country with his daughters. Confused by the exchange and not knowing whom to believe, Jenkins turned down the offer to be taken from Korea that day.[8]

Realizing that their meeting had come to an end, Koizumi beckoned to one of his diplomats, who proposed that the family meet in a third country to discuss the matter. Jenkins liked the idea, and the meeting was set in Indonesia. While arrangements were being made, Jenkins still harbored the thought that Hitomi wanted to come back to Korea. Still, if his wife wanted the family to live in Japan, he would acquiesce to her wishes.

On 8 May 2004 a chartered All Nippon Airways plane flew Jenkins and his daughters to Jakarta, Indonesia. As they deplaned, Hitomi greeted him with great affection amid a bevy of reporters and photographers. During their bus ride to a hotel, Hitomi told him that she had never wanted to return to Korea and that all the talk about being held against her will by the Japanese was *Gae-so-ri* (that is, dog talk). At that moment Jenkins made the decision that he and his daughters would not return to North Korea. During their stay in Jakarta, Jenkins got a telephone call from his sister Pat in Weldon, North Carolina. Their fifteen minutes of conversation, often interrupted by crying, was filled with family updates. His two sisters had passed away, but his four others were doing well, as was his brother, Gene. His mother could be heard in the background asking when he was coming home. He told his sister that he loved her and would talk to her soon.

While in Jakarta, Jenkins began to have prostate problems again, and he was visited daily by Japanese doctors. Weeks went by while diplomacy progressed. Finally it was time to go, and before leaving the hotel, Hitomi and Jenkins met with the three-man North Korean delegation and told it of their decision. The exchange was filmed so the Koreans couldn't assert later that the family had been kidnapped by the Japanese. On 18 July the family flew to Tokyo. Jenkins was taken immediately to a hospital to repair the surgery performed in North Korea.

While in the hospital Jenkins began to think about his legal problems and the court-martial he would soon face. He had decided to plead guilty to all charges. However, he was soon contacted by letter by a member of the Trial Defense Services (TDS), who advised him that they would provide him with an independent lawyer. Jenkins had no idea that such an army branch existed. TDS does what a public defender's office does for civilians accused of crimes in the United States who cannot afford their own lawyers. A few days later, he got a call from Capt. James Culp, an army officer stationed in Seoul, South Korea, who worked for TDS and had been assigned his case. Culp was a skilled and experienced lawyer. He had a thorough understanding of the Korean culture and was familiar with what was happening in the isolated North. He convinced Jenkins that he worked for his client and not the army. Jenkins had been accused of desertion, aiding the enemy, soliciting others to desert, and encouraging disloyalty. He and Culp spent endless hours together as Jenkins related his experiences in North Korea. Finally, with his defense case in hand, Culp met with the army prosecutor, Capt. Seth Cohen, at Camp Zama and got a verbal commitment that he was willing to accept a pretrial agreement sentencing Jenkins to a maximum of thirty days in jail.[9]

After reporting to Camp Zama, Jenkins immediately noticed the many changes that had taken place during the years he had been away from the army. In the 1960s there had been very little familiarity between officers and enlisted men. All that had changed. In past days army men had been paid in cash; now money was deposited in bank accounts. After he reported to Camp Zama he opened his first bank account.

Even though he knew that Jenkins had done a traitorous act for which he was and would be forever remorseful, Culp didn't judge Jenkins, and they became good friends. Culp escorted the family around the base, and Brinda and Mika took an immediate liking to him. The family's first look at the Post Exchange was an exciting experience for them. In Pyongyang the foreigners' stores shelves were mostly empty, but here in Japan the shelves were abundantly supplied with food, clothing, electronics, and cosmetics. It wasn't long before both daughters were convinced that leaving the austere darkness of Korea had been the best decision their parents had ever made. They were overjoyed to find a wondrous new world.

On 3 November 2004 a nervous, uniformed Jenkins walked into an army courtroom. Even though he had received a pretrial agreement of thirty days' imprisonment, he wasn't sure what would happen in court. The process he faced was called a "providence inquiry," wherein a judge decides whether one is really guilty of the crimes one has confessed to. The procedure took a full day, and at the end of it the judge sentenced Jenkins to six months in jail but recommended to Jenkins' commanding general that he throw out the sentence entirely, for clemency's sake. Her recommendation was denied, and that meant that Jenkins would have to serve his pretrial agreement of thirty days' imprisonment. That night he was flown to the brig at Yokosuka Naval Base. He was released five days short of his sentenced time for good behavior.

Charles Robert Jenkins now lives with his family in Mano on Sado Island, Japan. At this writing he's seventy-five years old.[10]

15

2nd Lt. William Calley
WAR CRIMES, COVER-UP—1968–1971

> *Some people think that the Japanese committed atrocities, that the Germans committed atrocities, that the Russians committed atrocities, but that the Americans don't commit atrocities. Well, this just isn't so. American troops are as capable as any other of committing atrocities.*—Robert Rheault, 1970, former commander of U.S. Special Forces, Vietnam[1]

On the morning of March 16, 1968, there were 700 residents of the hamlet of My Lai 4 in the Quang Ngai Province of South Vietnam. Beginning at about 7:30 a.m., 105 soldiers of Charlie Company, 1st Battalion, 20th Infantry Regiment (C-1/20), 11th Light Infantry Brigade, moved unopposed into the hamlet. By noon of March 16, 1968, the hamlet of My Lai 4 no longer existed. Huts were burned, livestock killed, wells poisoned and approximately 500 villagers lay dead under smoke-filled skies. Several female villagers were raped before they were murdered. The victims were primarily women and children and the elderly, all unarmed civilians.

The Army investigated the incident, and four officers and nine enlisted men were charged with the massacre. Some individuals, no longer subject to military jurisdiction, escaped being charged, and twelve other officers were charged with covering up the massacre. Most of the cases were dismissed. Of the twenty-five charged, only five were tried. Four were acquitted. On September 4, 1969, the Army charged Second Lieutenant William Calley with responsibility for the massacre and ordered a court-martial. Lieutenant Calley would be the sole participant convicted of the murders.[2]

Considered a monster by some, a martyr by others and a victim by still others, William Law Calley, Jr., was born in Miami, Florida, on June 8, 1943, the son of a World War II navy veteran and prosperous machine salesman. Sociable as a child growing up in a home with three sisters, he was nicknamed "Rusty" by family and friends for his reddish-brown hair. A poor student, he had to repeat the seventh grade and was sent away to a military school, Georgia Military Academy, after being caught cheating.

After graduating Edison High School in Miami, Calley enrolled briefly in Palm Beach Junior College, but dropped out after a semester of poor grades. A variety of low-skill jobs followed, including bellhop, dishwasher and a job with the railroad. He was wandering the western part of the country when he got a notice from his draft board. He left California to return to Florida when his car broke down in Albuquerque, New Mexico. Out of money, he enlisted in the army on July 26, 1966.[3]

After basic training at Fort Benning, Georgia, Private Calley was transferred to Fort Lewis, Washington, to train as a clerk typist. While there, he applied for, and was accepted to, Officers Candidate School (OCS) in March 1967. With the conflict in Vietnam in high gear, there was a continuous need for infantry platoon leaders and the 16-week officer training course at Ft. Benning, Georgia, was accelerated to get officers into the field as rapidly as possible.

Upon graduating OCS Class #51 on September 7, 1967, Calley was commissioned a Second Lieutenant (#05347602) and was sent to Schofield Barracks, Hawaii, assigned as the 1st platoon leader, Charlie Company, First Battalion, Twentieth Infantry Regiment, 11th Infantry Brigade. The unit trained for several months in Hawaii before being sent to Vietnam as arriving on December 1, 1967.

With no activity, his unit was left guarding various positions. Calley concerned himself with shooing away Vietnamese children and keeping his men from utilizing the services of the local prostitutes. Calley was unable to command the respect of either his subordinates or his superiors who rated him "average" on his Officer Evaluation Reports (OER). His platoon was almost universally hostile, considering him either inept or incompetent or a glory hungry martinet. His immediate superior, Captain Ernest Medina, the company commander, contemptuously referred to Calley as "Lieutenant Shithead" or "Sweetheart" in front of his platoon.

The days of inactivity came to a close when Charlie Company was transferred to northern Quang Ngai in late January 1968, and assigned to Task Force Baker, a 500-man strike force, part of the 23rd Infantry "Americal" Division. Their mission was to "pacify" the Viet Cong.

In the spring of 1967, as large numbers of North Vietnamese crossed the demilitarized zone into South Vietnam, U.S. forces began operations in the Quang Ngai Province near the northeast coast of South Vietnam. The area was believed to be a stronghold for the Viet Cong, and Task Force

(TF) Oregon began search and destroy operations to eliminate Viet Cong influence in the region. On September 25, 1967, Task Force Oregon was re-designated the 23rd Infantry (Americal) Division. In December, Charlie Company was sent to assist units operating in Quang Ngai.

In order to fill a tactical void by the withdrawal of a Korean Marine Brigade, Task Force (TF) Barker was created. Named for its commander, Lieutenant Colonel Frank A. Barker, the battalion-sized unit was made up of one rifle company from each of the 11th Brigade's battalions: Alpha Company, 3rd Battalion, 1st Infantry (A-3/1) under the command of Captain William C. Riggs; Bravo Company, 4th Battalion, 3rd Infantry (B-4/3) under the command of Captain Earl Michles; and Charlie Company, 1st Battalion, 20th Infantry (C-1/20) under the command of Captain Ernest L. Medina.

U.S. forces were frustrated in attempting to fight an "invisible" enemy and on two previous operations, February 12 and 23, Charlie Company had taken casualties from snipers, bombs, and booby-traps. This, combined with the impossibility of distinguishing friend from foe, led many Americans to feel hostility and contempt toward all Vietnamese. In addition, morale was low because there was a lack of clear objectives and a poorly defined mission in the conflict. All of these elements would influence the actions of Charlie Company.

On March 14, a squad from C Company ran into a booby trap, killing Sgt. George Fox, a popular sergeant, blinding another and seriously injuring two others. The following day, March 15, the new 11th Brigade commander, Colonel Oran Henderson, on his first day in command visited TF Barker headquarters at LZ (Landing Zone) Dottie to brief Barker and his officers regarding an upcoming tactical operation, a three-day search and destroy mission in the area, codenamed Operation Muscatine.

Henderson informed them that the target was Son My Village, located within the Son Tinh District of the Quang Ngai Province. It was believed to be sheltering and assisting the 48th VC Local Force (LF) Battalion. Although no operational plan was committed to paper, the plan was to sweep through the area and aggressively press and eliminate the 48th LF. Henderson was followed by an intelligence briefing by Lieutenant Colonel Barker who advised his company commanders that "most in Son My were VC (Viet Cong) or VC sympathizers." The civilians would have gone to market by 7:00 a.m. Operation Muscatine was to commence at 7:25 a.m.[4]

The plan was for a preparatory artillery barrage after which Charlie Company would air-assault into the LZ west of My Lai 4 and sweep east, followed by Bravo Company which would either reinforce Charlie Company or combat assault south of My Lai 1, depending on circumstances. Alpha Company would assume blocking positions north of Son My. Both Bravo and Charlie Companies would then push the 48th LF south to the Tra Khuc River where they would be trapped, blocked by the South China Sea to the east.

That evening, after a memorial service for the previous day's casualty, Captain Medina briefed Charlie Company about the operation planned for the following morning in Tu Cung, a subhamlet of My Lai Village, noted on American military maps as My Lai 4. Some soldiers recalled Medina saying words to the effect that they were to kill everything in My Lai, though Medina would later deny saying that, stating he only "fired them up" for the mission, telling them they could expect "a hell of a good fight." Medina made it clear he wanted hooches burned, livestock slaughtered, wells collapsed, crops ruined, foodstuffs destroyed and tunnels filled in. Accounts differ on his instructions regarding the treatment of noncombatants. Medina later testified that he advised them to use common sense, and that if they were engaged by weapons they could shoot back, but as Sgt. Kenneth Hodges recalled, "It was clearly explained that there were to be no prisoners. The order that was given was to kill everyone in the village. Someone asked about women and children. And the order was 'everyone in the village'... it was quite clear no one in the village was to be spared."[5]

Calley later testified that he clearly recalled Medina saying that any civilians would be clear of the area, and that anyone remaining would be the enemy. Medina emphasized the need for speed and aggressive action as they moved through the hamlets destroying everyone and everything, allowing no one behind them, neutralizing the enemy as they advanced to Pinkville.[6]

The operation began on March 16 as planned, with Alpha Company in place by 7:25 a.m. as artillery and helicopter gunships prepped Charlie Company's LZ. Barker circled overhead in the command-and-control helicopter, even as Henderson and his command group arrived overhead in a second helicopter.

At 7:22 a.m., nine helicopters, carrying the 1st and 2nd platoons departed LZ Dottie as Delta Company, 6th and 11th Artillery Battalion fired into Son My to clear a landing zone. Calley was in one of the first helicopters that landed, as his 1st Platoon was tasked with securing the LZ. By 7:40 a.m., Calley's platoon was on the ground west of My Lai 4 and moved into defensive positions to secure the LZ. Second Lieutenant Stephan Brooks moved the 2nd Platoon to the northwest edge of the village for the same purpose, but there was no sign of any enemy resistance, and the rest of 2nd and 3rd Platoons were on the ground by 7:50 a.m. and moving east. Also on the ground was Sgt. Ron Haberle, an Army photographer.

Calley's platoon and the 2nd Platoon moved into My Lai 4 to eliminate any resistance while Second Lieutenant Jeffrey LaCrosse's 3rd Platoon was held in reserve, to follow behind and burn the village and kill the livestock.

The 1st Platoon entered My Lai at 8:00 a.m. with Sgt. David Mitchell's 1st squad in the lead, followed by Calley with 24 men, followed by Sgt. L. G. Bacon's squad with Sgt. Isaiah Cowan's squad bringing up the rear. As they moved through the southern portion of the sub-hamlet, soldiers were involved in the widespread killing of Vietnamese, almost exclusively old men, women, children, and infants. Most of the inhabitants not immediately killed were rounded up into two groups. One group of 70–80 civilians were taken to a large ditch east of My Lai 4 and later shot. A second group of 20–50 was taken south of the hamlet and shot along a trail. Smaller groups were killed within the village itself. Photos taken by army photographer Ronald Haeberle of bodies in a ravine would later be splashed across front pages the world over.

The 2nd Platoon moved through the northern half of My Lai 4 and the hamlet of Binh Tay north of My Lai 4, killing a minimum of 60–70 civilians, and engaging in numerous rapes. After securing the LZ, the 3rd Platoon followed, setting hooches ablaze, killing cows, water buffalos, pigs, chickens and ducks as well as rounding up and killing 7–12 women and children. An order to stop the killing was received by the 2nd Platoon at approximately 9:20 a.m., but by the time 1st Platoon acknowledged receipt of a second, repeated order to cease the killing, they had already completed the sweep.[7]

Lieutenant Jeffrey LaCross' 3rd Platoon continued the killing. As they moved through the village burning huts and killing livestock, they gathered a group of 10 women and children and a few soldiers began to sexually abuse a 15-year-old Vietnamese girl. Just after army photographer Sergeant Ron Haeberle took a picture of the group, they were shot down and killed. That photo became an icon of the My Lai massacre.

Nguyen Hieu, a 23-year-old male, testified to the Peers Commission, "When the Americans came to my house, my mother came out of the house and the Americans then raped my mother and they shot her ... they shot my sister and two children." Nyugen Bat, 43, testified, "When I saw the Americans, they were coming and shooting people in the hamlet....

The first group came to shoot, and the second group came to burn the house." Pham Thi Thuam, a 30-year-old widow, recalled that she and her six-year-old daughter were pushed into the ditch just before the firing started, but hid beneath dead bodies and pretended to be dead, surviving several volleys of shots. Her father, sister, younger brother and three nephews were not as fortunate. Phuong Thi Moi, 13, Do Thi Man, 12, and Do Thi Nguyen, 10, were all found naked inside their homes, their vaginas ripped open. Army investigators estimated a minimum of twenty Vietnamese females were raped and murdered, almost half under the age of 15.[8]

Since Charlie Company had met with no resistance, Bravo 4/3 made a combat assault into an LZ south of My Lai 1 between 8:15–8:30 am, and also met little opposition. 1st Platoon secured the bridge over the My Khe River, then advanced into My Khe 4, opening fire and killing several noncombatants, with some estimates as high as 90. The company reported 38 VC KIA, although the Peers Report concluded it was highly unlikely that any were Viet Cong. Charlie Company departed My Lai 4 in the early afternoon and moved northeast to link up with Bravo 4/3 and took up night defensive positions. The operation continued until March 19.

Some Americans freely participated in the killing, some participated when ordered, some refused to obey orders to kill civilians but didn't object or try to stop the killings, and some took steps to actively prevent the killings.

Private First Class Dennis Conti, a grenadier in 1st Platoon was guarding detained villagers with Private Paul Meadlo when at approximately 9:00 a.m., Calley approached them. Conti later testified:

> Lieutenant Calley came out and said take care of these people. So we said, okay, so we stood there and watched them. He went away, then he came back and said, "I thought I told you to take care of these people." We said, "We are." He said, "I mean, kill them." I was a little stunned and I didn't know what to do. He said, "Come around this side. We'll get on line and we'll fire into them." I said, "No, I've got a grenade launcher. I'll watch the tree line." I stood behind them and they stood side by side. So they—Calley and Meadlo—got on line and fired directly into the people.... Meadlo fired a little bit and broke down. He was crying. He said he couldn't do any more. He couldn't kill any more people. He couldn't fire into the people any more. He gave me his weapon.... I said I wouldn't. "If they're going to be killed, I'm not going to do it. Let Lieutenant Calley do it," I told him. So I gave Meadlo back his weapon. At that time there was only a few kids still alive. Lieutenant Calley killed them one-by-one. I saw a group of five women and six kids—eleven in all—going to a tree line. "Get 'em! Get 'em! Kill 'em!" Calley told me. I waited until they got to the line and fired off four or five grenades. I don't know what happened.[9]

Private First Class Vardado Simpson, a rifleman with the 2nd Squad, 3rd Platoon, tortured by guilt, readily confessed to CID investigators: "I killed about eight people that day. I shot a couple of old men who were running away. I also shot some women and children. I would shoot them as they ran out of huts or tried to hide.... I shot them, the lady and the little boy. He was about two years old." He also testified to what he witnessed: "I saw Wright, Hutto, Hudson, Rucker and Mower go into a hut and rape a 17 or 18-year-old girl. I watched from the door. When they got done, they all took their weapons ... and fired into the girl until she was dead."[10] (Diagnosed as paranoid in 1982, Simpson committed suicide in May 1997.)

Private First Class Herbert L. Carter, a "tunnel rat" in the 1st Squad, 1st Platoon, was a witness to the killings, but testified that he refused to take part:

> [We] had rounded up a group of people. Meadlo was guarding them.... Calley came up and said that he wanted them all killed. I was right there within a few feet when he said this. There were about 25 people in this group. Calley said, "When I walk away, I want them all killed." Meadlo and Widmer fired into this group.... Cowan was there and fired into the people too, but I don't think he wanted to do it. There were others ... but I don't remember who. Calley had two Vietnamese with him at this time and he killed them too.... I didn't want to get involved and I walked away ... they were mostly women and children.... They weren't trying to escape or attack or anything. It was murder![11]

He also explained how he was wounded.

> Widmer came up and asked to borrow my pistol. I gave it to him. I saw a little boy there—wounded, I believe in the arm—and Widmer walked up close to the kid and shot him ... [he] said something like, "Did you see me shoot that son-of-a-bitch?" Stanley said something about how it was wrong. My gun had jammed when Widmer shot the kid ... then Widmer gave me my pistol back and walked off. I was trying to clear it when it accidentally went off and I was shot in the left foot ... the only people I killed in Vietnam, I killed in combat. I didn't kill any women or kids or unarmed persons at all, ever.[12]

Carter was flown out by helicopter, the only casualty in Charlie Company that day. Some sources say the wound was intentionally self-inflicted.

Some soldiers actively tried to help the Vietnamese. Pham Ky, 34, his wife, his 72-year-old mother and his three young daughters were taken from a bunker by three soldiers, one of whom was black. They took them to the southeastern edge of the village and told them to flee across the fields. They arrived safely at the village of Son Hoi.[13]

A few soldiers made an effort to stop the killing. Warrant Officer (WO1) Hugh Thompson was assigned as a pilot with Company B, 123rd Aviation Battalion flying a OH-23 *Raven*, a reconnaissance helicopter. Aboard his aircraft was his crew chief, Specialist 4th Class Glenn Andreotta and a gunner, Specialist 4th Class Larry Coburn.

Hugh "Buck" Thompson was born in Atlanta, Georgia, on April 15, 1943, and raised by strict Baptist parents. He dropped out of Troy State University to volunteer for the U.S. Navy in 1961 and served with a Seabee construction unit from 1961 to 1964. He returned home to Georgia and ran a funeral home until enlisting in the U.S. Army in 1966, Wanting to fly, he was trained as a helicopter pilot at Ft. Wolters and Ft. Rucker and arrived in Vietnam in late December 1967 as part of the 161st Assault Helicopter Company, which was reorganized into the 123rd Aviation Battalion of the 23rd Americal Division in January 1968.

He recalled the mission to support Task Force Baker on the morning of March 16, 1968: "We were to provide reconnaissance for a ground operation that was going on in My Lai 4, better known as 'Pinkville.' ... I flew a scout helicopter covered by two gunships that flew cover. My job was to recon in front of the friendly forces and draw fire, telling them where the enemy was."[14]

Larry Coburn, the gunner, also recalled in a later interview:

> Early in the morning we were one of the first American units on station ahead of the Americans that would be inserted on the ground. It started out as a routine air support and reconnaissance mission, but as the day progressed, we noticed obviously that we weren't receiving any fire. Our job was to fly low level and try to entice people into giving up their positions by firing on us. And that wasn't happening. We saw people leaving the village. It was a Saturday morning, so it wasn't uncommon for the people to go to market on Saturday morning. So we thought it was good that these women and children and elderly people were leaving the area. And as we progressed around the perimeter of the area that the troops were being inserted into, we found nothing, as far as resistance. At some point we had to go refuel. And it was so quiet that morning that we didn't even call a backup team to cover us while we were refueling.[15]

They left to refuel and upon returning at about 9:00 a.m., Thompson was surprised by what they saw:

> We kept flying back and forth, in front and in the rear, and it didn't take very long until we started noticing the large number of bodies everywhere. Everywhere we'd look, we'd see bodies. These were infants, two-, three-, four-, five year-olds, women, very old men, no draft-age people whatsoever. That's what you look for, draft-age people.... There was not the first weapon captured, to my knowledge, that day. I think a count has been anywhere from two to four hundred, five hundred bodies—it was that many. I think that's a small count, including the three villages that were hit.[16]

Thompson flew over a wounded girl lying in the road. He radioed for help, and marked her position with smoke. As they hovered, they observed an infantry captain approach her, nudge her with his foot, step back and shoot her. (Captain Medina would later be identified as the officer, but would testify that she was going for a weapon when he shot her.) Outraged, Thompson radioed back reporting "needless and unnecessary killings," reports certain to be monitored by higher command.

Thompson flew over an irrigation ditch filled with bodies of women, children and old men and observed that some were still moving. Thompson landed his helicopter and dismounted. Sgt. Mitchell, the 1st Platoon squad leader, came over. Thompson asked him whether any help could be provided to the people in the ditch and the sergeant replied that the only way to help them was to put them out of their misery. An officer, later identified as Lieutenant Calley, came up, and Thompson confronted him.

> THOMPSON: What's going on here, Lieutenant?
> CALLEY: This is my business.
> THOMPSON: What is this? Who are these people?
> CALLEY: Just following orders.
> THOMPSON: Orders? Whose orders?
> CALLEY: Just following…
> THOMPSON: But, these are human beings, unarmed civilians, sir.
> CALLEY: Look Thompson, this is my show. I'm in charge here. It ain't your concern.
> THOMPSON: Yeah, great job.
> CALLEY: You better get back in that chopper and mind your own business.
> THOMPSON: You ain't heard the last of this![17]

Thompson took off again, and Andreotta reported that Mitchell was now firing into the people in the ditch. Coburn recalled:

> Mr. Thompson landed by the ditch, where there were probably 150–200 people dead or dying. There was an American soldier standing there. We actually landed the aircraft, because the communication was so bad. He physically got out of the aircraft, went over and spoke to the soldier and explained to him these were obviously civilians. There were no weapons captured. There were no draft age males. These were civilians. We need to help them out. And the soldier agreed and said he'd help them out, and as we lifted off again, we heard automatic weapons fire, and he was firing into the ditch again.[18]

Flying over the northeast corner of the village, Andreotta spotted a group of civilians, several of them children, fleeing into an earthen-type shelter, pursued by American troops. Afraid of another massacre, the crew again took action.

> He [Thompson] landed the aircraft in between the advancing American troops and the people in the bunker, went over and spoke to a lieutenant and told him—or asked him how we could get these people out of the bunker. They were obviously civilians. And the lieutenant replied he'd get them out with hand grenades.

Mr. Thompson, who was outranked by this lieutenant, actually gave the lieutenant an order, told him to keep his people in place. He had a better idea, and I think he told him, "If you fire on these people when I'm getting them out of the bunker, my people will fire on you." So he went over to the bunker himself and coaxed the villagers out.[19]

In interviews with author Trent Angers years later, Thompson recalled that he landed his helicopter between the bunker and soldiers, then turned to Addreotta and Coburn and told them that if the Americans began shooting the villagers or him that they should fire their M-60 machine guns at the Americans. "Y'all cover me! If these bastards open up on me or these people, you open up on them. Promise me!" He then dismounted to confront the 2nd Platoon's leader, Stephen Brooks.

As Thompson stated to the Peers Inquiry in 1970, "I set down ... got out of the aircraft and talked with this lieutenant, and told him there were some women and kids in that bunker over there and could he get them out. He said the only way to get them out was with a hand grenade. I told him to just hold [his] men where they were, and I'd get the kids out."[20]

Thompson's testimony made no mention of his threat to shoot Americans, stating only, "When I got out of the helicopter, I told my crew chief and gunner to make sure I was covered real close," but his testimony was ambiguous as to who he needed protection from, claiming only that he didn't want to get caught in a crossfire. Given that he was still in uniform and subject to military justice, a reluctance to admit an order to fire on American troops is understandable. He also testified, "To the best of my knowledge today, sir, there were no words that I can recall between myself and the man who appeared to be the lieutenant."[21]

Thompson approached the bunker on foot and using hand signals coaxed nine civilians, four adults and five children, to come out. He made contact with Warrant Officer Dan Millians in one of the UH-1 Huey gunships flying escort, and convinced him to land and evacuate the civilians. It took two trips to evacuate them to the vicinity of Highway 521 near Hoa My.

Returning to base for refueling, Thompson flew over the ditch again and Andreotta yelled that he saw movement among the bodies. Thompson again landed and his crew dismounted and searched among the bodies, rescuing a small boy, bloody but unhurt. They flew him to a nearby hospital orphanage and left him in the care of a nun. (Thompson and Colburn would reunite with the boy when they returned to My Lai in 2001).

Angry and frustrated, Thompson returned to LZ Dottie around 11 a.m. and reported his observations, shouting and using the word "murder," to his company commander, Major Frederick Watke, and his complaints were verified by other pilots and crewmen present over My Lai. He estimated the killed at well over a hundred. Watke met with the commander of TF Barker, and advised him of the allegations. Barker immediately departed in his helicopter, and Watke assumed that the matter would be attended to.

Later that day, Watke met again with Barker who advised him that he could find nothing to substantiate Thompson's accusations. Watke later testified that, convinced that Barker was lying, he reported the incident to his battalion commander, Lieutenant Colonel John L. Holladay, at about 10 p.m.

Due to the late hour, it wasn't until the following morning, March 17, that Holladay and Watke met with the Assistant Division Commander, Brigadier General George H. Young. There are differences in recollections as to what was discussed. Holladay and Watke are clear that they alledged "lots of unnecessary killings ... mostly women, children and old men," that these killings were confirmed not only by Thompson, but other aviation personnel over My Lai, and that a confrontation had taken place between aviation and ground forces.

Young asserts that he was never advised of any unnecessary killings of noncombatants by Watke or Holladay, and he later testified that it was his impression that the confrontation was the major concern, resulting from an incident in which civilians had been caught in a crossfire between U.S. and enemy forces. This is what he later testified he reported to the Division Commander, Major General Samuel W. Koster, at about noon. This conflicts with statements made by Koster to the Army Criminal Investigation Division (CID) in which he stated he had been advised of some indiscriminate shooting of civilians. Koster subsequently directed Young to have Colonel Henderson, 11th Brigade Commander, conduct a thorough investigation.[22]

At 9 a.m. on the 18th, Young met with Colonel Henderson, Lieutenant Colonel Barker, Lieutenant Colonel Holladay and Major Watke at LZ Dottie and advised them that General Koster was directing Henderson to conduct an investigation. Watke repeated the allegations related by Thompson and others. When the meeting concluded, Henderson began his investigation by interviewing Thompson and two other aviation personnel. Although he later testified he spoke with them for "only a few minutes," others recall the meeting lasting for almost an hour. Thompson testified that he advised Henderson of the captain shooting the young girl, the bodies in the ditch, the bunker and the officer who indicated a grenade would get the civilians out, and of the rescued boy.

Henderson continued his investigation by meeting with Captain Medina, whose explanation of civilian casualties he considered "suspicious" and meeting with 30–40 soldiers in a group and asking them collectively if anyone had witnessed any atrocities. Not surprisingly, none stated they had. He concluded his "investigation" with a brief flight over the area. (Note that within the Peers summary itself, the use of the word "investigation" in the report is always in quotations and called Henderson's efforts "little more than a pretense of an investigation and had as their goal the suppression of the true facts concerning the events of March 16."[23])

On March 19, Henderson reported orally to Young and Koster on his findings, in which he deliberately misrepresented the scope of his investigation, and stated that although some twenty civilians had been killed by either artillery or gunships, there was no basis in fact as to the allegations made by Thompson. This oral report satisfied Koster, and no further action was taken until mid–April 1968 when information arrived at Division Headquarters from Vietnamese sources.

A report had proceeded up channel from the Son My Village Chief to the Son Tinh District Chief, to the Quang Ngai Province Chief, with copies to the 2nd ARVN Division and U.S. advisory teams, alleging that U.S. forces had committed mass murder in the Son My village on March 16. VC propaganda also circulated alleging the mass killing of 500 civilians at Son My. This resulted in Koster ordering Henderson to submit a written copy of his oral report.

On April 24, 1968, Henderson issued a written report on the events of March 16th in which he reported:

> The result of this operation were 128 VC soldiers KIA. During the preparatory fires and the ground action by attacking companies 20 noncombatants caught in the battle area were killed. U.S. Forces suffered 2 KIA and 10 WIA by booby traps and 1 man slightly wounded in the foot by small arms fire.... Interviews with LTC Frank A. Barker, TF Commander; Major Charles C. Calhoun, TF S3; Captain Ernest L. Medina, CO Co C, 1–20; and Captain Earl Michles, CO Co B, 4–3 revealed that at no time were civilians gathered together and killed by U.S. soldiers.

The report ended with:

> It is concluded that 20 noncombatants were inadvertently killed when caught in the preparatory fires and in the cross fires of the U.S. and VC forces on 16 March 1968. The allegation that U.S. forces shot and killed 400–500 civilians is obviously a Viet Cong propaganda move to discredit the United States in the eyes of the Vietnamese people in general and the ARVN soldier in particular.[24]

Koster later testified that he found Henderson's report "unacceptable" and ordered Young and Colonel Nels A. Parson, the Division Chief of

Staff, to conduct a formal investigation. Young and Parson denied ever receiving such orders. Koster and Henderson agreed an investigation was conducted and a report submitted by Barker, but no evidence exists that any such report was ever prepared. As the Peers Report later concluded, "Within the Americal Division, at every level from company to division, actions were taken or omitted which together effectively concealed the Son My incident." This included failure to report, and the omission and suppression of key information.

Despite regulations that required that possible war crimes be reported immediately up the chain of command, Koster took no further action. Officially, the military, and U.S. newspapers reported My Lai as a successful combat operation. Sgt. Jay Roberts, a reporter assigned to the 11th Brigade accompanied Charlie Company during the assault on My Lai and witnessed numerous killings, yet the press release he wrote on March 18 transformed a massacre into a "battle": "Infantrymen from Task Force Barker raided a VC stronghold known as 'Pinkville' six miles northeast of Quang Ngai, killing 128 in a running battle. The action occurred in the coastal town of My Lai where, three weeks earlier, another company of the brigade's Task Force Barker fought its way out of a VC ambush, leaving 80 enemy dead."

Colonel Barker's Combat Action Report of March 28 reads like a piece of bad fiction: "The initial [artillery/gunship] preparation resulted in 68 VC KIA's in the enemy's combat outpost positions. Co. C then immediately attacked to the east receiving enemy small arms fire as they pressed forward.... One platoon from Company B flanked the enemy positions and engaged one enemy platoon resulting in 30 enemy KIA's.... Co B and C received sporadic sniper fire throughout the day." Barker's report counted 128 enemy KIA and eleven VC captured, as well as one M-1 rifle, 2 M-1 carbines, and 18 grenades.[25]

And that is where the matter rested, as the nation's attention turned towards President Johnson's decision not to run for re-election, the assassinations of Martin Luther King and Robert Kennedy, protests over civil rights and a growing anti-war movement. In November 1968, Specialist 4th Class Tom Glen, a 21-year-old mortarman in the 11th Brigade wrote a letter to General Creighton Abrams, the new commander of all U.S. forces in Vietnam, in which he accused the Americal Division of "routine brutality" against Vietnamese civilians and captives and "indiscriminate killing" and rumors of a massacre, although he did not specifically mention My Lai.

Glen wrote "The average GI's attitude toward and treatment of the Vietnamese people all too often is a complete denial of what our country is attempting to accomplish.... Too many American soldiers seem to discount their very humanity.... Vietnamese flee from Americans who for mere pleasure, fire indiscriminately into Vietnamese homes and without provocation or justification shoot at the people themselves." He spoke of "severe beatings and torture" as the usual means of questioning suspects, and regretted that "racial intolerance and disregard for justice" was becoming a prototype of the American soldier.[26]

The letter was turned over to the deputy assistant chief of staff for operations (G-3) at division headquarters at Chu Lai who was instructed to investigate the allegations in the letter. The officer, Major Colin Powell, was new to the division, having arrived in July 1968, on his second tour of duty in Vietnam.

Powell had risen to the rank of Cadet Colonel in the ROTC program at City College of NYC, and was commissioned a second lieutenant in the Army upon his graduation in 1958. After assignments with the 3rd Armored Division in Germany and at Ft. Devens, Massachusetts, Powell was sent to Vietnam.

Captain Powell arrived in the A Shu Valley at the height of the monsoon season, on January 17, 1963. Densely forested and near the border with Laos, the valley was alive with NVA and VC guerrillas, and Powell was assigned as an advisor to a 400-man ARVN (Army Republic of Vietnam) unit. Soon after his arrival, Powell went on an extended patrol with the unit, where he learned that the ARVN strategy for dealing with the VC was to destroy rural villages and relocate the population to isolate the guerrillas. Many advisors complained that this was creating support for the enemy they were trying to defeat. As Powell later recounted in his book, *My American Journey*: "We burned down the thatched huts, starting the blaze with Ronson and Zippo lighters. Why were we torching houses and destroying crops? Ho Chi Minh had said the people were like the sea in which his guerrillas swam.... We tried to solve the problem by making the whole sea uninhabitable."[27]

Powell spent six months in the jungle searching out the elusive Viet Cong, until he stepped on a punji stake, a sharpened, dung-poisoned bamboo spear buried in the ground. The resulting infection and swelling in his right foot forced his evacuation to a hospital in Hue. Following his recovery, Powell spent the remainder of his tour assigned on the operations staff at ARVN division headquarters until his return to the states in late autumn, 1963. Assignments to the Advanced Infantry Officers School and the Command and General Staff College followed. Upon his return to Vietnam, Powell, now a major, had been assigned as executive officer of 3/1 Infantry,

11th Light Infantry Brigade (LIB) at Duc Pho, but the Americal division commander in Chu Lai, Major General Charles Getty selected Powell to take charge of operations and planning on his divisional staff. It would be Powell's responsibility to investigate the validity of charges made in Glen's letter.

By all appearances, Powell's investigation was, at best, cursory. He never interviewed Glen, nor did anyone else. His investigation seems to have consisted only of speaking to some of Glen's superior officers, who stated that Glen was rarely near enough to the front lines to know what he was talking about. Satisfied, Powell drafted his report, dated December 13, 1968, stating that there was no evidence of a pattern of brutality towards Vietnamese civilians and noted that all division soldiers had attended an hour-long class on the treatment of prisoners under the Geneva Convention. He wrote, "There may be isolated cases of mistreatment of civilians and POWs ... this by no means reflects the general attitude throughout the Division. In direct refutation of this [Glen's] portrayal is the fact that relations between Americal soldiers and the Vietnamese people are excellent." Powell also criticized Glen for not reporting earlier and for not being specific enough. It appears his report was exactly what his superiors wanted to hear and no further action was taken nor inquiries made.[28]

It was another letter that would finally bring the My Lai massacre into the light, this one written by a former soldier, Ron Ridenhour, who had heard only secondhand rumors of a massacre, and undertook his own investigation.

Ron Ridenhour had been drafted in March 1967, and after basic training he was sent to Schofield Barracks, Hawaii, in September 1967. Ridenhour was assigned to the 30-man 70th Infantry Detachment (LRRP), part of the 11th LIB, which was scheduled to deploy to Vietnam in December. Ridenhour was trained for long range reconnaissance patrols, but just prior to departure, the unit was disbanded because the brigade was under strength, and most of the men were transferred to Charlie Company, 1/20th Infantry. Ridenhour was assigned to the aviation section of Headquarters Company (HHC), 11th LIB where he flew as a door-gunner aboard helicopters providing light cover for infantry operations in the southernmost sectors of the I Corps area of operations, near the northern border of South Vietnam.

Late in April 1968, a disagreement with a superior led to his volunteering for assignment with the 51st Infantry Detachment, the division LRRP, and he was awaiting orders when he ran into PFC "Butch" Gruver who had been with him in 70th Infantry in Hawaii. "He had been assigned to 'C'

Company 1st of the 20th until April 1st when he transferred to the unit that I was headed for. During the course of our conversation he told me the first of many reports I was to hear of 'Pinkville.'" Gruver went on to relate details about a search and destroy mission Charlie Company had participated in the previous month. As Ridenhour described it in his letter:

> The other two companies that made up the task force cordoned off the village so that Charlie Company could move through to destroy the structures and kill the inhabitants. Any villagers who ran from Charlie Company were stopped by the encircling companies. I asked "Butch" several times if all the people were killed. He said that he thought they were men, women and children. He recalled seeing a small boy, about three or four years old, standing by the trail with a gunshot wound in one arm. The boy was clutching his wounded arm with his other hand, while blood trickled between his fingers. He was staring around himself in shock and disbelief at what he saw. "He just stood there with big eyes staring around like he didn't understand; he didn't believe what was happening. Then the captain's RTO (radio operator) put a burst of 16 (M-16 rifle) fire into him." It was so bad, Gruver said, that one of the men in his squad shot himself in the foot in order to be medivaced out of the area so that he would not have to participate in the slaughter.[29]

Gruver also told Ridenhour that although he hadn't seen it himself, he heard that one of the officers, "Lieutenant Kalley," had gathered several groups of civilians "of both sexes and all ages" and machine-gunned them. "We massacred this whole village. We just lined them up and killed them…. Men, women and kids. Everybody, we killed them all." Initially skeptical that American soldiers would do such a thing, much less that an officer would order it, Ridenhour decided to inquire further.

> It's hard for me to really describe exactly what my reaction was, because it's difficult to, the language doesn't quite, at least I haven't found a way to capture it, but it was I guess you would say, an epiphany. It was an instantaneous recognition and collateral determination that this was something too horrible, almost, to comprehend and that I wasn't gonna be a part of it. Just simply having the knowledge, I felt, made me complicit, unless I acted on it.
>
> So I started to act on it, and I spent the remainder of my time in Vietnam trying to locate people who had been there and of course part of it was easy because I was going straight to the divisional LRRP Company. Four or five people who had been my friends in Hawaii and had gone to Charlie Company had transferred into the divisional LRRP Company within a week or ten days after the massacre. I was able to go in and talk with them and two of them were very good friends.[30]

He spoke with Private First Class Mike Terry, a friend that went back to basic training, and PFC William Doherty who both corroborated Gruber's account, adding details of their own involvement. "I'd ask them, 'Hey, man what happened at Pinkville?' And it would be like lancing a boil. I mean, if you asked them, they were compelled to talk. They couldn't stop talking. They were horrified that it had occurred, that they had been there, and in the instances of all of these men, that they had participated in some way." Ridenhour was further convinced when, upon running into Sgt. Larry LaCroix at the USO in Chu Lai, LaCroix told him that he had witnessed Lieutenant Calley gun down at least three separate groups of villagers. "It was terrible. They were slaughtering the villagers like so many sheep."[31]

Ridenhour went to the division historical section and found the official report of the battle at My Lai, noting 128 VC killed. He noted the coordinates of the village, dates, and specific details. He was determined to cause an investigation into the massacre, but needed to find a witness that hadn't participated. That man was Private First Class Michael Bernhardt.

Bernhardt had refused to participate in the massacre, and was warned by Medina after the battle "not to do anything stupid like write your Congressman." With nine months left in-country, Bernhardt assured him that wasn't his intention, but his requests for transfer were always denied. As Ridenhour later stated:

> Every time they thought an ambush was coming, they'd send him up to the front of the line, where they thought the ambush was gonna be. He walked point in all the dangerous places and in the last four months he got jungle rot so bad, he could barely walk and they wouldn't let him out of the field. Finally, with about three weeks to go, he just jumped on a supply chopper as it was lifting off and without anybody's permission and went into the infirmary, the aid station, at the 11th brigade headquarters at Duc Pho.... Two days after he went into the brigade aid station he was at 2nd Surgical Hospital in Chu Lai, which is where I was then and we were all ready to come home. He and I talked for about thirty minutes and we realized that we felt the same way about it.[32]

Once he was out of the Army, Ridenhour drafted a letter dated March 29, 1969, detailing everything he had learned and he sent copies to President Nixon, the State Department, the Secretary of Defense, Melvin Laird, the Joint Chiefs of Staff, the Pentagon and thirty members of Congress, including Senators Edward Kennedy, Barry Goldwater, Eugene McCarthy and William Fullbright, and Rep. Mo Udall of Arizona, an anti-war Congressman from his home state, who called on the House Armed Services Committee to request the Pentagon to initiate an investigation into the matter. Whether through the urging of Congress, or on its own, the Pentagon ordered an investigation.

On April 12, Colonel Howard Whittaker was ordered by the Army Chief of Staff, General William C. Westmoreland to investigate the allegations in Ridenhour's letter, and he departed for Chu Lai, Vietnam, to begin the inquiry. Almost immediately, Whitaker reported to Washington that there might be substance to the charges, and that Charlie Company veterans should be interviewed.

On April 23, the Office of the Inspector General began a full inquiry and Colonel William Wilson was assigned as primary investigator. Wilson, a World War II veteran and Green Beret, was highly regarded, and considered a "no-nonsense" choice. He held a face to face interview with Ridenhour at the end of April, followed by one with LaCroix on May 2. LaCroix admitted that there had been "unnecessary killings" and mentioned that a helicopter pilot, Hugh Thompson, had filed a complaint, a fact that Wilson was unaware of. In mid–May, during an interview with Medina, he learned that Henderson had been ordered to conduct an investigation, and Wilson interviewed Henderson on May 26. Henderson claimed he ordered Barker to make a formal investigation, but no record was found. Henderson blamed the missing report on the disorganization of the Chu Lai headquarters following Barker's death in a helicopter mid-air collision on June 13, 1968. Also killed was Bravo Company commander, Captain Michles. Their deaths significantly hindered the investigation and prosecution.

On June 5, Calley was identified as a suspect in the inquiry and was recalled to Fort Benning from Vietnam. On June 13, Thompson identified Calley in a line-up as an officer present at My Lai. On July 17, Wilson took testimony from PFC Paul Meadlo, who admitted his guilt. Wilson presented his findings in a report to the Inspector General in Washington, D.C., and on August 4, the investigation was ordered to be turned over to the Army CID, with Chief Warrant Officer Andre Feher in charge of the investigation. Additional witnesses were interviewed, including Army photographer Sgt. Haeberle who showed Feher personal photos he had taken in My Lai, the first hard evidence of a massacre.[33]

On September 5, 1969, the day before he was to be discharged from the Army, Calley was charged with six counts of premeditated murder and the Army announced in a press release that Calley was being retained due to an ongoing investigation. Five days later, the story went public when NBC News reported that Calley was under investigation for the premeditated murder of Vietnamese civilians. The story drew little attention. His platoon sergeant, David Mitchell, was also charged with murder on October 28.

On November 11, investigative reporter Seymour Hersh was granted an interview with Calley at Fort Benning, Georgia. Headlined "Lieutenant Accused of Murdering 109 Civilians," the story ran on November 13 in the *St. Louis Post Dispatch*. In it, he reported, "Calley has formally been charged with six specifications of mass murder. Each specification cites a number of dead, adding up to the 109 total, and charges that Calley did 'with premeditation murder.... Oriental human beings, whose names and sex are unknown, by shooting them with a rifle.' The Army calls it murder; Calley, his counsel and others associated with the incident describe it as a case of carrying out orders." It was a foreshadowing of the defense that those accused of the murders would use.[34]

The story was quickly picked up by major news agencies like *Time*, *Newsweek*, the *New York Times*, and network TV. The story became the focus of a nation that was rapidly polarizing into two camps, one supportive of involvement in the war and the other opposed to it. Hersh's three-part series would win him the Pulitzer Prize in 1970.

On November 21, Staff Sgt. David Mitchell, then assigned to Charlie Company, 5/6th Infantry with the 1st Armored Division at Ft. Hood, was charged with assault for his actions at My Lai, the first enlisted man to be charged.

On November 24, 1969, Gen. William C. Westmoreland ordered an investigation, to focus on a possible cover-up by the military commanders while the CID concurrently carried on with investigating criminal charges. He placed Lieutenant General William R. Peers in charge of the investigation. Peers, a former corps commander in Vietnam had a reputation for being objective and possessing high integrity. It became known as the Peers Inquiry, and its finding the Peers Report. That same day, charges against Calley were referred for a General Court Martial.[35]

Two days later, in a hearing before the House and Senate Armed Forces Committee, Secretary of the Army Stanley Resor testified on what was known at that point about the alleged massacre at Son My, advised them of Peers' appointment and presented copies of Sgt. Haberle's photos taken at My Lai on March 16.

From December 3 through December 26, the Peers Commission took testimony from 39 witnesses, including Chief Thompson, Captain Medina, Major Watke, Private First Class Colburn, Colonel Henderson and Generals Young and Koster, as well as Captain Eugene Kotouc, and Warrant Officer Don Millians. Peers' thirteen-person staff eventually grew to 80 investigators, and Peers himself returned to Vietnam to interview U.S. military personnel, American civilian personnel, Vietnamese government officials, officers from the Army of the Republic of Vietnam, and Vietnamese civilians living in Son My. He was unable to locate any formal report by Barker or anyone else on the incident.

In the interim, on December 5, *Life* magazine printed in color, and CBS on its *Evening News* broadcast, images of the Haberle photos which caused a media frenzy of interest in the story, and public uproar as the massacre was increasingly covered in newspapers, radio and television. Even President Nixon felt obligated to comment, acknowledging that a massacre had occurred, but stating his confidence that such acts were unusual. Concurrently, the investigation was expanded as the Peers investigation identified ten possible suspects and the CID investigation concluded that members of Charlie Company killed 347 civilians, including women and children, and that 45 Charlie Company soldiers were guilty of crimes ranging from violation of the rules of war to murder.[36]

On February 12, 1970, as a result of the investigation into the events at My Lai, Army investigators uncovered evidence of a second massacre in the neighboring village of My Khe, and charged 1st Lieutenant (now Captain) Thomas K. Willingham, a platoon leader in Bravo Company, with the murder of between 90–100 civilians, including women and children. Willingham had falsely claimed to investigators that his men came under fire and killed 39 enemy combatants, stating he had no knowledge of any "unnecessary killings."

On March 7, 1970, the Peers Inquiry completed taking testimony after finishing its 399th interview. The report was scheduled to be delivered to Gen. Westmoreland a week later, on March 14. In the interim, on March 10, Captain Medina was charged with the premeditated murder of four civilians and assault on a fifth civilian.

On March 14, 1970, the Peers Inquiry issued its Summary of Findings, and concluded:

1. During the period of 16–19 March 1968, troops of Task Force Barker massacred a large number of Vietnamese nationals in the village of Son My.
2. Knowledge as to the extent of the incident existed at Company level, at least among the key staff officers and commander at the Task Force Barker level, and at the 11th Brigade command level.
3. Efforts at the Americal Division command level to conceal information concerning what was probably believed to be the killing of 20–28 civilians actually resulted in the suppression of a war crime of far greater magnitude.
4. The commander of the 11th Brigade, upon learning that a war crime had probably been committed, deliberately set out to conceal the fact from proper authority and to deceive his commander concerning the matter.
5. Investigations concerning the incident conducted within the

Americal Division were superficial and misleading and not subjected to substantive review.
6. Efforts were made at every level of command from company to division to withhold and suppress information concerning the incident at Son My.
7. Failure of Americal Division headquarters personnel to act on information received from GVN/ARVN officials served to suppress effectively information concerning the Son My incident.
8. Efforts of the Americal Division to suppress and withhold information were assisted by U.S. officers serving in advisory positions with Vietnamese agencies.

The following day, March 15, pressured by a pending expiration of a two-year statute of limitations, the Army charged 25 officers and men for their part in the My Lai massacre. Four officers and nine enlisted men were charged with murder and assault, and another twelve officers were charged with crimes related to the cover-up.

In addition to Calley, Willingham and Medina, one other officer, Captain Eugene M. Kotouc, the division intelligence officer, was accused of killing two suspected Viet Cong during an interrogation, and charged with murder.

Along with Staff Sgt. Mitchell, eight other enlisted men, Sgt. Kenneth Hodges, Sgt. Charles Hutto, Sgt. Esquivel Torres, Specialist 4th Class William Doherty, Specialist 4th Class Robert T'Souvas, Corporal Kenneth Schiel, Private Max Hutton and Private Gerald Smith, were charged with numerous crimes including rape, assault and murder. The Army wanted to bring charges against an additional twenty-two soldiers, but were unable to legally do so because they had already been discharged from the Army.[37]

Additionally, twelve officers were charged with violations ranging from failure to obey orders to dereliction of duty, false swearing and failing to report. These officers included Generals Koster and Young; Colonel Robert B. Luper, the 6th Bn/11th Artillery commander; Colonel Nels A. Parson Jr., the 23rd Infantry Division chief of staff; Lieutenant Colonel David C. Gavin and Lieutenant Colonel William D. Guinn, advisers serving with the South Vietnamese; Major Charles C. Calhoun, executive and operations officer of Task Force Baker, Major Robert W. McKnight, the brigade operations officer; Major Frederic W. Watke, commander of CO. B, 123rd Aviation Bn; 1st Lieutenantt Kenneth W. Boatman, an artillery forward observer, and 1st Lieutenant Dennis H. Johnson, assigned to the 52nd Military Intelligence Detachment. Both Boatman and Johnson had been subsequently promoted to captain. Additionally, both Medina and Willingham were also charged in the cover-up.[38]

In the end, as a result of Congressional interference and the reluctance of some commanders to prosecute offenders, military prosecutors would find that the charging of individuals with crimes would be infinitely easier than obtaining convictions.

On June 9, 1970, charges of murder and conspiracy were dropped against Captain Thomas K. Willingham. Citing "uncooperative witnesses" and "contradictory testimony," Army lawyers dropped all charges in the interest of justice.

On June 23, the Army dismissed court-martial charges against Young, Parson and McKnight after Lieutenant General Jonathan O. Seaman, the 1st Army Commander at Ft. Meade, Maryland, to whom the charges had been referred for investigation determined that the charges were "unsupported by the evidence."[39]

The following month, on July 28, General Seaman announced his decision to proceed with Article 32 hearings for seven officers: Colonel Henderson, Lieutenant Colonels Guinn and Gavin, Majors Calhoun and Watke and Captain Johnson. Cover-up charges against Colonel Luper and Captain Boatman were dismissed. Article 32 proceedings commenced at Ft. Meade beginning in August.[40]

The following month, on August 19, 1970, charges of rape and assault with intent to commit murder were dropped against Staff Sgt. Kenneth Hodges, due to "insufficient evidence." He was subsequently honorably discharged at the "convenience of the government," an action he unsuccessfully fought. On September 4, 1970, charges against Corporal Schiel were dropped after his Article 32 investigation determined there was insufficient evidence to proceed with a court-martial.

The first soldier brought to trial for the My Lai massacre was Staff Sergeant David Mitchell, a squad leader in Calley's platoon, who was charged with assault with intent to kill 30 civilians. The trial began on October 19, 1970, at Fort Hood, Texas.

The prosecution's case was hampered by a decision of the judge, Lieutenant Colonel George R. Robinson, to exclude four prosecution witnesses, ruling that they could not testify unless the defense received access to statements made in previous testimony before a House of Representatives subcommittee investigation of event at My Lai. The Herbert Committee refused to declassify or release testimony by Thompson and other aviators present at My Lai, and they were not allowed to testify. After calling only three witnesses, including a former radio operator, Charles Sledge, who testified seeing Mitchell fire into the irrigation ditch, the prosecutor, Captain Michael Swan, rested his case the following day, on October 20, after only six hours of testimony.[41]

The defense, led by civilian attorney Ossie Brown, pointed out discrepancies in Sledge's prior testimony, and called eight witnesses who testified that Mitchell was not at the ditch, and Mitchell himself testified "*I shot at no one.*" On November 20, the jury of seven officers, six of whom were Vietnam veterans, acquitted Mitchell on all charges.

On January 6, 1971, General Seaman announced the dismissal of charges against Guinn, Gavin, Watke and Calhoun, four of the officers charged in the cover-up, citing "insufficient evidence." That same day, the second court-martial of an enlisted soldier, Sgt. Charles Hutto, began at Fort McPherson. Accused of assault with intent to murder six civilians, Hutto admitted to killing unarmed civilians with his M-60 machinegun stating, "It was murder. I wasn't happy about shooting all the people.... I didn't agree with all the killing, but we were doing it because we had been told." The defense based its case on the fact that Hutto was only following orders, and that since he believed that the Army would only give him legal orders, he was not guilty of assault with intent to kill.[42]

The trial judge, Colonel Kenneth Howard, in his instructions declared that a superior's order to kill unarmed civilians was illegal, but stated that the question was the accused's ability to decide for himself whether the order was illegal. After two hours of deliberation, the six-officer jury, all combat veterans found Hutto not guilty on January 14.

Another soldier, Private Gerald A Smith, was brought to trial at Ft. Riley, Kansas, the day after Hutto's court-martial began, on January 7, 1971. Charged with premeditated murder and indecent assault, the charges were dismissed by the convening authority on January 22, reasoning that "the possibility of conviction [had been] diminished by the acquittal of Sgt. Hutto" and "other considerations bearing upon their prospective merit." One of the other "considerations" was the prosecution's inability to locate a key witness. A day earlier, on January 21, charges were dropped against Specialist Doherty.[43]

The following week, on January 29, the same day that charges were dismissed against MGen. Koster, four enlisted men, Sgt. Torres, Specialist T'Souvas, and Private Hutson, had all charges withdrawn, the last enlisted men charged. Because the dismissal of charges for insufficient evidence did not create immunity from future prosecution, many participants were less than forthcoming as witnesses in those few cases that later came to trial.

In the interim, following several pre-trial motions, the court-martial of Calley began at Ft. Benning, Georgia, on November 17, 1970, under extensive media coverage. Charged with 109 counts of premeditated murder under Article 118 of the Uniform Code of Military Justice, there were four specifications:

> Specification 1: In that First Lieutenant William L. Calley, Jr. ... did, at My Lai 4, Quang Ngai Province, Republic of South Viet-Nam, on or about 16 March 1968, with premeditation, murder an unknown number, not less than thirty, Oriental human beings, males and females of various ages, whose names are unknown, occupants of the village of My Lai 4, by means of shooting them with a rifle.
> Specification 2: In that First Lieutenant William L. Calley, Jr ... did, at My Lai 4, Quang Ngai Province, Republic of South Viet-Nam, on or about 16 March 1968, with premeditation, murder an unknown number, not less than seventy, Oriental human beings, males and females of various ages, whose names are unknown, occupants of the village of My Lai 4, by means of shooting them with a rifle.
> Specification 3: In that First Lieutenant William L. Calley, Jr ... did, at My Lai 4, Quang Ngai Province, Republic of South Viet-Nam, on or about 16 March 1968, with premeditation, murder one Oriental male human being, whose name and age is unknown, by shooting him with a rifle.
> Specification 4: In that First Lieutenant William L. Calley, Jr ... did, at My Lai 4, Quang Ngai Province, Republic of South Viet-Nam, on or about 16 March 1968, with premeditation, murder one Oriental human being, an occupant of the village of My Lai 4, approximately two years old, by shooting him with a rifle.

Major General Orwin K. Talbott, the convening authority at Ft. Benning selected Colonel Reid Kennedy as the military judge. A panel of twenty-five officers was examined before six officers were finally selected to serve as the jury. All were combat veterans, and five had seen service in Vietnam. Colonel Clifford H. Ford, a combat veteran of World War II, was the only one of the six not a veteran of Vietnam. Major Charles C. McIntosh had two Silver Stars for combat in Korea and Vietnam and Major Walter Kinard had earned both a Silver and Bronze Star in Vietnam. Major Carl Bierbaum had flown helicopters, Captain Harvey Brown had served as an advisor and Captain Ronald Salem had led a platoon in combat.[44]

The prosecution was assigned to Captain Aubrey Daniel, a University of Richmond Law School graduate who was drafted six months after graduation and applied for a direct commission in the Judge Advocate General's Corps. His only background in military law was a two-week abbreviated course on the UCMJ prior to his assignment to Fort Benning. He was assisted by Captain John Partin.[45]

Besides his military counsel, Major Kenneth Raby, Calley hired a civilian, George Latimer, to present his defense. Latimer, a distinguished jurist, had previously served as a Justice of the Utah Supreme Court and on the United States Court of Military Appeals in Washington, D.C., the nation's highest military court. He was also a combat veteran having served with the 40th Infantry Division in the South Pacific during World War II. He participated in four assault landings, and was the division chief of staff, rising to the rank of colonel. Also on the defense team was Richard B. Kay and Brookes S. Doyle Jr.

Although Calley's original defense had been that the casualties had been caused by accidental aerial assaults, the new defense alluded to inadequate training, and diminished capacity due to stress and marijuana use, but primarily rested on the defense of superior orders, i.e., that he was following the orders of his superior Captain Medina, Charlie Company commander.

Firm in the belief in Calley's guilt, Daniel's focus was his duty to prosecute Calley, not the others involved and not the war. "I undertook the prosecution of the case without any ulterior motives for personal gain, either financial or political. My only desire was to fulfill my duty as a prosecutor and to see that justice was done in accordance with the laws of the nation."[46]

The prosecution was hampered by the fact that many of the soldiers were now civilians and beyond the reach of the military and that others still in the military were reluctant to testify due to the possibility of prosecution. Nevertheless, Daniel's case was presented methodically and effectively.

Daniel first called Haberle, whose photographs conclusively proved that a massacre had taken place, and Thompson who could with certainty place Calley at the scene of the massacre. Robert Maples, an M-60 gunner, testified that he witnessed Calley and Meadlo firing into a group of civilians in the eastern drainage ditch, and that he had refused to participate. Dennis Conti testified that he was ordered to round up people, mostly women and children, and bring them back to Calley on the trail south of the hamlet. Calley ordered him to make them "squat down and bunch up so they couldn't get up and run." Minutes later, he testified, Calley and Paul Meadlo "fired directly into the people." He also testified that he refused to fire at civilians.

The final prosecution witness, possibly the most damning, was Paul Meadlo. Meadlo, who had been granted immunity, had previously refused to testify claiming 5th Amendment protections. Threatened by the judge with contempt, he testified in a flat voice about how he had gathered up between 30–50 men, women and children, which he insisted on characterizing as Viet Cong, south of the hamlet. He was approached by Lieutenant

Calley who said, "You know what to do with them, Meadlo," and he testified, "I assumed he wanted me to guard them. That's what I did."

When Calley returned he said, "How come they're not dead?" Meadlo replied, "I didn't know we were supposed to kill them," and Calley said, "I want them dead." He then described how he and Calley emptied several magazines into the people in the ditch. Meadlo also testified how they had fired into people in the eastern drainage ditch. Following Meadlo's testimony, the prosecution rested.

The defense was brief, and ineffective. Latimer's defense hinged on two main premises; that the stress of combat, especially with an "invisible" enemy, sufficiently impaired Calley's thinking to the point that he was incapable of premeditated murder and that Calley was following the orders of his superiors.

One the first point, Latimer called New York psychiatrist Albert LaVerne, who testified that Calley's judgment was impaired on the morning of March 16, 1968, and that Calley "was compelled to carry out [Captain Medina's] order without challenging that order." But under Daniel's cross-examination, LaVerne admitted that Calley was conscious of his actions, that he knew right from wrong, and that he wasn't neurotic or psychotic.

As to the second point, Latimer had Calley take the stand to testify. In attempting to justify the shooting of women and children, Calley stated that "everyone was a potential enemy and that men and women were equally dangerous. The Vietnamese women, for some reason, are better shots than the men are.... Children were used to throw hand grenades or plant mines. It was essential that troops in Viet Nam put out of their minds the World War II and Korean concept of giving candy and chewing gum and things to children. The Communists used that American philosophy against us."[47]

Under Latimer's direct examination, Calley testified that although he remembered taking a class on the Geneva Convention, he couldn't recall any of it and that he was never instructed that he had the choice of refusing an order that he considered illegal. He did recall learning that "all orders were to be assumed legal, that the soldier's job was to carry out any order given him to the best of his ability."

Calley testified regarding Captain Medina's briefings that "we would have to neutralize My Lai completely, not let anyone get behind us. He said it was completely essential that we not lose our momentum of attack.... I believe somebody asked if that meant women and children. He said that meant everything."[48]

Calley also testified to shooting people and giving the orders to "waste" civilians:

CALLEY: I gave the order to take those people through the ditch and had also told Meadlo if he couldn't move them, to waste them, and I directly—other than that, there was only that one incident. I never stood up there for any period of time. The main mission was to get my men on the other side of the ditch and get in that defensive position, and that is what I did, sir.
DANIEL: Now, why did you give Meadlo a message or the order that if he couldn't get rid of them to waste them?
A: Because that was my order, sir. That was the order of the day, sir.
Q: Who gave you that order?
A: My commanding officer, sir.
Q: He was?
A: Captain Medina, sir.
Q: And stated in that posture, in substantially those words, how many times did you receive such an order from Captain Medina?
A: The night before in the company briefing, platoon leaders' briefing, the following morning before we lifted off and twice there in the village.

In essence, Calley testified that he was ordered to kill the enemy, and that he followed his orders. "I never sat down to analyze it, men, women, and children. They were enemy and just people."

Under Daniel's cross-examination, Calley admitted that there was no enemy fire, that he had fired at "people" and the "enemy," and that "I didn't discriminate between individuals in the village, sir. They were all the enemy, they were all to be destroyed, sir."

In his final address to the jury, Daniel invoked the memory of Abraham Lincoln's order to Union troops during the Civil War: "Men who take up arms against one another in public do not cease on this account to be moral human beings, responsible to one another and to God."

In his instructions to the jury, Kennedy advised,

> The acts of a subordinate done in compliance with an unlawful order given him by his superior are excused and impose no criminal liability upon him unless the superior's order is one which a man of ordinary sense and understanding would, under the circumstances, know to be unlawful, or if the order in question is actually known to the accused to be unlawful.
>
> If you find beyond reasonable doubt, on the basis of all the evidence, that Lieutenant Calley actually knew the order under which he asserts he operated was unlawful, the fact that the order was given operates as no defense.

The jury deliberated for 79 hours and 57 minutes over thirteen days before reaching a verdict. On March 21, 1971, Calley was found guilty of the premeditated murder of 22 civilians, thus bringing to an end the longest court-martial in American military history. Upon hearing the verdict, Calley stood erect and saluted the jury.[49]

The following day, Calley read a statement to the court prior to sentencing, in which he asserted that he had only done as he'd been trained to do.

If I have committed a crime, the only crime I've committed is in judgment of my values. Apparently I valued my troops' lives more than I did that of the enemy.

When my troops were getting massacred and mauled by an enemy I couldn't see, I couldn't feel and I couldn't touch—that nobody in the military system ever described them as anything other than Communism. They didn't give it a race, they didn't give it a sex, they didn't give it an age. They never let me believe it was just a philosophy in a man's mind. That was my enemy out there.

And when it became between me and that enemy, I had to value the lives of my troops—and I feel that was the only crime I have committed. Yesterday, you stripped me of all my honor. Please, by your actions that you take here today don't strip future soldiers of their honor, I beg of you.

But not one shot was fired at Calley's men, there were no casualties, there was no battle, and the court failed to see how killing old men, women and children worked to protect American soldiers. Following his statement, Calley was sentenced to life imprisonment at hard labor.

The sentence generated an enormous response from the American public with many expressing the belief that Calley was a scapegoat who only carried out orders from above. The White House received 5,000 telegrams which ran 100 to 1 in favor of clemency. So great was the outcry that on April 1, 1971, President Nixon ordered Calley released from the stockade and placed under house arrest pending his appeal. The American Legion raised money for his appeal. Draft Board members resigned. Veterans turned in their medals. Flags were flown at half-mast in Indiana and Georgia Governor Jimmy Carter urged his constituents to drive for a week with their headlights on in protest of the sentence.

On April 29, 1971, Captain Eugene Kotouc was cleared by a court-martial at Fort McPherson, Georgia, on charges of assault and murder. The following month, on May 19, Generals Koster and Young were stripped of their Distinguished Service Medals and Koster was reduced in rank to Brigadier General. Young retired from the Army shortly after receiving the censure, and Koster resigned as Superintendant at West Point, where he'd graduated as part of the Class of 1942, to become deputy commander at Maryland's Aberdeen Proving Ground, in charge of Army weapons testing. He retired from the Army in 1973.

On August 20, 1971, the Third Army Commanding General, Major General Albert O'Connor, reduced Calley's sentence of life imprisonment to twenty years. The case was still pending reviews by the U.S. Court of Military Review and the U.S. Court of Military Appeals before final review by the president.

Three days earlier, on August 16, 1971, the court-martial of Captain Medina got underway at Fort McPherson, Georgia. Medina, the sixth and final soldier and second officer to be tried for the murders at My Lai, was charged with murder of 102 Vietnamese civilians. Additionally, he was accused of participating in the cover-up, but those charges were later dropped because of an expired statute of limitations.[50]

The judge, Colonel Kenneth Howard, empaneled a jury of five combat officers to hear the case.

The prosecutor, Major William G. Eckhardt, allowed that while Medina might not have specifically ordered the murder of civilian noncombatants, he was aware of the killings and chose not to intervene, which made him guilty of the murders under the doctrine of "command responsibility." Under this doctrine, a commander can be held criminally punishable for *inaction*, that is, failing to intervene once he has knowledge of criminal acts. The key element is knowledge. Additionally, Medina was charged with killing a woman, a young boy and assaulting a prisoner.

The position of the defense was that Medina didn't order the killings, was unaware that the killings were going on, and that he ordered the killings to cease once he became aware of them.

None of the prosecution's fifty witnesses could place Medina at the scene, except one, John M. Smail, an assistant machine-gunner in Charlie Company. Smail testified that Medina's command group was passing through his area when a young boy of five or six emerged from the brush, face and hands bleeding, and was shot by the last member of the party, radioman Frederick Widner, in Medina's presence. Frank D. Beardslee, Barker's driver, testified that he witnessed Medina fire two shots over a prisoner's head. And the prosecution was unable to get the results of a polygraph admitted that indicated that Medina became aware of the killings at between 8 a.m. and 9 a.m., not the 10–10:30 a.m. he later testified to.[51]

Medina was defended by F. Lee Bailey, a noted criminal attorney who succeeded in getting key prosecution witnesses excluded from testifying and keeping damaging evidence like the Haberle photographs from the jury. Bailey addressed each of the prosecution's points in presenting his defense.

With regards to Medina being responsible for the actions of his men, and thus being culpable in their murdering of civilians, Bailey pointed out that all the witnesses were uncertain regarding the exact timing of the mass killings and the cease-fire order. This was important to the defense, because the judge, Colonel Howard, would later instruct the jury that Medina could not be held liable for killings that were committed by his men before he was aware of what was going on.

Medina defended the shooting of the woman, explaining that he had orders from his brigade commander to round up enemy weapons, and when a helicopter dropped a smoke signal to indicate the location of an armed suspect, Medina had rushed to the location where he saw a Vietnamese in black pajamas. It was a woman, and there was no weapon. Medina was turning back when he saw "what he believed to be movement" by the woman, and he "instinctively turned and shot," Medina immediately notified the brigade commander, Colonel Henderson, of the incident and Henderson radioed back: "I understand; these things happen."

Medina also testified that he was acting on instinct when he ordered his men to shoot at a Vietnamese figure moving in the grass. He countermanded the order and lowered his rifle when he saw that the target was a child, but it was too late and someone else shot the boy

Finally, on the charge of assaulting a prisoner, Medina testified that he merely fired twice over the man's head to frighten him and extract intelligence, as he had been told by a Vietnamese interpreter that the prisoner was "a ranking member of the Viet Cong" who might know the whereabouts of the 48th Viet Cong battalion, which had eluded them at My Lai.

In its final argument, Major Eckhardt ridiculed as "incredible" the defense's contention that Captain Medina had remained unaware of any large scale killings until it was too late since Medina had maintained continuous radio contact with his platoons during the action. He characterized Medina as an officer who had abrogated his responsibility, and who like Pontius Pilate "cannot wash the blood from his hands."

Medina heard himself described by Bailey in the defense summation as "no filthy felon" but "a disciplined commander who honored and loved the uniform he wore and the company it represented."[52]

Prior to the case being given to the jury, Colonel Howard reduced the charges of 102 counts of premeditated murder to manslaughter, and dismissed the charges regarding the killing of the young boy. On September 22, the jury deliberated for only 60 minutes before the president of the court, Colonel Wiliam D. Proctor, announced Medina's acquittal on all charges.

With the trial over, the Pentagon announced that although the My Lai investigation was not officially closed, no further action was pending. Of the 14 officers and enlisted men charged with murder at My Lai, eight had charges dismissed, five were acquitted, and only one—Calley—was convicted.

The last My Lai court-martial was that of Colonel Oran K. Henderson, which commenced at Ft. Meade, Maryland, on August 23, 1971. Charged with dereliction of duty for failing to investigate charges of a massacre, Henderson was the highest ranking officer, and the only officer charged in the cover-up, to be brought to trial. Following some delays and pre-trial motions, the trial resumed on September 7.

The judge, Colonel Peter S. Wondolowski, empaneled a jury of two generals and five colonels to hear the case, with Major General Charles N. Mount Jr. selected as president of the court. Major Carroll J. Tichenor presented the government's case while Henderson was represented by a civilian lawyer, Henry Rothblatt, assisted by his military lawyer, Lieutenant Colonel Frank Dorsey.

Henderson was charged with failure to properly investigate the allegations of a massacre, violating regulations requiring the reporting of possible war crimes, and lying under oath to a Pentagon inquiry into the massacre.

Citing Henderson's report on the events of March 16, in which he described the event as a combat action in which 128 Viet Cong were killed and in which 20 civilians were killed by artillery or helicopter gunships, Tichenor suggested that Henderson lied and concealed facts, and conducted a superficial investigation because he feared that disclosure of the facts would negatively impact his career and his chances for promotion to general.[53]

The defense maintained that Henderson, a wounded combat veteran of three wars, was misled by subordinates, primarily Medina, and that although Thompson testified that he met with Henderson on March 18, 1968, and made him aware of his confrontation with Calley, Medina's shooting of a woman, and observing numerous bodies, General Young supported Henderson in his testimony that no allegations were made. Additionally, Medina, now out of the Army, testified that he concealed information regarding the killings from Henderson.

After 62 days and 106 witnesses, in a court-martial that equaled Calley's in duration, the case was sent to the jury which deliberated for four hours over two days, before acquitting Henderson on all charges regarding the cover-up. Henderson's court-martial was the last prosecution by the government over the events at My Lai.[54]

Although the court-martials were finished, the case of the My Lai Massacre was far from over. Two weeks after the verdict in the Calley Court-Martial, a Harris Poll found that for the first time, the majority of Americans now opposed the war in Vietnam, while at the same time an overwhelming majority disapproved of the verdict. The political Right Wing was disgusted by Calley's conviction while the political Left Wing believed Calley a scapegoat to avoid the blame going higher up the chain of command. And the antiwar movement began to characterize all soldiers as "baby-killers."

As his case worked its way through the courts, Calley remained under house arrest at Ft. Benning, living in a small apartment where he cooked his own meals, watched television, and answered his mail. The prosecutor, Aubrey Daniels, wrote a highly publicized letter to President Nixon critical of his releasing Calley to house arrest stating his shock that "people across this nation have failed to see the moral issue, that it is unlawful for an American soldier to summarily execute unresisting men, women and babies."

On February 16, 1973, the U.S. Army Court of Military Review upheld Calley's conviction and sentence, an action repeated by the U.S. Court of Military Appeals on December 31, 1973. The Secretary of the Army, Howard Calloway, reviewed and approved both the sentence and findings on April 17, 1974, but in a separate action reduced his sentence to ten years, making him eligible for parole in six months. On May 3, President Nixon announced he had reviewed the case and would not take any further action.[55]

In the interim, on February 11, 1974, Calley requested a writ of Habeas Corpus from the Federal District Court in Columbus, Georgia, additionally asking for bail and a temporary restraining order to prevent his transfer to Leavenworth Federal Penitentiary. On February 27, Judge Robert Elliott granted the restraining order and released Calley on his own recognizance.

Almost immediately, the Army appealed and on June 13, 1974, a judge on the 5th Circuit Court of Appeals ordered Calley returned to Army custody and on June 27, Calley was transferred to the Military Prison at Ft. Leavenworth, Kansas. Other than a day in the stockade at Ft. Benning, it was the first time Calley was incarcerated following the verdict in March 1971.

On September 25, 1974, Judge Elliott overturned Calley's conviction and ordered him released stating that Calley had been denied a fair trial which had been prejudiced by pretrial publicity. "Never in the history of the military justice system, and perhaps in the history of American courts, has any accused ever encountered such intense and continuous prejudicial publicity." Elliott also cited the government's denial of Calley's request to subpoena Secretary of Defense Melvin Laird and Gen. Westmoreland as defense witnesses, Congress' refusal to release testimony taken in its investigation into My Lai, and inadequate notice of charges.

The Army ultimately appealed and won a reversal of Elliott's decision and a reinstatement of the verdict, but by that time, the Army had already paroled Calley on November 19, 1974. Army Secretary Calloway had signed an order on October 30 granting Calley's parole based on his good behavior and completion of one third of his sentence. In the end, Calley served forty months of his life sentence, thirty-five of which were under house arrest in his own quarters.[56]

It is ironic that while many considered Calley a hero and celebrated his release, the real heroes of the massacre at My Lai went unacknowledged and were at times vilified for their actions. Many felt they had betrayed the Army and American soldiers fighting in Vietnam.

Hugh Thompson, the helicopter pilot who initially reported the killings, was awarded the Distinguished Flying Cross and his crew Bronze Stars for saving the lives of Vietnamese civilians "in the face of hostile enemy fire" and "transporting a Vietnamese child caught in an intense crossfire." Disgusted by the fabrication, feeling that his commanding officers were trying to buy his silence, Thompson threw away the citation. He remained to fly combat missions following My Lai, but without adequate cover. As his gunner stated in an interview for *60 Minutes* in 2004, "He didn't have any adequate cover in my opinion. Instead of being followed by two armed gun ships, he had another scout helicopter.... It seemed like he was really going out on a limb."[57]

Thompson's OH-23 helicopter was hit by enemy fire on eight occasions, causing the loss of his aircraft four times. On the last incident, he broke his back in the crash and was evacuated to Japan. During his rehabilitation, news of the massacre went public and Thompson was called to testify at the Peers Inquiry and before Congress, where Congressman L. Mendel Rivers, chairman of the House Armed Services subcommittee, stated that there had been no massacre and it was Thompson who should be punished for My Lai, for ordering guns turned on American soldiers.

Thompson returned to duty at Ft. Rucker, Alabama, as an instructor-pilot where he was given a direct commission as a captain. While at Rucker, he received death threats, hate mail, found mutilated animals left on his porch, and was socially ostracized. Other assignments included Ft. Jackson, South Carolina; Korea; Ft. Ord, California; Ft. Hood, Texas; and Hawaii before retiring from the Army as a major in November 1983.

Thompson took a job flying helicopters for an oil company in Louisiana and volunteered as a veterans counselor for the Louisiana Department of Veteran Affairs. It took thirty years before his actions were recognized.

On March 6, 1998, at a ceremony at the Vietnam Veterans Memorial in Washington, D.C., Major General Mike Ackerman, himself a Vietnam veteran, presented the Soldier's Medal to Thompson, his gunner Larry Colburn and posthumously to Glenn Andreotta, the crew chief, stating, "It was the ability to do the right thing, even at the risk of their personal safety that guided these soldiers to do what they did." The Soldier's Medal is the highest award for valor not involving combat, and the citation read in part: "for heroism above and beyond the call of duty while saving the lives of at least 10 Vietnamese civilians during the unlawful massacre of non-combatants by American forces at My Lai" and that they "landed in the line of fire between American ground troops and fleeing Vietnamese civilians to prevent their murder."

Thompson was invited to speak on professional military ethics at the Naval Academy in 2003, at West Point in 2005 and at the Air Force Academy, Quantico Marine Base and the U.S. Army School of the Americas. He died of cancer in Alexandria, Louisiana, on January 6, 2006, at age 62. He was buried with full military honors in Layfayette, Louisiana, including a three-volley salute and a helicopter fly-over.

Glenn Andreotta only survived My Lai by about three weeks. Assigned as a crew chief with B Company, 123rd Aviation Battalion, he was killed in action on April 8, 1968, while flying an armed reconnaissance mission aboard an OH-6 helicopter piloted by 1Lieutenant Barry Lloyd.

Flying about 10 kilometers south of Quang Ngai City, Andreotta was killed by small arms fire, taking a single shot to the head. Ground fire brought down the aircraft and the gunner, SP5 Charles M. Dutton, was shot and killed in the wreckage. Lloyd was thrown free of the aircraft and survived to be rescued by another helicopter. Andreotta is remembered on panel 48E of the Vietnam Wall.

Larry Colburn left the Army, married and had a son, Conner, before starting a medical supply business in Canton, Georgia. A little more than a week after accepting the Soldier's Medal in Washington, D.C., Colburn traveled with Thompson to My Lai on March 16, 1998, for a ceremony marking the 30th anniversary of the massacre. They both returned to My Lai three years later in 2001 for the dedication of the My Lai Peace Park where they were reunited with Do Ba, the boy they'd rescued from the ditch 33 years earlier. Following Thompson's death in 2006, Colburn returned alone to My Lai in 2008, on the 40th anniversary.

When asked in a 2009 interview if he would have fired on American soldiers, Colburn replied, "I may have been able to create a diversion somehow. Unless they fired on me, I don't think I could have. I would have probably died there. I couldn't turn a gun on an American soldier.... I remember thinking, 'How did we get into this? How did I end up here?' And to be absolutely honest with you, the first thing I thought of was my mother. 'Oh my God, Mom, get me out of here.' But, trying to think what she would want me to do, and she would've wanted me to do exactly what Mr. Thompson was doing."[58]

Because of the Army's decision not to undertake a definitive body count, the number of civilians killed at My Lai can never be determined with certainty. Estimates vary, with 347 and 504 being the most commonly cited figures. The My Lai Peace Memorial lists 504 names, with ages ranging from one to 82 years. One U.S. Army investigation arrived at the lower figure of 347 deaths, the official U.S. estimate.

On August 20, 2009, at a Kiwanis Club meeting in Columbus, Georgia, Calley, the only individual convicted for the murders in My Lai, publicly apologized for the first time and he expressed his remorse at what happened. "I feel remorse for the Vietnamese that were killed, for their families, for the American soldiers involved and their families." But the apology was marginalized when he again tried to justify his actions through obedience to orders, as he stated, "If you are asking why I did not stand up to them when I was given the orders, I will have to say that I was a second lieutenant getting orders from my commander and I followed them—foolishly, I guess."[59]

Chapter Notes

Preface

1. Randy James, "A Brief History of the Court Martial," *Time*, 18 November 2009.
2. Maj. Gen. Kenneth J. Hodson, "Perspective: The Manual for Courts-Martial—1984," *Military Law Review* 57 (Summer 1972).

Chapter 1

1. *New York City Department of Parks and Recreation*, http://www.nycgovparks.org/parks/bowlinggreen/history.
2. John Rubino, "Hyperinflation History: The Continental," http://dollarcollapse.com/articles/hyperinflation-history-the-continental/.
3. John Edwin Bakeless, *Turncoats, Traitors and Heroes: Espionage in the American Revolution* (Boston: Da Capo, 1988), 97–102.
4. Ibid., 97.
5. Donald N. Moran, "A Brief History of the Commander-in-Chief Guards with Roster," *Revolutionary War Archives*, http://www.revolutionarywararchives.org/guards-link/120-a-brief-history-of-the-commander-in-chief-guards-with-roster.
6. Ibid.
7. Bakeless, *Turncoats, Traitors and Heroes*, 98.
8. "Samuel Fraunces: Black Man or White Man?" *The President's House in Philadelphia*, http://www.ushistory.org/presidentshouse/history/fraunces.htm.
9. Carlos E. Godfrey, *The Commander-in-Chief's Guard: Revolutionary War* (Clearfield, Utah: Clearfield, 2000), 27.
10. Ibid., 104.
11. Bakeless, *Turncoats, Traitors and Heroes*.
12. *American Archives*, series 4, vol. 6, *Court Martial for the trial of Thomas Hickey and others* (Transcript), Northern Illinois University Libraries, http://lincoln.lib.niu.edu/cgi-bin/amarch/getdoc.pl?/var/lib/philologic/databases/amarch/.17512.
13. Ibid.
14. Ibid.
15. Ibid.
16. Ibid.
17. Bakeless, *Turncoats, Traitors and Heroes*, 107.
18. Godfrey, *Commander-in-Chief's Guard*, 33.
19. Thomas Miner, "Thomas Hickey and the Plot against Washington," *Hornpipe* Magazine, 5 March 2010.
20. Godfrey, *Commander-in-Chief's Guard*.
21. Alan Axelrod, *The Complete Idiot's Guide to the American Revolution* (New York: Alpha Books, 1999).

Chapter 2

1. George E. Buker, *The Penobscot Expedition: Commodore Saltonstall and the Massachusetts Conspiracy of 1779* (Annapolis, MD: Naval Institute Press, 2002).
2. Louis Arthur Norton, *Captains Contentious: The Dysfunctional Sons of the Brine* (Columbia: University of South Carolina Press, 2009).
3. Ibid.
4. "Biography of Paul Revere," Paul Revere Heritage Project, http://www.paul-revere-heritage.com/biography/pre-revolution-activities.html.
5. David Hackett Fischer, *Paul Revere's Ride* (New York: Oxford University Press, 1995).
6. Ibid.
7. Ibid.
8. Charles Ferris Gettemy, *The True Story of Paul Revere: His Midnight Ride, His Arrest and Court-Martial, His Useful Public Services* (New York: Little, Brown & Co., 1912).
9. Belle Moses, *Paul Revere: The Torch Bearer of the Revolution* (New York: D. Appleton & Co., 1912; Wright Press, 2007).
10. *The Proceeding of the General Assembly and of the Council of the State of Massachusetts*

Bay relating to the Penobscot Expedition and the orders of the Continental Navy Board to the Commander of the Naval Forces—Report of the committee appointed to inquire into the Cause of the Failure of the said Expedition (Boston: J. Gill, Printer to the General Assembly, 1782).
11. Norton, *Captains Contentious*.
12. Gardner W. Allen, *A Naval History of the American Revolution: Chapter XII, The Penobscot Expedition 1779* (Boston: Houghton, 1912), http://americanrevolution.org/navindex.html.
13. *The Proceeding of the General Assembly and of the Council of the State of Massachusetts Bay relating to the Penobscot Expedition and the orders of the Continental Navy Board to the Commander of the Naval Forces—Report of the committee appointed to inquire into the Cause of the Failure of the said Expedition*.
14. Buker, *The Penobscot Expedition*.
15. Allen, *A Naval History*.
16. Letter of Paul Revere to the Boston (MA) *Gazette*, August 9, 1779.
17. Williams and Chase, *History of Penobscot, Maine, with Illustrations and Biographical Sketches* (Cleveland, OH: Williams, Chase & Co., 1882), p. 89, quoting William D. Williamson's *History of Maine*. Williamson got this casualty information directly from General Wadsworth.
18. Allen, *A Naval History of the American Revolution*.
19. Norton, *Captains Contentious*.
20. Ibid.
21. Ibid.
22. Gettemy, *The True Story of Paul Revere*.
23. Massachusetts Archives, Vol. 145, p. 237.
24. Revere's letter to the Council, Massachusetts Archives, Vol. 226, p. 254; also Vol. 175, p. 545.
25. Gettemy, *The True Story of Paul Revere*.
26. Massachusetts Archives, Vol. 145, p. 375
27. Massachusetts Archives, Vol. 176, p. 109
28. Gettemy, *The True Story of Paul Revere*.

Chapter 3

1. "USS *Somers*," *Dictionary of American Naval Fighting Ships*, Naval Historical Center, http://www.history.navy.mil/danfs/s15/somers-ii.htm.
2. Robert McHenry, ed., *Webster's American Military Biographies* (New York: Dover, 1984).
3. David Howe, "Essay on the Legal Aspects of the *Somers* Affair and Bibliography," Naval Historical Center, http://www.history.navy.mil/wars/somers.htm.
4. Alexander S. Mackenzie and James Fenimore Cooper, *Proceedings of the naval court martial in the case of Alexander Slidell, a Commander in the Navy of the United States, &c., Including the Charges and Specifications of Charges Preferred Against Him by the Secretary of the Navy. To which is Annexed an Elaborate Review by James Fenimore Cooper* (New York: Henry G. Langley, 1844). Cornell University Library (2009)
5. Howe.
6. Ibid.
7. Ibid.
8. Ibid.
9. "USS *Somers*," *Dictionary of American Naval Fighting Ships*, Naval Historical Center, http://www.history.navy.mil/danfs/s15/somers-ii.htm.

Chapter 4

1. Douglas V. Meed, *The Mexican War 1846–1848* (Oxford, U.K.: Osprey, 2002), 26.
2. Edward S. Wallace, "The Battalion of Saint Patrick in the Mexican War," Society for Military History *Military Affairs* 14, no. 2 (Summer 1950), 85–91.
3. Ibid.
4. Ibid.
5. Jeffrey L. Hanson, "The Saint Patricks Battalion of the Mexican-American War: Why They Deserted Just to Fight On" (honors thesis, Southern Illinois University, Carbondale, 2003), available at http://opensiuc.lib.siu.edu/cgi/viewcontent.cgi?article=1323&context=uhp_theses, p. 5.
6. James Callaghan, "The San Patricios," *American Heritage* 46, no. 7 (November 1995).
7. "Skirmish at Rancho de Carricitos, Texas: The Thornton Affair, 25 April 1846," *Roll of Honor: U.S. Battle Casualties of Minor Actions*, http://www.dmwv.org/honoring/other.htm.
8. "The Mexican War," Lone Star Internet, http://www.lone-star.net/mall/texasinfo/mexicow.htm.
9. Lawrence Cress and George Wilkins, *Dispatches from the Mexican-American War* (Norman: University of Oklahoma Press, 1999).
10. Callaghan, "San Patricios."
11. Meed, *Mexican War*, 48–49.
12. Peter F. Stevens, *The Rogue's March: John Riley and the St. Patrick's Battalion* (Washington, D.C.: Brassey's, 1999), 195.
13. Ibid., 209–16.
14. Fairfax Downey, "Tragic Story of the San Patricio Battalion," *American Heritage* 6, no. 4 (June 1955).
15. Jaime Fogarty, "The San Patricio Battalion: The Irish Soldiers of Mexico," *Voices of Mexico* (April–June 2000).
16. Meed, *Mexican War*, 57.
17. Callaghan, "San Patricios."

18. Fogarty, "San Patricio Battalion."
19. Pam Nordstrom, "San Patricio Battalion: The Irish Fight for Mexico," *Handbook of Texas Online*, http://www.tshaonline.org/handbook/online/articles/qis01.
20. Stevens, *Rogue's March*, 248.
21. Niles National Register, s.v. "9 October 1847," http://nilesregister.com.
22. Stevens, *Rogue's March*, 262.
23. Ibid., 264–64.
24. Ibid., 264.
25. Wallace, "Battalion of Saint Patrick in the Mexican War," 85–91.
26. Stevens, *Rogue's March*, 292.

Chapter 5

1. John A. Marshall, *American Bastille: A History of the Illegal Arrests and Imprisonment of American Citizens during the Late Civil War* (n.p.: T. W. Hartley, 1869), 71–90.
2. *History of Huntington County Indiana; From the Earliest Time to the Present, With Biographical Sketches, Notes, Etc., Together With a Short History of the Northwest, the Indiana Territory, and the State of Indiana* (n.p.: Walsworth, 1887), 514–15.
3. Allan Nevins, "The Case of the Copperhead Conspirator," *University of Minnesota: Department of Sociology*, http://www.soc.umn.edu/~samaha/cases/milligan_copperhead_conspirator.htm.
4. Ibid.
5. Curtis A. Bradley, "The Story of Ex Parte Milligan: Military Trials, Enemy Combatants and Congressional Authorization," *University of Virginia: School of Law*, http://www.law.virginia.edu/pdf/workshops/0708/bradley.pdf, p. 12–13.
6. Ibid.
7. *Ex Parte Milligan 71 U.S. 2 (4 Wall) 1866*.
8. Bradley, "Story of *Ex Parte Milligan*," p. 9–10.
9. Ibid., p. 16.

Chapter 6

1. James M. Page and Michael J. Haley, *The True Story of Andersonville Prison: A Defense of Major Henry Wirz* (n.p.: Neale, 1908; General Books, 2009), 183.
2. Ibid., 183–84.
3. Terry G. Scriber and Theresa Arnold-Scriber, *The Fourth Louisiana Battalion in the Civil War: A History and Roster* (Jefferson, NC: McFarland, October 2007), 15.
4. Page and Haley, *True Story of Andersonville Prison*, 186.
5. Robert McHenry, *Webster's American Military Biographies* (New York: Dover, 1978), 485.
6. David J. Coles, ed., *Encyclopedia of the American Civil War: A Political, Social, and Military History* (New York: W. W. Norton, 2002), 48–51.
7. Page and Haley, *True Story of Andersonville Prison*, 186.
8. John W. Chambers, ed., *Oxford Companion to American Military History* (Oxford: Oxford University Press, 1999), 560.
9. Ken Burns, *The Civil War: The Complete Text of the Bestselling Narrative History of the Civil War—Based on the Celebrated PBS Television Series* (New York: Vintage, MTI edition, September 1994), 285.
10. "Andersonville Prison," *Civil War Trust*, http://www.civilwar.org/education/history/warfare-and-logistics/warfare/andersonville.html.
11. Samuel S. Boggs, *Eighteen Months a Prisoner under the Rebel Flag* (Whitefish, Mont.: Kessinger, 2008), 35–36.
12. Ibid.
13. Page and Haley, *True Story of Andersonville Prison*, 166–67.
14. Norton Parker Chipman, *The Tragedy of Andersonville: Trial of Captain Henry Wirz, the Prison Keeper* (Whitefish, Mont.: Kessinger, 2008), 46–49.
15. Ibid.
16. Ibid.
17. Carfy Mulligan, ink drawings of prisoner, counsel, and court, *Boston Advertiser*, 21 August 1865.
18. "The Rebel Assassins. Trial of Henry Wirz, the Andersonville Jailor," special dispatch, *New-York Times*, 21 August 1865, http://www.nytimes.com/1865/08/22/news/rebel-assassins-trial-henry-wirz-andersonville-jailor-meeting-organization.html.
19. Mulligan, ink drawings.
20. General Court Martial Orders No. 607, War Department, *Adjutant-General's Office, Washington, D.C., 6 November 1865*, available at http://www.civilwarhome.com/chargesandspecifications.htm.
21. Carolyn Kleiner, "The Demon of Andersonville," *Legal Affairs* (September/October 2002).
22. Ibid.
23. Bill Carnes and Troy Drew, "The Trial of Captain Henry Wirz: A Brief Summary," http://law2.umkc.edu/faculty/projects/ftrials/wirz/INTRO.HTM.
24. William Marvel, *Andersonville: The Last Depot* (Chapel Hill: University of North Carolina Press, 2006), 244–46.
25. Page and Haley, *The True Story of Andersonville Prison*, 191–204.

26. Ibid.
27. Page and Haley, *True Story of Andersonville Prison*, 205–6.
28. Kleiner, "Demon of Andersonville."
29. Page and Haley, *True Story of Andersonville Prison*, 212–15.
30. "Execution of Wirz; Closing Scenes in the Life of the Andersonville Jailor," New York Times, 10 November 1865, http://www.nytimes.com/1865/11/11/news/execution-wirz-closing-scenes-life-andersonville-jailor-farewell-interview-with.html.
31. "The Final Intercession for Wirz: His Counsel Has an Interview with the President," *New York Times*, 11 November 1865, http://www.nytimes.com/1865/11/11/news/final-intercession-for-wirz-his-counsel-has-interview-with-president-letter-wirz.html.
32. Ibid.
33. "Execution of Wirz."
34. Joan M. Dixon, *The Civil War Years, vol. 2, July 1, 1863–December 31, 1865*, National Intelligencer Newspaper Abstracts Special Edition (Berwyn Heights, Md.: Heritage Books, 2009).
35. Page and Haley, *True Story of Andersonville Prison*, 221.
36. "The Prison Camp at Andersonville: Rock Island Prison," National Park Service Civil War Series, http://www.nps.gov/history/history/online_books/civil_war_series/5/sec6.htm.

Chapter 7

1. Todd S. Purdum, "115 Years Late, He Won His Bars," *New York Times*, 30 July 1995.
2. John F. Marszalek, Jr., *Assault at West Point: The Court Martial of Johnson Whittaker* (New York: Collier Books, 1972), 43.
3. Chambers, Oxford Companion to *American Military History*, 585.
4. Marszalek, Jr., Assault at West Point, 36.
5. Capt. Matt Oliver, "Society's Sacrifice: The First Black Cadet at West Point, James Webster Smith" (history paper, LD 720, U.S. Military Academy, n.d.), available at http://digital-library.usma.edu/libmedia/archives/toep/first_black_cadet_wp_james_webster_smith.pdf, p. 5–7.
6. Ibid.
7. Ibid., p. 3–4.
8. Thomas J. Fleming, *West Point: The Men and Times of the United States Military Academy* (New York: William Morrow, 1969).
9. Oliver, "Society's Sacrifice," p. 5–7.
10. Ibid.
11. William P. Vaughn, "West Point and the First Negro Cadet," *Military Affairs* (October 1971), 100–102.

12. Gail L. Buckley, *American Patriots: The Story of Blacks in the Military from the Revolution to Desert Storm* (New York: Random House, 2002), 120–22.
13. John F. Marszalek Jr., "A Black Cadet at West Point," *American Heritage* 22, no. 5 (August 1971).
14. Ibid.
15. Ibid.
16. Ibid.
17. Records of the Office of the Judge Advocate, QQ1858 Part 1, 9–10 April 1880, National Archives and Records Administration, College Park, Md.
18. Marszalek, "Black Cadet at West Point."
19. Marszalek, *Assault at West Point*, 63.
20. Ibid., 72.
21. Ibid., 73.
22. Marszalek, *Assault at West Point*, 116.
23. Records of the Office of the Judge Advocate.
24. Marszalek, "Black Cadet at West Point."
25. Marszalek, *Assault at West Point*, 153.
26. John T. Hubbell and James W. Geary, eds., *Biographical Dictionary of the Union: Northern Leaders of the Civil War* (Westport, Conn.: Greenwood, 1995), 53–54.
27. Ibid., 517–18.
28. "Brig. Gen. E. V. Sumner Dies: Veteran of Civil and Indian Wars, Was 77 Years Old," *New York Times*, 25 August 1912.
29. "The Court-Martial Meets and Adjourns for Two Weeks," *New York Times*, 21 January 1881.
30. General Court-Martial Orders, No. 18, Headquarters of the Army, Adjutant General's Office, Washington, D.C., 22 March 1882, U.S. Army Center of Military History, Fort McNair, Washington, D.C.
31. "West Point's First Black Cadet Gets Commission," *Jet*, 13 October 1997.

Chapter 8

1. "Buffalo Soldiers," http://www.africanamericanhistoryonline.com/buffalosoldiers.php.
2. Ben Fogelberg, *Western Voices: 125 Years of Colorado Writing* (Golden, Colo.: Fulcrum, for the Colorado Historical Society, 2004), 266.
3. Garna L. Christian, *Black Soldiers in Jim Crow Texas, 1899–1917* (College Station: Texas A&M University Press, 1995), 174.
4. Walter C. Rucker and James N. Upton, *Encyclopedia of American Race Riots* (Westport, Conn.: Greenwood, 2006), 77–83.
5. "24th Infantry Regiment (Deuce Four)," http://www.25thida.org/24thinf.html.
6. Rucker and Upton, *Encyclopedia of American Race Riots*, 283–86.

7. Tabitha C. Wang, "East St. Louis Race Riot: July 2, 1917," *BlackPast.org: Remembered and Reclaimed*, http://www.blackpast.org/aah/east-st-louis-race-riot-july-2-1917.
8. Martha Gruening, "Houston: An NAACP Investigation," Crisis, November 1917, http://books.google.com/books?id=O1oEAAAAMBAJ&pg=PA14&dq=Houston+Gruening&hl=en&ei=gu1UTPiBLJGWsgOt5LTaAg&sa=X&oi=book_result&ct=result&resnum=3&ved=0CC8Q6AEwAg#v=onepage&q&f=false, p. 14–19.
9. Ibid.
10. "Army Riot at Houston Cost [sic] 17 Lives: Negro Troops Ordered Out of State, Congress Will Take Up Race Question," *New York Times*, 25 August 1917.
11. Bruce A. Glasrud and Michael N. Searles, *Buffalo Soldiers in the West: A Black Soldiers Anthology* (College Station: Texas A&M University Press, 2007), 197–211.
12. Ibid.
13. Christian, *Black Soldiers in Jim Crow Texas*, 153–55; "Army Riot at Houston Cost 17 Lives."
14. Christian, *Black Soldiers in Jim Crow Texas*, 153–55.
15. Ibid.
16. "Rioters to Face Military Court: Negro Soldiers Involved in the Houston Murders to Be Dealt with under Army Law," *New York Times*, 26 August 1917.
17. Ibid.
18. Rucker and Upton, *Encyclopedia of American Race Riots*, 287–88, 576.
19. Ibid.
20. Robert V. Haynes, "A Night of Violence: The Houston Riot of 1917," *Southwestern Historical Quarterly* 76 (1973), 418–39.
21. Rucker and Upton, *Encyclopedia of American Race Riots*.
22. Haynes, "Night of Violence," 418–39.
23. Rucker and Upton, *Encyclopedia of American Race Riots*, 287–88, 576.
24. Glasrud and Searles, *Buffalo Soldiers in the West*, 197–211.

Chapter 9

1. "FBI History: Famous Cases," *George John Dasch and the Nazi Saboteurs*, http://www.fbi.gov/about-us/history/famous-cases/nazi-saboteurs/george-john-dasch-and-the-nazi-saboteurs.
2. Harvey Ardman, "World War II: German Saboteurs Invade America in 1942," *World War II*, 12 June 2006, http://www.historynet.com/world-war-ii-german-saboteurs-invade-america-in-1942.htm.
3. Alex Abella and Gordon Scott, *Shadow Enemies: Hitler's Secret Terrorist Plot against the United States* (Guilford, Conn.: Globe Pequot, 2003), 66.
4. W. A. Swanberg, "The Spies Who Came In from the Sea," *American Heritage* 21, no. 3 (April 1970).
5. Pierce O'Donnell, *In Time of War: Hitler's Terrorist Attack on America* (New York: New Press, 2005), 28.
6. Abella and Scott, *Shadow Enemies*, 20–24.
7. Ibid.
8. O'Donnell, *In Time of War*, 32–33.
9. Ibid.
10. "Counter-Intelligence in WW II: CI Reader Volume 2, Chapter 1," *National Counter-Intelligence Center*, http://www.fas.org/irp/ops/ci/docs/ci2/2ch1_d.htm.
11. Ibid.
12. Ibid.
13. Louis Fisher, *Military Tribunals: The Quirin Precedent* (Washington, D.C.: Library of Congress, Congressional Research Service, 26 March 2002).
14. Michael Dobbs, *The Nazi Raid on America* (New York: Random House, 2005), 67–68.
15. Ibid., 67–68.
16. "U-202," *U-Boat.net*, http://www.Uboat.net/boats/u202.htm.
17. Ardman, "German Saboteurs Invade America in 1942."
18. Eastern Sea Frontier War Diary, chap. 4, June 1942, 1–12, Military Reference Branch, National Archives and Records Administration, College Park, Md.
19. Abella and Scott, *Shadow Enemies*, 9.
20. "US Coast Guard Oral History Project: John C. Cullen," *United States Coast Guard*, http://www.uscg.mil/history/weboralhistory/CullenJohn03302006.pdf, p. 9–10.
21. David Alan Johnson, *Betrayal: The True Story of J. Edgar Hoover and the Nazi Saboteurs Captured During WWII* (New York: Hippocrene Books, 2007), 77.
22. "German Espionage and Sabotage against the U.S. in World War II," Eastern Sea Frontier War Diary, http://www.history.navy.mil/faqs/faq114-3.htm.
23. Johnson, *Betrayal*, 92–94.
24. "German Espionage and Sabotage against the U.S. in World War II."
25. Ibid.
26. Johnson, *Betrayal*, 78.
27. Fisher, *Military Tribunals*.
28. Johnson, *Betrayal*, 152.
29. Fred L. Borch, "Sitting in Judgement," *Prologue* (Summer 2009), http://www.loc.gov/rr/frd/Military_Law/pdf/Sitting-in-Judgment.pdf, p. 36–37.
30. Fisher, *Military Tribunals*.
31. In 10 USC § 821 (1994), Congress takes

notice of the law of war in this manner: "The provisions of this chapter conferring jurisdiction upon courts-martial do not deprive military commissions, provost courts, or other military tribunals of concurrent jurisdiction with respect to offenders or offenses that by statute or by the law of war may be tried by military commissions, provost courts, or other military tribunals."
32. Fisher, *Military Tribunals*.
33. Ibid.
34. Gary Cohen, "The Keystone Kommandos," *Atlantic Monthly*, February 2002.
35. *Ex Parte Quirin 317 US.1*: Brief in Support of Petition for Writ of Habeas Corpus.
36. Ibid.
37. *Ex Parte Quirin 317 US.1*: Respondent's answer to Petitions.
38. Swanberg, "Spies Who Came In from the Sea."
39. Abella and Scott, *Shadow Enemies*, 196.
40. "Nazi Saboteurs Electrocuted," *Milwaukee Journal*, 8 August 1942.
41. "U-202."
42. "U-584," *U-Boat.net*, http://www.uboat.net/boats/u584.htm.

17. "Court Martial at Fort Lawton," Seattle Post Intelligencer, 21 November 1944.
18. Casey McNerthney, "Apology 64 Years in the Making for Black Soldiers Wrongfully Convicted," *Seattle Post Intelligencer*, 23 July 2008.
19. Ibid.
20. Moreo, *Riot at Fort Lawton*, 28.
21. "28 Convicted by Court Martial," *Milwaukee (Wisc.) Journal*, 18 December 1944.
22. "Negro Asks Support to End Racial Bias," *Christian Science Monitor*, 20 December 1944.
23. Hamann, *On American Soil*, 299.
24. "Desegregation of the Armed Forces," Harry S. Truman Library and Museum http://www.trumanlibrary.org/whistlestop/study_collections/desegregation/large/index.php.
25. "Black Soldiers' Convictions in WWII May Be Up for Review," *Seattle Times*, 9 June 2006.
26. Kim Murphy, "Justice, 64 Years Later," *Los Angeles Times*, 27 July 2008.
27. Keith Ervin, "Army Apologizes to Soldiers Convicted after Fort Lawton Riot," *Seattle Times*, 27 July 2008.

Chapter 10

1. Jack Hamann, *On American Soil: How Justice Became a Casualty of World War II* (Chapel Hill, N.C.: Algonquin Books, 2005), 43–44.
2. "Record Army Trial Opens: 42 Are Accused in Camp Rioting," *Miami (Fla.) News*, 25 November 1944.
3. Dominic Moreo, *Riot at Fort Lawton* (n.p.: iUniverse [privately published], 2005), 13.
4. Ibid., 43.
5. "Record Army Trial Opens."
6. Moreo, *Riot at Fort Lawton*, 144.
7. Ibid., 25.
8. Investigation of Attack on Italian Service Unit Personnel by American Soldiers at Ft. Lawton Washington, file 333.9, Ft. Lawton—Formerly Confidential General Correspondence 1939–47, Record Group 159, Records of the Inspector General, National Archives and Records Administration, College Park, Md.
9. Ibid.
10. Moreo, *Riot at Fort Lawton*, 65.
11. Hamann, *On American Soil*, 112.
12. "Put Down Italian Prisoner Riot," *Ellensburg (Wash.) Daily Record*, 18 August 1944.
13. Hamann, *On American Soil*, 118.
14. Ibid.
15. Ibid., 277.
16. "Negro Soldiers Plead Not Guilty in Court Martial: All charged with Rioting, Three Face Murder Charges," *Spartanburg (S.C.) Herald Journal*, 17 November 1944.

Chapter 11

1. "Port Chicago Naval Magazine Explosion on 17 July 1944: Court of Inquiry: Finding of Facts, Opinion and Recommendations," *Naval History and Heritage Command*, http://www.history.navy.mil/faqs/faq80–4a.htm.
2. Ibid.
3. Christopher Bell and Bruce A. Elleman, *Naval Mutinies of the Twentieth Century: An International Perspective* (New York, Routledge, 2003), 159–75.
4. "Port Chicago Naval Magazine Explosion on 17 July 1944."
5. "African Americans at War," in *The Oxford Companion to World War II*, ed. I. C. B. Dear and M. R. D. Foot (Oxford, U.K.: Oxford University Press, 1995).
6. Robert L. Allen, *The Port Chicago Mutiny: The Story of the Largest Mass Mutiny Trial in U.S. Naval History* (Berkeley, Calif.: Heyday Books, 2006), 30–31.
7. "Port Chicago Naval Magazine Explosion on 17 July 1944."
8. Ibid.
9. Ibid.
10. Ibid.
11. Ray Jones and Joe Lubow, *Disasters and Heroic Rescues of California: True Stories of Tragedy and Survival* (Guilford, Conn.: Globe Pequot, 1 January 2006), 89–97.
12. "Port Chicago Naval Magazine Explosion on 17 July 1944."

13. Ibid., [emphasis added].
14. Allen, *Port Chicago Mutiny*, 95.
15. Ibid., 84.
16. Ibid., 85.
17. Leonard F. Guttridge, *Mutiny: A History of Naval Insurrection* (Annapolis, Md.: Naval Institute Press, 2006), 204–15.
18. "Hugo Wilson Osterhaus," *Arlington National Cemetery*, http://www.arlingtoncemetery.net/hwosterhaus2.htm.
19. Allen, *Port Chicago Mutiny*, 122.
20. Guttridge, *Mutiny*, 204–15.
21. Allen, *Port Chicago Mutiny*, 118.
22. "50 Navy Men Sentenced on Mutiny Count," *Milwaukee (Wisc.) Journal*, 18 November 1944.
23. "Sentences of 86 Seamen on Coast, Guam Voided" *(Baltimore, Md.) Afro-American*, 12 January 1946.
24. Ibid.
25. "Navy Reviews Courts Martial of Black Sailors," Tuscaloosa (Ala.) News, 6 January 1994; Bell and Elleman, *Naval Mutinies of the Twentieth Century*, 159–74.
26. "Navy Won't Overturn the Courts-Martial of 258 Black Sailors in World War II," Philadelphia Inquirer, 7 January 1994.
27. "The Nation," *Baltimore (Md.) Sun*, 7 January 1994.
28. Katherine Bishop, "Exoneration Sought in Mutiny of '44," *New York Times*, 12 August 1990.
29. Ibid.
30. William Glaberson, "Old Sailor Turns to Clinton to Lose Label of a Mutineer," *New York Times*, 23 June 1999.
31. William Glaberson, "Sailor from Mutiny in '44 Wins a Presidential Pardon," *New York Times*, 24 December 1999.

Chapter 12

1. Jonathan Sutherland, *African-Americans at War: An Encyclopedia* (Santa Barbara, Calif.: ABC-CLIO, December 2003), vol. 1.
2. Gail Buckley, *American Patriots: The Story of Blacks in the Military from the Revolution to Desert Storm* (New York: Random House, 2001), 282–84.
3. Gar Smith, "The Real Story of the Tuskegee Airmen," *The Berkeley Daily Planet*, February 17, 2012. http://www.berkeleydailyplanet.com/issue/2012-02-17/article/39323.
4. Lynn M. Homan and Thomas Reilly, *Tuskegee Airmen: American Heroes* (Mount Pleasant, S.C.: Arcadia, November 1998), 27.
5. Sutherland, *African-Americans at War*.
6. Ibid.
7. Maj. John D. Murphy, "The Freeman Field Mutiny: A Study in Leadership" (research paper AU/ACSC/0429/97–03, Air Command and Staff College, Maxwell Air Force Base, Ala., 1997).
8. Alan L. Gropman, *The Air Force Integrates 1945–1964*, Special Studies (Washington, D.C.: Office of Air Force History and Museums, June 1986).
9. Ibid.
10. Lt. Col James C. Warren, *The Tuskegee Airmen Mutiny at Freeman Field* (Vacaville, Calif.:, Conyers, 1995), 21–22.
11. Ibid., 22–24.
12. Gropman, *Air Force Integrates 1945–1964*.
13. Warren, *Tuskegee Airmen Mutiny at Freeman Field*, 26.
14. Ibid., 25.
15. Al Siebert, "A Brief History on Freeman Field," *Freeman Field Flying Association*, www.freemanfield.org/images/data/freemanhistory.pdf, p. 1–3.
16. Warren, *Tuskegee Airmen Mutiny at Freeman Field*, 30.
17. Murphy, "Freeman Field Mutiny."
18. Sutherland, *African-Americans at War*.
19. J. Todd Moye, *Freedom Flyers: The Tuskegee Airmen of World War II* (Oxford, U.K.: Oxford University Press, 2010), 129.
20. Warren, *Tuskegee Airmen Mutiny at Freeman Field*, 6–8.
21. Ibid.
22. Lynn M. Homan and Thomas Reilly, *Black Knights: The Story of the Tuskegee Airmen* (Gretna, La.: Pelican, January 2001), 190.
23. Cited in (among other sources) Gropman, *Air Force Integrates 1945–1964*, 23.
24. Moye, *Freedom Flyers*, 135.
25. Ibid., 137.
26. Warren, *Tuskegee Airmen Mutiny at Freeman Field*, 102.
27. Ibid., 137.
28. Sutherland, *African-Americans at War*.
29. Warren, *Tuskegee Airmen Mutiny at Freeman Field*, 154.
30. Ibid., 138.
31. Homan and Thomas Reilly, *Black Knights*, 203.
32. Herbert M. Frisby, "Record of Court-Martial of Godman Field Officers Reads Like a Novel" *(Baltimore, Md.) Afro-American*, 14 July 1945.
33. Herbert M. Frisby, "Two Cleared: Third Faces Trial Today" *(Baltimore, Md.) Afro-American*, 3 July 1945.
34. Lawrence P. Scott and William M. Womack, *Double V: The Civil Rights Struggle of the Tuskegee Airmen* (East Lansing: Michigan State University Press, 1998), 247.
35. Richard Goldstein, "Alfred McKensie, Who Fought for Rights, Dies at 80," *New York Times*, 11 April 1998.

Chapter 13

1. Chambers, *Oxford Companion to American Military History*.
2. William Bradford Huie, *The Execution of Private Slovik* (New York: Dell, 1954), 103.
3. Ibid., 154.
4. 28th Infantry Division Association, http://28thinfantrydivisionassoc.org/historic_events.html.
5. Huie, *Execution of Private Slovik*, 132–34.
6. Ibid., 141.
7. Benedict B. Kimmelman, "The Example of Private Slovik," *American Heritage* 38, no. 6 (September/October 1987).
8. Garry Henbest, "Henbest Took Private Slovik's Confession: Southwest Missouri Man Witness to Infamous Desertion Case," *Springdale (Ark.) Morning News*, 17 July 2006.
9. Huie, *Execution of Private Slovik*, 152–54.
10. Ibid., 150.
11. Ibid.
12. Ibid., 154.
13. Charles B. MacDonald, *The Battle of the Huertgen Forest* (Philadelphia: University of Pennsylvania Press, 2003), 196.
14. "The Fight for Hurtgen Forest," *U.S. Army Medical Department, Office of Medical History*, http://history.amedd.army.mil/booksdocs/wwii/HuertgenForest/HF.htm.
15. Dr. Jerold E. Brown, *Combined Arms in Battle Since 1939* (Fort Leavenworth, Kans.: U.S. Army Command and General Staff College, 1992), chap 11 (Discipline).
16. Huie, *Execution of Private Slovik*, 169.
17. Ibid., 170.
18. Ibid., 177.
19. "Eddie Slovik Court Martial: 1944: Case Reviewed Extensively," *Law Library: American Law and Legal Information*, http://law.jrank.org/pages/2983/Eddie-Slovik-Court-Martial-1944-Case-Reviewed-Extensively.html.
20. Charles Whiting, *America's Forgotten Army: The True Story of the U.S. Seventh Army in World War II* (New York: St. Martin's, 2001), 150.
21. Huie, *Execution of Private Slovik*, 200–204.
22. Whiting, *America's Forgotten Army*, 153.
23. Huie, *Execution of Private Slovik*, 235.
24. "Private Slovik Finally Rejoins Beloved Bride Antoinette," *Houston (Tex.) Chronicle*, 12 July 1987.
25. Huie, *Execution of Private Slovik*, 190–92.
26. Whiting, *America's Forgotten Army*, 153.

Sidebar

1. "Civil Trials for Civilians," *Time*, 21 November 1955.
2. Elizabeth Dinan, "Portsmouth Attorney Pens Book of Military Murder in South Korea: Attorney Shares Tale of Korean War Incident," *Seacoastonline*. http://www.seacoastonline.com/articles/20100613-NEWS-6130334.
3. "*Toth v. Quarles:* A Death in Korea, a Gap in Jurisdiction," *Law Library: American Law and Legal Information*, http://law.jrank.org/pages/13647/Toth-v-Quarles.html [hereafter "A Gap in Jurisdiction"].
4. "Supreme Court Sets Toth Hearing for October 10," *Pittsburgh (Pa.) Press*, 17 September 1955.
5. "Toth Freed by Supreme Court: Oakland Ex-GI Will Not Face Court Martial," *Pittsburgh (Pa.) Post Gazette*, 8 November 1955.
6. *Toth V. Quarles*. 350 U.S. 11 (1955).
7. "A Gap in Jurisdiction."

Chapter 14

1. Charles Robert Jenkins and Jim Frederick, *The Reluctant Communist: My Desertion, Court Martial and Forty-Year Imprisonment in North Korea* (Berkeley: University of California Press, 2009), 76.
2. Ibid., 9.
3. Graeme Wood, "The U.S. Soldier Who Defected to North Korea," *Atlantic*, September 2013.
4. Jenkins and Frederick, *Reluctant Communist*, 94–97.
5. John M. Glionna, "Second Life of G.I. Who Deserted to North Korea," *Los Angeles Times*, 16 July 2009.
6. Ibid.
7. Adam Westlake, "North Korean Abductee Calls for the Release of Other Japanese Nationals," *Japan Daily Press*, 8 October 2012.
8. Sarah Buckley, "North Korea's Mystery Guest (Charles Robert Jenkins)," *BBC Online*, 2 June 2004, http://www.freerepublic.com/focus/f-news/1146241/posts.
9. Jenkins and Frederick, *Reluctant Communist*, 179–80.
10. Blaine Harden, "American Freed by N. Korea Relishes Celebrity in Japan," *Washington Post*, 6 April 2008.

Chapter 15

1. Grace Sevy, ed., *The American Experience in Vietnam: A Reader* (Norman Press, 1989).
2. James S. Olson and Randy Roberts, *My Lai: A Brief History with Documents* (Bedford/St. Martin's; illustrated edition, 1998).
3. "An Average American Boy?" *Time*, Dec. 5, 1969.
4. Summary Report, Peers Commission,

Department of the Army Review of the Preliminary Investigations in the My Lai Incident.
  5. Michael Bilton and Kevin Sim, *Four Hours in My Lai* (Viking Adult, 1992).
  6. Olson and Roberts.
  7. Summary Report, Peers Commission
  8. Summary of Rapes, Peers Commission, *Department of the Army Review of the Preliminary Investigations in the My Lai Incident.*
  9. Testimony of Dennis Conti, Peers Commission.
  10. Statement of Varnado Simpson to Reis R. Kash, CID on November 9, 1969, at Jackson, Mississippi. My Lai Investigation File # 69-CID0011-00069, Ft. Belvoir, VA.
  11. Statement of Herbert Carter, My Lai Investigation File #69-CID0011-00074 Ft. Belvoir, VA.
  12. Ibid.
  13. "The Villagers of My Lai," University of Missouri Kansas City, http://www.law.umkc.edu/faculty/projects/ftrials/mylai/myl_bvillagers.htm.
  14. Hugh Thompson, My Lai 25 Years After: Facing the Darkness, Healing the Wounds, Conference at Tulane University, New Orleans, December 2, 1994.
  15. "Hugh Thompson's Crewmember Remembers Helping to Stop the My Lai Massacre," *Democracy Now*, National Public Radio, January 18, 2006.
  16. Hugh Thompson, My Lai 25 Years After: Facing the Darkness, Healing the Wounds, Conference at Tulane University, New Orleans, December 2, 1994.
  17. Trent Angers, *The Forgotten Hero of My Lai: The Hugh Thompson Story* (Acadian House Publishing, 1999).
  18. "Hugh Thompson's Crewmember Remembers Helping to Stop the My Lai Massacre."
  19. Ibid.
  20. Testimony of Hugh Thompson Jr, Peers Commission.
  21. Ibid.
  22. Summary Report, Peers Commission.
  23. Ibid.
  24. Joseph Goldstein, Jack Schwartz, and Burke Marshall, *The My Lai Massacre and Its Cover-up: Beyond the Reach of the Law. The Peers Report with a Supplement and Introductory Essay on the Limits of Law* (New York: The Free Press, 1976).
  25. LTC Barker's Combat Action Report to 11th Bde HQ, dated March 28, 1968.
  26. Robert Parry, *Colin Powell and the Lessons of My Lai*, www.consortiumnews.com/2009/090409.html.
  27. Colin Powell, *My American Journey: An Autobiography* (New York: Random House, 1995).

  28. Robert Parry, *Colin Powell and the Lessons of My Lai.*
  29. Ronald Ridenhour, Letter of March 29, 1969, sent to the President, Congress et al., http://www.law.umkc.edu/faculty/projects/ftrials/mylai/ridenhour_ltr.html.
  30. Ronald Ridenhour, My Lai 25 Years After: Facing the Darkness, Healing the Wounds, Conference at Tulane University, New Orleans, December 2, 1994.
  31. Riddenhour, Letter.
  32. Ronald Ridenhour, My Lai 25 Years After: Facing the Darkness, Healing the Wounds, Conference at Tulane University, New Orleans, December 2, 1994.
  33. My Lai timeline, http://www.pbs.org/wgbh/americanexperience/features/timeline/mylai-massacre/.
  34. Seymour Hersh, "Lieutenant Accused of Murdering 109 Civilians," *St. Louis Post-Dispatch*, November 13, 1969.
  35. Captain Norman G. Cooper, "My Lai and Military Justice—To What Effect," *Military Law Review* Vol. 59, Winter 1973.
  36. My Lai timeline, http://www.pbs.org/wgbh/americanexperience/features/timeline/mylai-massacre/.
  37. *Toth v. Quarles. 350 U.S. 11 (1955)* (See Sidebar)
  38. "14 Army Officers Charged in My Lai Massacre 'Cover-up,'" Daytona Beach (FL) *Morning Journal*, March 18, 1970.
  39. "Charges Dropped for Three," *Tri-City Herald* (WA), June 23, 1970.
  40. Seymour M. Hersh, "The Investigation of Son My," *The New Yorker*, Jan. 29, 1972.
  41. "One Not Guilty for My Lai," *Time*, November 30, 1970.
  42. "A Question of Orders," *Time*, January 25, 1971.
  43. Captain Norman G. Cooper, "My Lai and Military Justice—To What Effect?" *Military Law Review* Vol. 59, Winter 1973.
  44. "Jury Selected," *Spokesman Review* (Spokane WA), Nov. 17, 1970.
  45. "The Nation: Portrait of a Prosecutor," *Time*, April 19, 1971.
  46. Michael R. Belknap, *The Vietnam War on Trial: The My Lai Massacre and the Court-Martial of Lieutenant Calley* (University of Kansas Press, 2002).
  47. "The Nation: Who Is Responsible for My Lai?" *Time*, March 8, 1971.
  48. Ibid.
  49. Lawrence Rockwood, *Walking Away from Nuremberg: Just War and the Doctrine of Command Responsibility* (University of Massachusetts Press, 2007).
  50. Homer Bigart, "Prosecution Says That Medina Chose Not to Intervene at My Lai," *New York Times*, August 17, 1971.

51. Homer Bigart, "Medina Is Placed at Slaying Scene," *New York Times*, August 19, 1971.
52. Homer Bigart, "Medina Found Not Guilty of All Charges on My Lai," *New York Times*, September 23, 1971.
53. David Goeller, "Colonel Henderson Is Acquitted of My Lai Cover-up Charges," *Washington Post*, December 18, 1971.
54. Ibid.
55. "General Lauds Decision to Trim Calley Sentence," *Chicago Tribune*, April 18, 1974.
56. "Ex Army Lt. Calley Wins Parole After Long Battle," *The Bryan (OH) Times*, November 9, 1974.
57. Rebecca Leung, "An American Hero, Vietnam Veteran Speaks Out About My Lai," CBS Worldwide, http://www.cbsnews.com/stories/2004/05/06/60minutes/main615997.shtml.
58. Interview with Larry Coburn, *The American Experience—My Lai*, PBS, http://www.pbs.org/wgbh/americanexperience/featu res/interview/mylai-colburn/.
59. "Calley Apologizes for Role in My Lai Massacre: After Nearly 40 Years of Silence, Convicted Ex-Army Officer Says He's Sorry," Associated Press, August 21, 2009.

Bibliography

Abella, Alex, and Gordon Scott. *Shadow Enemies: Hitler's Secret Terrorist Plot Against the United States*. Globe Pequot, 2003.

African Americans at War. The Oxford Companion to World War II. Oxford University Press, 1995.

Allen, Robert L. *The Port Chicago Mutiny: The Story of the Largest Mass Mutiny Trial in U.S. Naval History*. Berkeley, CA: Heyday Books, 2006.

Angers, Trent. *The Forgotten Hero of My Lai: The Hugh Thompson Story*. Acadian House Publishing, 1999.

Ardman, Harvey. "World War II: German Saboteurs Invade America in 1942." *World War II* magazine, Feb. 1997.

Bakeless, John Edwin. *Turncoats, Traitors and Heroes: Espionage in the American Revolution*. Da Capo Press, 1988.

Belknap, Michael R. *The Vietnam War on Trial: The My Lai Massacre and the Court-Martial of Lieutenant Calley*. University of Kansas Press, 2002.

Bell, C., and Bruce A. Elleman. *Naval Mutinies of the Twentieth Century: An International Perspective*. Routledge, 2003.

Bigart, Homer. "Prosecution Says That Medina Chose Not to Intervene at My Lai." *New York Times*, August 17, 1971.

Bilton, Michael, and Kevin Sim. *Four Hours in My Lai*. Viking Adult, 1992.

Bishop, Katherine. "Exoneration Sought in Mutiny of '44." *New York Times*, August 12, 1990.

Boggs, Samuel S. *Eighteen Months a Prisoner Under the Rebel Flag*. Kessinger Publishing, 2008.

Buckley, Gail. *American Patriots: The Story of Blacks in the Military from the Revolution to Desert Storm*. New York: Random House, 2001.

Buker, George E. *The Penobscot Expedition: Commodore Saltonstall and the Massachusetts Conspiracy of 1779*. Annapolis, MD: Naval Institute Press, 2002.

Callaghan, James. "The San Patricios." *American Heritage Magazine* Volume 46, Issue 7, November 1995.

Chambers, John Whiteclay, II, ed. *The Oxford Companion to American Military History*. New York: Oxford University Press, 1999.

Chipman, Norton Parker. *The Tragedy of Andersonville: Trial of Captain Henry Wirz, the Prison Keeper*. Kessinger Publishing, 2008.

Christian, Garna L. *Black Soldiers in Jim Crow Texas, 1899–1917*. College Park: Texas A&M University Press, 1995.

Cohen, Gary. "The Keystone Kommandos." *Atlantic Monthly*, February 2002.

Coles, David J., ed. *Encyclopedia of the American Civil War: A Political, Social, and Military History* W. W. Norton & Company, 2002.

Cooper, Captain Norman G. "My Lai and Military Justice: To What Effect." *Military Law Review* Vol. 59, HQ Dept of the Army, Washington, D.C., Winter 1973.

Cress, Lawrence, and George Wilkins. *Dispatches from the Mexican-American War*. Norman: University of Oklahoma Press, 1999.

Dobbs, Michael. *The Nazi Raid on America*. Random House, 2005.

Downey, Fairfax. "Tragic Story of the San Patricio Battalion." *American Heritage Magazine*, Volume 6, Issue 4, June 1955.

Fantina, Robert. *Desertion and the American*

Soldier, 1776–2006. Algora Publishing, 2006.

Fisher, Louis. *Military Tribunals: The Quirin Precedent.* Congressional Research Service (CRS), Library of Congress. March 26, 2002.

Fogarty, Jaime. "The San Patricio Battalion: The Irish Soldiers of Mexico." *Voices of Mexico Magazine,* National University of Mexico, April-June 2000

Fogelberg, Ben. *Western Voices: 125 Years of Colorado Writing.* Fulcram Publishing, Colorado Historical Society, 2004.

Frisby, Herbert M. "Record of Court-Martial of Godman Field Officers Reads Like a Novel." *Afro-American* (Baltimore, MD), July 14, 1945.

Gettemy, Charles Ferris. *The True Story of Paul Revere: His Midnight Ride, His Arrest and Court-Martial, His Useful Public Services.* Little Brown & Co., 1912.

Glaberson, William. "Old Sailor Turns to Clinton to Lose Label of a Mutineer." *New York Times,* June 23, 1999.

Glaberson, William. "Sailor from Mutiny in '44 Wins a Presidential Pardon." *New York Times,* December 24, 1999.

Glasrud, Bruce A., and Michael N. Searles. *Buffalo Soldiers in the West: A Black Soldiers Anthology.* Texas A&M University Press, 2007.

Glionna, John M. "Second Life of G.I. Who Deserted to North Korea." *Los Angeles Times,* July 16, 2009.

Godfrey, Carlos E. *The Commander-In-Chief's Guard: Revolutionary War.* Clearfield, Co.: 2000.

Goeller, David. "Colonel Henderson Is Acquitted of My Lai Cover-up Charges." *Washington Post,* December 18, 1971.

Goldstein, Joseph, Jack Schwartz, and Burke Marshall. *The My Lai Massacre and Its Cover-up: Beyond the Reach of the Law. The Peers Report with a Supplement and Introductory Essay on the Limits of Law.* New York: The Free Press, 1976.

Gray, Valerie A. *The Court Martial Trial of West Point Cadet Johnson Whittaker.* Enslow Publishers, 2001.

Gropman, Alan L. *The Air Force Integrates 1945–1964.* Special Studies—Office of Air Force History and Museums, June 1986.

Gruening, Martha. "Houston—An NAACP Investigation" *The Crisis Magazine,* November 1917.

Guttridge, Leonard F. *Mutiny: A History of Naval Insurrection.* Annapolis, MD: Naval Institute Press, 2006.

Hamann, Jack. *On American Soil: How Justice Became a Casualty of World War II.* Algonquin Books, 2005.

Hanson, Jeffrey L. "The Saint Patrick's Battalion of the Mexican-American War: Why They Deserted Just to Fight On." Honor Thesis, Southern Illinois University, Carbondale, 2003.

Haynes, Robert V. *A Night of Violence: The Houston Riot of 1917.* Baton Rouge: Louisiana State University Press, 1976.

Hersh, Seymour. "Lieutenant Accused of Murdering 109 Civilians." *St. Louis Post-Dispatch,* November 13, 1969.

Hodson, Kenneth J. "The Manual for Courts-Martial—1984." *Military Law Review,* Summer 1972.

Homan, Lynn M., and Thomas Reilly. *Black Knights: The Story of the Tuskegee Airmen.* Pelican Publishing, 2001.

Homan, Lynn M., and Thomas Reilly. *The Tuskegee Airmen.* Arcadia Publishing, 1998.

Hubbell, John T., and James W. Geary, eds. *Biographical Dictionary of the Union: Northern Leaders of the Civil War.* Westport, CT: Greenwood Press, 1995.

Huie, William Bradford. *The Execution of Private Slovik.* Dell Publishing, 1954.

Investigation of Attack on Italian Service Unit Personnel by American Soldiers at Ft. Lawton Washington. File 333.9, Ft. Lawton—Formerly Confidential General Correspondence, 1939–47. Record Group 159, Records of the Inspector General, NARACP.

James, Randy. "A Brief History of Military Commissions." *Time,* May 18, 2009.

Jenkins, Charles Robert, and Jim Frederick. *The Reluctant Communist: My Desertion, Court Martial and Forty-Year Imprisonment in North Korea.* University of California Press, 2009.

Johnson, David Alan. *Betrayal: The True Story of J. Edgar Hoover and the Nazi Saboteurs.* New York: Hippocrene Books, 2007.

Jones, Ray, and Joe Lubow. *Disasters and Heroic Rescues of California: True Stories of Tragedy and Survival.* Globe Pequot; 1st edition, 2006.

Kimmelman, Benedict B. "The Example of Private Slovik." *American Heritage Magazine* Vol. 38, Issue 6, Sept./Oct. 1987.

Kleiner, Carolyn. "The Demon of Andersonville." *Legal Affairs Magazine*, Sept./Oct. 2002.

Mackenzie, Alexander S., and James Fenimore Cooper. *Proceedings of the naval court martial in the case of Alexander Slidell, a Commander in the Navy of the United States, & Including the Charges and Specifications of Charges Preferred Against Him by the Secretary of the Navy. To which is Annexed an Elaborate Review by James Fenimore Cooper.* New York: Henry G. Langley, 1844. Cornell University Library, 2009.

Marshall, John A. *American Bastille: A History of the Illegal Arrests and Imprisonment of American Citizens during the Late Civil War.* T. W. Hartley, 1869.

Marszalek, John F., Jr. *Assault at West Point: The Court Martial of Johnson Whittaker.* Collier Books, 1972.

Marszalek, John F., Jr. "A Black Cadet at West Point." *American Heritage Magazine*, Vol. 22, Issue 5, August 1971.

Marvel, William. *Andersonville: The Last Depot.* University of North Carolina Press, 2006.

McHenry, Robert, ed. *Webster's American Military Biographies.* Dover, 1984.

McNerthney, Casey. "Apology 64 Years in the Making for Black Soldiers Wrongfully Convicted." *Seattle Post-Intelligencer*, July 23, 2008.

Meed, Douglas V. *The Mexican War, 1846–1848* Osprey Publishing, 2002.

Miller, Frederic, Agnes Vandome, and John McBrewster. *Henry Wirz.* VDM Publishing House, 2009.

Miller, Robert. *Shamrock and Sword: The Saint Patrick Battalion in the U.S.-Mexican War* Norman: University of Oklahoma Press, 1989.

Moses, Belle. *Paul Revere: The Torch Bearer of the Revolution.* D Appleton & Co., 1912; Wright Press, 2007.

Moye, J. Todd. *Freedom Flyers: The Tuskegee Airmen of World War II.* Oxford University Press, 2010.

Murphy, Maj. John D. "The Freeman Field Mutiny: A Study in Leadership." Research Paper AU/ACSC/0429/97-03, Air Command and Staff College, 1997.

Norton, Louis Arthur. *Captains Contentious: The Dysfunctional Sons of the Brine.* University of South Carolina Press, 2009.

O'Donnell, Pierce. *In Time of War: Hitler's Terrorist Attack on America.* The New Press, 2005.

Olson, James S., and Randy Roberts. *My Lai: A Brief History with Documents.* Bedford/St. Martin's; illustrated edition, 1998.

Page, James M., and Michael J. Haley. *The True Story of Andersonville Prison: A Defense of Major Henry Wirz.* Neale Publishing, 1908; General Books, 2009.

Port Chicago Naval Magazine Explosion on 17 July 1944: Court of Inquiry: Finding of Facts, Opinion and Recommendations. U.S. Naval Historical Center.

Powell, Colin. *My American Journey: An Autobiography.* Random House, 1995.

Ridenhour, Ronald. My Lai 25 Years After: Facing the Darkness, Healing the Wounds. Conference at Tulane University, New Orleans, December 2, 1994.

Rockwood, Lawrence. *Walking Away from Nuremberg: Just War and the Doctrine of Command Responsibility.* University of Massachusetts Press, 2007.

Rucker, Walter C., and James N. Upton. *Encyclopedia of American Race Riots.* Greenwood, 2006.

Scott, Lawrence P., and William M. Womack. *Double V: The Civil Rights Struggle of the Tuskegee Airmen.* Michigan State University Press, 1998.

Sevy, Grace, ed. *The American Experience in Vietnam: A Reader.* Norman Press, 1989.

Stevens, Peter F. *The Rogue's March: John Riley and the St. Patrick's Battalion.* Washington D.C.: Brassey's, 1999.

Sutherland, Jonathan. *African-Americans at War: An Encyclopedia, Vol. 1.* ABC-CLIO, 2003.

Swanberg, W.A. "The Spies Who Came in from the Sea." *American Heritage Magazine*, Vol. 21, Issue 3, April 1970.

Thompson, Hugh. My Lai 25 Years After: Facing the Darkness, Healing the Wounds. Conference at Tulane University, New Orleans, December 2, 1994.

Vaughn, William P. "West Point and the First Negro Cadet." *Military Affairs*, Oct. 1971.

Wallace, Edward S. "The Battalion of Saint

Patrick in the Mexican War." *Military Affairs*, Society for Military History, Volume 14, Issue 2, Summer 1950.

Warren, Lt. Col James C. *The Tuskegee Airmen Mutiny at Freeman Field*. Vacaville, CA: Conyers, 1995.

Westlake, Adam. "North Korean Abductee Calls the Release of Other Japanese Nationals." *Japan Daily Press*, October 8, 2012.

Whiting, Charles. *America's Forgotten Army: The True Story of the U.S. Seventh Army in World War II*. St. Martin's Press, 2001.

Wood, Graeme. "The U.S. Soldier Who Defected to North Korea." *The Atlantic Magazine*, September 2013.

Index

Adams, John Quincy 37
Adams, Sam 12, 14, 15
HMS *Albany* 19
Ampudia, Gen. Pedro de 35
Andersonville 54–68
Andreotta, Spec. Glenn 210, 212, 213, 236, 237
Arista, Gen. Don Mariano 35–38

Bailey, F. Lee 232
Barker, Lt. Col. Frank A. 206, 208, 214–216, 223
Beauregard, Gen. P.G.T. 39
Berger, Ernest 99–127
Burger, Justice Warren 1
Butler, Gen. Benjamin 51, 57

Calley, 2Lt. William 204–238
Camp Logan 88–98
Carver, George Washington 161
Chesnut, Mary Boykin 70
Clinton, William "Bill" 69, 87, 160, 176
Coburn, Spec. Larry 210–213
Conti, PFC Dennis 209, 229

Dasch, George 99–127
Davis, Benjamin O. 162, 163, 173, 174
Davis, Justice David 51–52
Davis, Capt. George 39, 43
Davis, Jefferson 56, 62, 67, 70
Davis, Marion B. 186
Dawes, William 14–15
Dawkins, Henry 4
USS *Dolphin* 27
HMS *Duchess of Gordon* 4
Dunlap, James 3

Eisenhower, Dwight D. 186, 188, 189
USS *Enterprise* 195
Executive Order 9279 145

Flipper, Henry O. 73–74, 84
Forbes, Gilbert 5–7
Fort Lawton 128–142
Fraunces Tavern 6
Freeman Army Airfield 161–176

Gates, Gen. Horatio 12
Glen, Spec. Tom 216, 218
Gibbs, Captain Caleb 6

Haberle, Sgt. Ron 208, 222, 228, 232
Hancock, John 9, 12, 14–16, 25
Harvard University 70, 84, 87, 117, 119
Hasan, Maj. Nidal Malik 1
Haupt, Herbert Hans 99–127
Heinck, Heinrich 99–127
Henderson, Col. Oren 206, 207, 214–216, 221–222, 225, 233–234
Hickey, Thomas 3–9
Hodges, Sgt. Kenneth 207, 224–225
Hoover, J. Edgar 112–114, 118, 125–126
Howe, Lt. Gen. William 5

Jenkins, Sgt. Charles Robert 192–203
USS *John Adams* 28
Johnson, Andrew 51
Jones, Jacob 31
Jones, John Paul 11, 27
Jones, Pvt. William G. 128, 130–131
Jones, Pvt. William O. 135, 138, 141

Kerling, Edward 99–127
Ketcham, Issac 4, 5, 7, 8
King George III 3
Koster, Maj. Gen. Samuel 214–216, 222, 225, 227, 231

Lee, Maj. Gen. Charles 6
Lee, Gen. Robert E. 39, 62
Lincoln, Abraham 37, 48, 51, 63, 67, 230
Lincoln, Robert Todd 86
Lynch, Pvt. Michael 4–7

Mackenzie, Alexander Slidell 26–33
McClellan, Gen. George B. 39
McLean, Brig. Gen. Frances 10
Meadlo, Pvt. Paul 209–210, 221, 228–230
Medina, Capt. Ernest 205–207, 212–215, 220–225, 228, 230–234
Michles, Capt. Earl 206, 215, 221
Milligan, Lambdin P. 47–53

254 Index

Neubauer, Herman Otto 99–127
USS *North Carolina* 27, 31

O'Brian, John Paul Jones 39
Operation Muscatine 206
Operation Pastorious 99–127

Parker, Capt. John 16
Peers Report 208, 209, 213, 215–216, 222–223, 236
Pinkville 207, 211, 216, 219
Port Chicago 143–160
USS *Potomac* 28
Powell, Adam Clayton 172
Powell, Maj. Colin 217, 218
USS *Pueblo* 195

Quiren, Richard 99–127

Reily, Capt. John Patrick 34–46
Revere, Paul 10–25
Ridenhour, Ron 218–221
Riggs, Capt. William C. 206
USS *Roanoke* 28
Roosevelt, Eleanor 155, 158, 173
Roosevelt, Franklin D. 99, 113–115, 120–123, 145, 156, 160–163, 172–173
Roosevelt, Theodore 84, 89

Saltonstall, Commodore Dudley 11, 17–23
San Patricios 34–46
USS *Sangay* 151
Santa Ana, Gen. Antonio Lopez de 39–40, 42, 44, 46
USS *Scholarie* 101

Scott, Winfield 39, 41–43, 44, 46
Sears, Capt. Clinton 84
Sears, Lt. Clinton B. 77
Sherman, William T. 59, 77, 78, 82
Slidell, John 26, 34–35
Slovik, Pvt. Eddie 177–189
USS *Somers* 26–33
Son My 206, 207, 215–216, 222–224
Spencer, Phillip 26–33
Stamp Act 3

Task Force (TF) Baker 205–206, 214, 216, 223
Taylor, Gen. Zachery 35, 37–39, 41
Theil, Werner 99–127
Thompson, Clinton 174–175
Thompson, WO1 Hugh 210–215, 221–222, 225, 228, 234, 236–237
Thoreau, Henry, David 37
Tyron, William 4

Washington, Booker T. 161
Washington, George 3, 5–9, 32
Washington, John 73, 97
Washington Lifeguards 4–6, 180
West Point 36, 56, 69–74, 76–80, 82–87, 96, 116–118, 164, 166, 232, 237
Whittaker, Cadet Johnson C. 69–87
USS *Wilson* 154
Winder, Gen. John Henry 56, 61, 62
Winder, Capt. Richard 62, 65
Winder, Gen., William Henry 56
Wirz, Maj. Henry 54–68

Young, Brig. Gen. George H. 222, 231

www.ingramcontent.com/pod-product-compliance
Ingram Content Group UK Ltd.
Pitfield, Milton Keynes, MK11 3LW, UK
UKHW041934140426
5217IPUK00014B/470